THE
MANNINGS

BALLANTINE BOOKS

NEW YORK

THE
MANNINGS

THE FALL AND RISE OF
A FOOTBALL FAMILY

Lars Anderson

Published in the United States by Ballantine Books,
an imprint of Random House, a division of
Penguin Random House LLC, New York.

BALLANTINE and the HOUSE colophon are registered
trademarks of Penguin Random House LLC.

Grateful acknowledgment is made to Malaco Records to
reprint an excerpt from "The Ballad of Archie Who"
by Lamont Wilson, copyright © Lamont Wilson.
Reprinted with permission by Malaco Records.

Library of Congress Cataloging-in-Publication Data
Names: Anderson, Lars.
Title: The Mannings : the fall and rise of a football family / Lars Anderson.
Description: First Edition. | New York : Ballantine Books, [2016] |
Includes bibliographical references and index.
Identifiers: LCCN 2016018007 (print) | LCCN 2016029392 (ebook) |
ISBN 9781101883822 (hardcover : acid-free paper) | ISBN 9781101883846 (ebook)
Subjects: LCSH: Manning, Archie, 1949- | Manning, Peyton. | Manning, Eli,
1981- | Manning family. | Football players—United States—Biography.|
Quarterbacks (Football)—United States—Biography.
Classification: LCC GV939.A1 A54 2016 (print) | LCC GV939.A1 (ebook) |
DDC 796.3320922 [B]—dc23 LC record available
at https://lccn.loc.gov/2016018007

Printed in the United States of America on acid-free paper

randomhousebooks.com

2 4 6 8 9 7 5 3 1

FIRST EDITION

Book design by Dana Leigh Blanchette

FOR MY LITTLE MAN, LINCOLN HENRY ANDERSON:
KNOW THAT DAD LOVES YOU, ALWAYS.

Contents

―――
―――

Peyton's Final Pass

Santa Clara, California. Winter 2016.

High above the grass football field in Santa Clara, California, the family fidgeted and fretted inside a luxury suite on the seventh level of Levi's Stadium. It was early in the evening of February 7, 2016. Archie, Olivia, Cooper, and Eli Manning peered through the gathering darkness down at the field, where the oldest player in the game—a thirty-nine-year-old man who just two months earlier Archie had believed would never take another NFL snap, a man in the deep winter of his career—was about to enjoy one last moment of summer.

With 3:08 remaining in Super Bowl 50, the Denver Broncos led the Carolina Panthers 22–10. Running back C. J. Anderson of the Broncos had just scored on a 2-yard touchdown plunge. Now Denver would try for a 2-point conversion. Lining up in the shotgun formation seven yards behind center, Peyton Manning received the snap. He took one step back, turned to his right, and flung a pass into the end zone.

As the ball spiraled through the cool California night, there were so many memories that filled the Manning family suite on the seventh level of the stadium.

There was Archie bringing little Peyton into the New Orleans Saints locker room when Peyton was five years old. Peyton and his older brother, Cooper, then seven, would hunt for the ankle-and-wrist tape that the players had discarded onto the floor. They'd wad the strips into their version of a football and then head out into the empty Superdome, where the boys played one-on-one football, their grunts and giggles rising into the far reaches of the stadium. Archie would sometimes join them, beginning Peyton's education in the art of throwing a football. Archie had been a constant presence in Peyton's life—he sat in the top row of the bleachers at his high school games with his bulky video camera resting on his right shoulder—because he vowed to be the father to his own kids that he didn't have.

There was Olivia driving her boys to hundreds of football practices in New Orleans. She would never forget the piles and piles of muddied clothes—and mounds of jockstraps—that she fed into their washing machine. Olivia, the dimple-cheeked, sweet-smiling, long-legged homecoming queen at Ole Miss in the fall of 1970, also was a fixture in the stands throughout Peyton's football career. It was likely that no mom in the history of the sport had watched her sons play more football games than Olivia, and just the sight of her in the stands was calming to all her children, but especially to Peyton, especially on those long-ago Friday nights at high school stadiums throughout Louisiana.

There was Cooper catching passes from Peyton in their one season together of high school football. The autumn of 1991 was the best time of Peyton's football life for one reason: he shared it with his big brother, Cooper, his best friend. Less than a year later Cooper would have to quit playing because of a spinal condition, and the words he would pen in a handwritten letter to Peyton—"I would like to live my dream of playing football through you"—would be the core inspiration to his younger brother for the next quarter century.

There was young Eli begging teenage Peyton to throw passes to him when Eli was eight years old. When thirteen-year-old Peyton finally caved in to his little brother's pestering, Peyton would grab a few pillows from a living room couch, stuff them into Eli's shirt, then go outside to the front lawn and rifle lasers at his brother, who would engulf the high-velocity balls in his padded chest before being knocked over like a bowling pin. The tourists on the buses that rolled by the Manning house in the Garden District on their way to see novelist Anne Rice's mansion down the street would wonder aloud, *Why is that bigger boy punishing that little one?*

At Levi's Stadium, the last throw of Peyton's career, for a 2-point conversion, flew 7 yards over the middle into the arms of wide receiver Bennie Fowler, sealing Denver's 24–10 win in Super Bowl 50. As soon as Fowler hauled in the pass, Peyton—who had made $247 million in NFL contracts alone, the most in league history—flashed a gleaming smile just like he used to when he threw touchdown passes in the front yard in games on First Street, which Archie filmed with his ever-present VHS camera.

Peyton was now the oldest quarterback ever to win the biggest game in American sports.

It ends for everybody. For Archie, who since 2014 has had neck and back surgeries and a knee replacement—the price of an NFL career—the end came in 1984 after thirteen NFL seasons and playing on teams that never had a winning record or advanced to the playoffs.

Father and mother sensed the end was coming for Peyton. Two weeks before Super Bowl 50, Archie and Olivia visited their middle son in Denver. On the eve of the AFC championship game between the Broncos and the Patriots—a game Denver would win 20–18 with Peyton contributing two touchdown passes—both parents grew emotional when they reflected on Peyton's career. Embracing his wife, his eyes wet, Archie told Olivia, "Hey, this really has been fun with this guy."

An hour after the AFC title game, Peyton joined his parents, family, and close friends—including four former receivers he had played with in Indianapolis—in his private suite in Mile High Stadium. Beers in hand, the stories flowing, they reflected on Peyton's career. Peyton understood he was no longer the player he once was—his arm was now more BB gun than howitzer—but there was a part of him that was as vibrant as ever, still crackling with curiosity, redlining at full power:

His mind.

As soon as the final pass was completed in Santa Clara, Archie and Olivia high-fived in the luxury suite. Cooper, always the most exuberant Manning brother, jumped around and beamed like he had just personally won the Super Bowl. Eli—who had made $188 million in NFL contracts alone, the second-highest total in league history—remained expressionless as he kept his eyes trained on his big brother down on the field. Eli, ever the quarterback, already was thinking about what Denver needed to do to close out the game, calculating clock management and the number of time-outs each team had. Archie was doing the same. For the father and the two youngest Manning boys, quarterbacking never really ends, whether in uniform or not.

After the final seconds ticked off the clock at Super Bowl 50, Peyton and Eli had combined to win four of the past ten Super Bowls. The brothers were two of twelve quarterbacks in NFL history to capture a pair of Vince Lombardi Trophies. Peyton alone was the only signal caller to guide two different teams to the sport's biggest prize.

But the legacy of Peyton ran far deeper than victories and Super Bowls. For nearly two decades Peyton was the face of the most popular sport in America. His five NFL MVP awards are a record. He is the NFL's all-time leader in passing yards (71,940) and touchdown passes (539). He threw for 4,000 yards in a season fourteen times, also an NFL record, which was important because Peyton's videogame-like numbers helped spur the rise in popularity of fantasy football in the mid 2000s. Peyton used his influence to change the game as well: in 2004 Peyton's incessant complaints of defensive backs not getting called for illegal contact—especially in the 2003 AFC championship game between the Colts and Patriots—was a major reason that the NFL tightened the rules on defensive backs, which in turned ushered in the era of high-flying passing attacks.

Peyton's obsessive study habits, his hallmark, elevated how NFL quarterbacks prepare for games. The most vital lesson Archie—who was sacked 396 times in the NFL, 11th most in history—taught young Peyton was that the best way to avoid injury was to know where his open receiver would be before the ball was even snapped. The only way to gain this knowledge, Archie stressed, was through film study of the opposing defense. So in his teen years, Peyton began viewing game film day and night. By the time he was in the NFL he would wear out the video-room interns by watching three seconds of a single play over and over for half an hour, analyzing every single movement of all twenty-two players, even studying quarterback kneel downs at the end of games. Peyton's mind was so sharp that, after winning MVP honors in Super Bowl XLI against the Bears in February 2007, he verbally recounted nearly every play of the Colts' 29–17 victory to an equipment manager a day later while flying to Hawaii for the Pro Bowl.

After Super Bowl 50, Peyton met his family outside the Broncos' locker room. Together they headed out into the night. Peyton wouldn't attend the team party at the Santa Clara Marriott. He celebrated this victory—his final victory—with those who mattered most.

Archie and Olivia still live in the same classic manor home in the Garden District on First Street in New Orleans where they raised their three sons. The house—a 5,000-square-foot 1844 Greek Revival—has soaring ceilings, wide-board wood floors, a swimming pool off the patio, four bedrooms upstairs, and formal living and dining rooms, a comfortable den, and an open country kitchen downstairs. It also features a manicured front yard and a backyard perfect for kids who love playing pickup football games. It is, in the words of a family friend, "the ideal place to raise three rambunctious boys."

In the Manning family scrapbooks are old yellowed photographs of Archie and Olivia with their small boys. So many times in the past few years, as the father and mother watched two of their sons play on television, they would recall where it all began. They'd be transported back through the mists of time to those afternoon games in the yard with Archie throwing the ball to his sons, to those Friday nights at Newman High where, under the amber glow of old high school stadium lights, they first watched Cooper, then Peyton, then Eli play football. Those had been the best of times, they would tell each other.

Archie and Olivia could still picture, on the grainy film of memory, the pure joy on the faces of their boys when they won a youth league football game and the head-shaking and dirt-kicking disappointment when they lost. But mostly, Archie and Olivia would remember that they were always together—as a family, five bound as one—sharing in the triumphs, the trials, and even the tragedies of football and life itself.

Archie and Olivia both would ask themselves: *Where did the time go? How did they grow up so fast?*

The Mannings bear the most esteemed name in the genteel South. In the world of football they are the equivalent to the Kennedys in politics and the Rockefellers in finance.

Family dynasties often clarify the values of their culture and their times. The Kennedys played touch football on the lawn of the compound in Hyannis Port, creating youthful, vibrant images that powerfully distilled the aspirations and hopes of millions in the 1960s. The Mannings cast a similar spell not only because Archie, Peyton, and Eli have been so absurdly good at football, but also because of what their story reveals about fatherhood, brotherhood, the South, and the lessons that sports can ultimately teach us.

To understand the ascendance of the Manning family, you first need to travel to where it all began—to the tiny Delta town of Drew, Mississippi. It's the spot where tragedy nearly destroyed this football family before it ever rose. Yet it's also the place where the seeds for all that would come were planted.

A reminder to us all that anything is possible.

THE
MANNINGS

CHAPTER 1

——

Desperate for a Hero

Parchman Farm, Mississippi. Summer 1961.

It was one of the scariest places in the South, a vast acreage of cotton and corn deep in the Mississippi Delta.

Beyond the two massive iron gates that served as the entrance to Parchman Farm, the sinners worked the fields at the old penal plantation during the day and prayed they wouldn't be attacked at night. They never knew what could leap from the shadows—a knife-wielding guard, an enraged bunkmate, a fellow inmate who had been driven to the brink of delirium. *Slavery,* the condemned said under their breaths at Parchman Farm, *couldn't have been this bad.*

Located nine miles down the road from the town of Drew in northwestern Mississippi, Parchman Farm was the state's oldest penitentiary. Built in 1909 on fifteen thousand acres, it was a prison that had no walls. Other than the maximum security unit that was known as "Little Alcatraz," Parchman didn't even have cells. Inmates were housed in military-style barracks they called "cages," where they would collapse onto rickety bunks after toiling from sunrise to sundown chopping timber, clearing ground, and picking cotton.

For decades the prison was a working farm that resembled an antebellum plantation, filled with black field hands (prisoners) and white foremen (guards). The leather strap, known as "Black Annie," was the ultimate symbol of discipline on the farm; when a convict didn't keep up with the line in the cotton fields, an overseer would grab Black Annie—three feet long, six inches wide—and administer a hellish whipping, cracking open bare flesh for all to see.

To make sure the prisoners didn't run, the guards had bloodhounds and specially trained German shepherds always at the ready. There were also gun-wielding marksmen who stood sentinel day and night. Called "headhunters" on the farm, the shotgun-toting guards rarely hesitated to fire on a fleeing convict. The only potential for escape came in the evenings when the chained inmates sang in unison about their backbreaking misery in the miles and miles of dusty, hot cotton fields. At Parchman, the blues came naturally.

One of the inmate-bluesmen was Bukka White, who, in the 1940s, served time for a shooting incident. One afternoon one of White's nephews, a young man named Riley B. King, visited his uncle at Parchman. Upon entering the front gate, Riley saw the terror in the eyes of the inmates.

The images of his trip to the Farm would stick with young Riley and become his artistic inspiration. He soon moved to Memphis and began picking at the guitar and singing at the Sixteenth Avenue Grill, earning the nickname "Blues Boy." He later shortened it to B.B. For the rest of his life B. B. King played the blues with the haunting desperation that he saw in the soul of his uncle at Parchman, as if every note he strummed was a scream for freedom.

In the spring of 1961—just as an earnest, redheaded boy celebrated his twelfth birthday that May by tossing around a football with his daddy in the family yard only nine miles down the road from the Farm—a group of civil rights activists from several Northern states rode interstate buses into the Deep South. The so-called Freedom Riders wanted to challenge the nonenforcement of two Supreme Court cases that ruled racial segregation in restaurants and on public buses were unconstitutional. The state governments of Alabama and Mississippi ignored the rulings, and the federal government refused to enforce them. So the Freedom Riders traveled in droves to the South.

The wick on the powder keg was lit. Mobs of angry Southerners, viewing this as another act of Northern aggression, surrounded the buses in the Alabama towns of Anniston, Birmingham, and Montgomery and attacked the Riders. Ross Barnett, the governor of Mississippi, agreed to protect the Riders as long as he could arrest them for disturbing the peace once they reached Jackson, Mississippi. By late June of '61 more than forty Freedom Riders were sent to Parchman. They were immediately assigned to chain gangs.

The Mississippi governor told the guards at Parchman to "break their spirit." Once the Riders arrived at the Farm, they were strip-searched, were allowed to shower only once a week, weren't given any mail, and slept in cells in which the lights were kept on twenty-four hours a day.

Twelve-year-old Archie Manning walked among the convicted at Parchman. A few of Archie's closest friends at Drew Junior High had parents who worked at the prison as administrators and lived in housing on the grounds. Archie occasionally spent the night with his friends at the Farm, and he would see the condemned up close, watching them toil in the fields and perform yard work around the employees' houses. One time Archie's Little League baseball team traveled to the Farm to play a squad of convicts; Archie's team won, but Archie understood the other team was on orders to lose the game.

Little Archie heard about the Freedom Riders at Parchman, but he was too young to fully understand why they were there. Archie was never scared of the prisoners—the boy had a fearless streak— but the mere presence of the prison was a daily reminder to Archie to always do right.

Citizens across the country were outraged at the treatment of the Riders at Parchman, where three hundred Riders would be imprisoned. Reporters and camera crews descended on the prison, which during the early days of the civil rights movement came to represent the brutality of the Old South.

America was beginning to boil. More than ever, Southerners were desperate for one of their own to rise up, for someone to spark those fading embers of greatness, someone to bring light to a place that was now growing dark, a hero to redeem them all.

They were looking for a kid from Drew.

CHAPTER 2

The Pee-Wee QB

Drew, Mississippi. Summer 1951.

The bolls of soft cotton blew out of Parchman Farm. When a dry wind stirred the parched fields, the cotton would drift like snowflakes southward down Highway 49 for nine miles to the corner of Third and Green Streets in Drew, to the little white house of Buddy and Jane Manning.

Prisoners escaped from Parchman a few times a year—the announcements would blare over the radio in Drew: "A convict is out! Lock your doors!"—but Buddy always told his two children and wife not to worry. "If he's out, he sure as heck ain't stopping in Drew," Buddy said. "He's leaving here, not staying." If Buddy's only son ever did get scared, he would dash into his backyard clubhouse with a sign on the door that read "No Girls Allowed."

In the 1950s and '60s, life in this Delta town of about two thousand moved slower than winter. Drew had three stoplights, two cafés, three service stations, two drugstores—where the sodas flowed from hand-pumped spigots—a dry cleaner, three churches, and one school. In the summers a frozen custard stand opened, where kids smothered their faces in eggs, cream, and sugar while shooting marbles. Two policemen patrolled during daylight; one night watchman relieved them once the lampposts flickered on.

Virtually every resident knew all their neighbors, and kids of all classes of life played together on sandlots and lawns. Drew was a kind of Mayberry, a wholesome-as-milk place where an adult could grab anyone's child by the arm, hand him or her a dollar and tell the youngster to head to the corner barbershop for a cut. It was a town where, after a rare winter storm, kids would sled around on top of old car hoods, a place where in the summers children would run around with toy walkie-talkies in their hands and play games like hide-and-seek and kick the can. If Drew was your home, no one was a stranger.

Drew was filled with farmers—at one point in the 1950s, Drew had more cotton gins than any town in America. The area was ideal for growing cotton. Lying in the heart of the Delta, Drew is nestled between the Sunflower River to the West and the Talla-hatchie to the East. The land was as fertile as any in the South and flat as an ironing board. On a clear day in Drew, the locals swore you could see all the way to the end of the earth.

The farmers liked to gather at the Case farm machinery shop, where Elisha Archibald Manning Jr.—whom everyone called "Buddy"—was the manager. Sipping nickel Cokes, the farmers would sit on a few stools at "the Case Place," as they called it, and trade gossip, offer predictions about the weather, and swap tales— some a little taller than others. Buddy wasn't a big talker, but ev-eryone seemed to like him. When the cost of a Coke ballooned from a nickel to a dime in the rest of the country, Buddy refused to raise his price. He didn't want his friends to suffer.

Standing only 5'7", Buddy was country tough. He grew up in

Crystal Springs, Mississippi, and was the youngest of five Manning children. Following the path of two older brothers, he played on the offensive line for his high school football team. Buddy was a scrapper, rarely shying away from a brawl. "When the fights broke out, Buddy was there," his high school yearbook noted. Buddy didn't share many stories about his football days—he believed life was to be lived, not reviewed—but all his friends knew that it was not a wise idea to raise a fist to the Case Place manager.

More than anything, Buddy valued hard work. He sold and leased farming equipment. He rarely missed a day of work, and always showed up wearing a straw hat and a shirt with two front pockets. He'd stuff one pocket with pens and the other with a lighter and his pack of Chesterfields, which Buddy smoked constantly. Buddy was particular about his work apparel: if he received a shirt with only one pocket as a birthday present, it wouldn't get hung in his closet; he'd exchange it for a two-pocket shirt. The man knew what he liked, was stubborn in his ways, and craved routine.

Sometimes Buddy's wife, Jane Manning, would accompany him when he made the rounds to customers' houses to collect debts. Nine years younger than her husband, Jane, whom everyone called "Sis," was an elegant woman who enjoyed writing letters to friends and family members in her immaculate longhand. A graduate of Union University in Jackson, Tennessee, Sis also could be as persistent as kudzu. No matter what anyone told her, she always left the keys in the ignition of her unlocked car in the driveway, because she'd rather a thief or an escaped convict from Parchman steal the car than enter the house to search for the keys.

Buddy earned about $6,000 a year. His income could have been higher, but Buddy despised shaking down his friends to force them to honor their payments. It wasn't in Buddy's bighearted nature to play the role of the heavy. By all accounts, when it came to friends, he could be too nice for his own good.

When Buddy and Sis drove to the different farmers to collect the debts, the visits were as much social calls as work. Sis would politely try to nudge Buddy's farming pals into opening their wallets, looking them dead in the eyes and asking them to pay for what her husband had leased to them. But many of the bills went unpaid because the farmers had spent their crop money on other things, like a brand-new television set that featured what in the late '50s was the newest innovation: a color picture. Sis would ask Buddy's customers to do the right thing and pay what they owed for their combines or tractors, but many didn't flinch at taking advantage of Buddy's good nature. Buddy chalked it up to the culture of the Delta, where some farmers viewed debt as a problem that could be dealt with down the road—or, if they were lucky, never at all.

Still, Buddy and Sis, a stay-at-home mom, managed to get by. They devoutly attended Drew Baptist Church—God was the center of their lives—and they were happily in love when they started a family. In 1947 Pamela Ann was born. Two years later, on May 19, 1949, Sis gave birth to a boy, Elisha Archibald Manning III. They called him Archie.

Almost as soon as he could crawl, that child had some sort of ball in his hands.

In Drew in the 1950s the seasons on the calendar were defined by athletics—fall was football, winter was basketball, spring was track, and summer was baseball. Games were the pride and passion of the folks in Drew, the common heartbeat in the community. And so it was fitting that after Archie was born, an old high school football coach who lived nearby walked over to the Manning house one evening and presented Buddy and Sis with a gift: a tiny football helmet and uniform for their eighteen-month-old son. In the sprawling story of the Manning football dynasty, this was the moment of genesis.

The Mannings' modest three-bedroom, one-bathroom home sat across the street from the high school, a small white stucco building. Soon after he could walk, little Archie would stand on the corner in his yard and watch members of the Drew High football team play games of touch football during P.E. class. The action mesmerized Archie, holding his gaze. He began to go to bed each night with a football cradled in his arms.

As Archie grew, his face conveyed a rural innocence—his freckles, his slight squint, and his red, combed-over hair gave him a Huck Finn quality—but there was also a sadness in his eyes, as if he was waiting for heartbreak. Yet when he flashed his little-boy grin—one so bright it would melt every heart in the room—suddenly he would appear to be the happiest child in all of Sunflower County.

Things came naturally to Archie. He could read, spell, and write before he entered grade school. He could throw a ball like it was an innate skill and swing a stick—later a baseball bat—with a big-leaguer's grace. Buddy could see that his only son was different than the other boys, and he repeatedly told Archie that he should never be conceited about the gifts his Maker had bestowed on him. Buddy emphasized that the difference between a successful man and a failed man was as thin as a stick of baseball-card bubblegum. Always be humble, Buddy implored, because God can take away all that He has given in a heartbeat. For young Archie, a child in the Bible Belt, it was as if these words thundered from the sky.

Buddy and Sis infused Archie's young life with discipline and routine. Archie never missed a Cub Scout meeting. He had dance lessons, piano tutorials, and Sunday afternoon piano recitals. He won the Junior Achievement Award given by the Drew Garden Club for an arrangement of flowers he had meticulously put together.

One of the few times Archie was ever physically punished as a child was when he failed to show up for a Sunday piano recital at four p.m.; Archie had been playing touch football at a friend's house. Buddy, who wasn't thrilled to be spending his own Sunday afternoon listening to piano, brought out the belt for the no-show Archie. Archie soon quit playing piano, though Buddy told him he would regret it. "Trust me, one day when you're older, you'll wish you can play," Buddy said. Archie would later admit that his father was right.

But the sun in Archie's solar system as a kid—the one thing that lit up his world like nothing else—was sports. When he was six years old he'd sit in his living room waiting for a Major League Baseball game to start on television—his favorite team was the St. Louis Cardinals, the big-league squad closest to Drew—and he'd get butterflies in his stomach, as if he were about to take the diamond himself. In the early mornings he'd carefully read the baseball box scores in the newspaper, analyzing the statistics as though he'd be tested on them later that day in grade school. When the *Sporting News* arrived in the mail, he'd grab the magazine and carefully scan every page, desperate for more information about his beloved Cardinals.

Summer Saturdays were Archie's favorite time of the year. In the morning he'd play baseball in a lot behind his house, a small patch of paradise that he and his friends had carved out of a fallow cotton field. They built a pitcher's mound, burlap sacks filled with dirt served as the bases, and Archie mowed a line deep in the outfield to signify the outfield fence. When Sis wasn't looking,

Archie raided the kitchen for a bag of flour, which he poured onto the dirt to make batters' boxes.

In the summer of 1961, as Archie and his buddies read about the Yankees' Roger Maris smashing a record 61 home runs, a local kid named Jerry Knox blasted 68 round-trippers in Archie's little park. In his mind, Archie would become a New York Yankee one day like Maris. He dreamed of how his scouting report would be read aloud over the radio as he strode onto the Yankee Stadium field in that towering cathedral in the South Bronx: *Archie Manning, shortstop, Drew, Mississippi. Bats left, throws right. Good speed, good arm, great bunter.*

Saturday afternoons were spent with his father. Buddy would shut down his Case farm machinery store early, and by noon he and his boy would be sitting in the living room, just the two of them, watching a baseball game. Even when they didn't talk—and Buddy never said much—young Archie felt closer to his dad on these afternoons than he did at any other time. This was the magic of sports—the power to bond, to bring together, to create shared history—and Archie understood it all before he was four feet tall.

Late summer and early fall days offered a double dose of sports for Archie. Baseball would seize his attention for a few years, but he gradually fell in deeper love with football. On Halloween night of 1959—Archie was ten—he and Buddy sat in their living room together, riveted to the crackling sounds pouring out of their transistor radio. Archie's favorite college football team, Ole Miss, was playing LSU. The third-ranked Rebels traveled to Baton Rouge on a foggy, wet night to face the top-ranked Tigers in what was the most important game of the entire '59 season—and one of the most significant in Mississippi history.

Young Archie's mind raced with the rise and fall of the crowd noise, with the images of dashing runs and arching passes painted by the resonant voice of announcer J. C. Polit. In the fourth quarter, with just over ten minutes to play and Ole Miss leading 3–0, LSU running back Billy Cannon fielded a bouncing punt on the Tigers' 11-yard line. Archie and Buddy heard it all: how Cannon ran right, broke up the field, evaded seven Ole Miss tacklers, and sprinted down the sideline into the end zone. As Polit yelled "Touchdown!" Archie sobbed into a pillow, his spirit crushed by what had transpired 280 miles away in the rain. LSU won 7–3 on that play by Cannon, which catapulted him to winning the Heisman Trophy.

Buddy went to bed, but Archie was too upset to drift into dreamland. So he stayed up late, scanning the AM radio dial for any game he could find—Rice, TCU, USC, it didn't matter, he just wanted more football. Then at midnight he found a rebroadcast of the Ole Miss–LSU game. Lying in his bed, he listened again, closing his eyes and imagining he was in the grandstands, hunkered down in the rain, watching the action. After the final whistle blew, this time in the small hours of the next day, Archie cried again—the devastation still as penetrating as it had been the first time he heard the outcome of that contest.

Like most boys with soaring imaginations, Archie and his friends created games to play. In the seventh grade, Archie played with high school boys in their own "bowl" games—the "Turkey Bowl" was on Thanksgiving afternoon, and the "Christmas Bowl" kicked off on December 25. The contests took place on the Drew High football field. Archie was the youngest, but he was also one of the quickest. Playing wide receiver, Archie felt so proud when he caught a deep ball, but when he dropped a pass he would be so upset with himself that he felt like running across the street and hiding in his backyard clubhouse. The twelve-year-old perfection-ist didn't tolerate mistakes.

For as long as he could remember, Archie wanted to play quar-terback, to have the ball in his hands and be the player who was the coach on the field. The only football bubblegum cards he kept were those of the star NFL signal callers—Johnny Unitas of the Baltimore Colts, Bobby Layne of the Detroit Lions, Y. A. Tittle of the San Francisco 49ers, and, his favorite, Charlie Conerly of the New York Giants, who earlier had played quarterback at Ole Miss. Archie was so enamored with the position that, while play-ing catch with himself in his yard—he could throw the ball re-markably high for a boy his age—he'd repeatedly look across the street at the high school to spot Ronnie Steed, Drew's starting quarterback. Steed was the epitome of 1950s cool to Archie, who would take note of what Steed was wearing and then, the next day, dress just like him.

Archie began playing organized football in the sixth grade on a squad that limited players to 120 pounds. His dad had only four rules for him: he could never quit, he could never talk back to the coach, he could never bad-mouth another player, and he couldn't "shine your ass," which meant he could never boast about anything he accomplished on the field. Archie obeyed, fearful of receiving the belt. Buddy didn't punish his son often, but if Archie stepped out of line, he would lash him with his belt. After little Archie stole some plums from the backyard of an elderly woman when he was in grade school, Buddy unloaded on Archie's rear end.

During the first preseason football practice, the coach lined up all the boys. Walking in front of them he said, "Okay, you're the fullback. . . . You're the halfback." Archie stood near the end of the line, afraid that he wouldn't be able to play quarterback, but too shy to speak up. Then as the coach neared him, one of the kids said, "Archie's got to play quarterback." The coach looked hard at Archie for one second . . . two . . . three. Finally, he said, "Okay, Archie, you're our quarterback." At that moment Archie felt like the luckiest kid in all of Drew.

The pee-wee coach allowed Archie to call his own plays, a common practice at the time. Archie was as skinny as chicken wire—he often forgot to eat because he was so consumed with practicing and playing football, which caused his older sister, Pam, to repeatedly remind Archie to stuff his face when at the dinner table— but Archie was also as quick as a cornered rabbit. His favorite play to call was a rollout to the right, which gave him the option to run or pass. He scored dozens of touchdowns on this simple play before he'd even reached puberty.

Even though he was just a kid, the strategy of football games fired Archie's imagination. He peppered his coaches with questions and could draw plays up in the dirt with the ease of a Charlie Conerly. Buddy nurtured his son's flowering football mind by becoming friends with the high school football coaches, who lived in housing near the school—and near the Mannings. Buddy would invite his neighbors over for dinner, and then let Archie talk on and on about football, the one subject that could strip him of his reticence. A coach gave him an old ball to play with, and starting in fifth grade, Archie became a regular at the Drew football games. Buddy didn't have time to drive to away games—he had to work—so he told Archie to ask his uncle Peyton for a lift.

Peyton, who lived on a nearby farm, would pick up Archie in his Studebaker, and together they would drive to different Delta towns for Friday night games. Sitting next to his uncle in the stands, the wooden lights above them illuminating the evening, Archie would be hypnotized by the action. He was enthralled by the chess-match strategy of the game, the violence, the battle of muscles and wills—it all stirred something inside him. That was what Archie wanted. That, he hoped, would be his future.

Uncle Peyton was always on his best behavior around Archie—he cut out the swearing and didn't take any nips out of his bourbon flask—and he frequently told his nephew how much fun he had at these high school games. Sometimes Peyton, who would never marry, wouldn't want the nights to end, and so he would take Archie to get a bite to eat before driving him home.

"Let's go on over to Cleveland and get us some breakfast," Peyton would say. The two would then drive to an all-night café in nearby Cleveland, Mississippi, and eat scrambled eggs and sausage. Then, around 11 p.m., Peyton would drop off his favorite nephew at his home in Drew.

Uncle Peyton and Archie sometimes also spent Saturdays together, walking up and down Main Street in Drew, Peyton buying Archie ice cream at the five-and-dime store. Other times Archie would go to Peyton's farm, and for three dollars a day, he would chop cotton with his favorite uncle.

The two grew close over the years. And there was just something about that name—Peyton—that was melodic and appealed to Archie's ear.

CHAPTER 3

"My Boy Will Be There"

Drew, Mississippi. Autumn 1953.

In careful handwriting, Archie wrote an essay for school when he was in ninth grade. The precise cursive letters on the three-line paper were delivered by a steady hand, as if done with a stencil and a focused, concentrated mind. Entitled *My Autobiography,* the essay read, "I am told I was born on Thursday, May 19, 1949. . . . Today I am 14 years old and in the ninth grade of Drew Junior High School. I have been blessed with a healthy body and mind. I stand five feet six inches tall and weigh one hundred-twenty pounds. . . . I don't know what I intend to be but plan to enter some college. I hope to be someone my friends, teachers, and parents won't be ashamed of."

In thought and action, Archie was a people pleaser. The last thing he wanted was to disappoint anyone. When his mom told him to do a chore—clean his room, take out the garbage, cut the grass—she didn't have to repeat her request. To his father's questions he replied "yes sir" or "no sir," and he looked him and other adults in the eyes when spoken to. At school he was the student who always did his homework; a pop quiz rarely caught him off guard.

In middle school Archie was popular among the boys—he had no interest in girls yet—and even more popular in the cafeteria, where he and Pam ate their lunches from paper sacks filled with food prepared by their mother, Sis, a skilled cook of Southern cuisine. The freezer at the Mannings was typically jammed full: aunts and uncles who lived on nearby farms raised cattle, and they would drop off cuts of beef, which Sis packed in the cold storage bin. Her soul food was so scrumptious that just the smell of it could lead a pack of kids to the Manning household. When Archie and Pam reached into their lunch sacks, kids stopped eating to see what they would pull out. Eyes bulged when they ate fried chicken or barbecued brisket accompanied with black-eyed peas or collard greens.

Attentive and soft-spoken, ninth-grade Archie was a favorite of his Sunday school teachers. Every Sunday, Archie, wearing a red blazer and white gloves, strode into First Baptist Church, located in the center of town. For thirteen straight years he never missed a session of Sunday school—the longest-standing record in Drew for perfect attendance—and after each class he was awarded an attendance pin. Like most things in life, Archie viewed his weekly trips to Sunday school as a competition; he wasn't going to let anyone else collect more attendance pins than him.

But Archie, like most energetic boys who loved games, was more interested in football than in faith. In the ninth grade he played backup quarterback on the Drew varsity team because Drew didn't have enough players to field a junior varsity squad. During practices fifteen-year-old Archie ran the scout team as its signal caller, replicating the plays of each upcoming opponent.

Archie was a wispy blur on the scout team, scrambling around the field like he was running from bullies at recess. He was so impressive that, late in the fall, the coach told him that he would put him in for a play in the next game. But the very next day at practice Archie was tackled by a varsity player and fell to the ground—hard. He broke his right arm, ending his season.

Archie had brittle bones. At the beginning of his sophomore year he stood six feet tall and weighed only 135 pounds. He contemplated quitting football because he doubted his body could hold up—plus, he enjoyed playing baseball and basketball just as much. But then Gerald Morgan, a Presbyterian minister, became the football coach at Drew. Employing his preacher's persuasion, Morgan convinced Archie to stick with football.

A former Ole Miss quarterback, Morgan liked what he saw in Archie: he was coordinated, could throw a beautiful spiral, and had natural running agility. But Archie recently experienced a growth spurt, which left his upper body underdeveloped and weak. Morgan told Archie to lift weights and to improve his throwing motion and his accuracy, patiently showing him how to do both. Every time Morgan asked Archie if he understood what he was teaching, Archie replied, "Yes, sir."

On Sundays after church most of Archie's friends cruised Drew in cars with their girlfriends, driving up and down the streets, occasionally racing one another, a typical teenage activity in the 1960s. But Archie, who rarely dated in high school, took his coach's instructions to heart. After Sunday school he went home, changed clothes, and headed straight to a vacant lot to play pickup football with kids, some older and some younger. Archie would volunteer to be the quarterback of both teams. For hours, he threw all types of passes—short lobs, deep rainbows, 15-yard darts, 20-yard floaters. He was determined to improve, one pass at a time.

Morgan didn't start Archie at the beginning of his sophomore season. After Drew lost its opening game 7–0—Archie sat on the bench the entire four quarters—Buddy walked over to Morgan. "Coach, my boy was gonna be the quarterback and you didn't even put him in the game," Buddy said.

"Archie is going to have to get stronger and faster," Morgan told Buddy. "He's got a lot of abilities, a lot of potential, but he's going to have to get faster if he's going to realize it."

Archie played sparingly during the remainder of the season. In one game he fumbled his first two snaps—he would settle down and later throw a touchdown pass—but Archie spent most of the fall standing next to Morgan on the sideline. Archie lived in the coach's shadow, watching *him* watch the game, trying to understand what an old quarterback like Morgan focused on from the moment each huddle broke to the blast of the whistle that signaled the end of the play. Archie also intently listened to every word issued from Morgan's lips, as if each syllable sprang from the good book itself.

Impressed by Archie's improved focus and resolve, Morgan started his sophomore quarterback in the season finale, a home game against rival Cleveland High, a school located fifteen miles away. Before kickoff the Cleveland coach strolled over to Morgan, asking for more benches for their sideline. The Cleveland squad boasted forty-five players; Drew had twenty. "We already gave you our bench," Morgan said. "We don't even have one."

"Well, we need one," the Cleveland coach insisted.

"Do you think I'm going to go into Drew to find you a bench?" Morgan asked. "I can't get you a bench." The Cleveland coach stormed away.

Before sending his young quarterback onto the field, Morgan gave Archie a pep talk, hoping to sprinkle pixie dust on his player. He told Archie that he believed in him, that the players believed in him. It was time, Morgan emphatically implored, for Archie to be a leader. The team was his—*now*.

Archie responded: facing a bigger, faster, stronger squad, Archie—for the first time in his young life—rose to the moment. He flung passes down the field with pinpoint accuracy and slipped past defenders as if he were slathered in bacon grease. Watching from the sidelines, standing by himself in his straw hat and double-pocketed work shirt, Buddy quickly realized that his boy had the makings of a special player. Buddy never showered Archie with praise—his parenting style was more tough love than show love—but now even the old man cracked a smile as he watched his son dazzle the home crowd by throwing two touchdown passes and running for another.

But Archie's efforts weren't enough: Cleveland won the game 35–21. After the final whistle blew Morgan still was upset with the Cleveland coach. As the two shook hands at midfield, a red-faced Morgan told the coach, "You did everything you could to run up the score on us in Drew. You write it down: we're going to kick your behind next year."

The Drew players saw the emotion in their coach before retreating to their locker room. As was his custom, Morgan turned off the lights and said a prayer in the dark with his boys. As Morgan spoke, he heard a few kids sniffling. He turned on the lights: three seniors were sobbing.

Archie told Buddy about the tears in the dark locker room. That evening Buddy walked over to Morgan's house. "The whole town has heard about the prayer meeting," Buddy said. "My boy will be there for whatever you want him to do. You want him to run track, lift weights, or whatever you want he will do. My boy will be there."

———

In the spring, when his afternoon baseball practices were over, Archie would walk over to the track to meet with Morgan. The runners had long since scattered, but Archie would spend about an hour a day one-on-one with Morgan, performing various sprints. Even after Morgan left, as the sun bled across the Western horizon, spreading its last light over the Delta, Archie would continue to run in the twilight. From across the street, Buddy could see the silhouette of his boy working to improve his speed.

For the first time in his life, Archie started lifting weights, focusing on increasing his arm strength and his leg strength and thickening his upper body. During the summer before Archie's junior year, Morgan hung an old rubber tire from one of the rusted goalposts on the Drew High football field. He then strung a volleyball net behind the tire. Morgan instructed Archie to throw balls through that tire from every angle—and every yardage—on the field.

As always, Archie obeyed his coach. "A lot of kids I have to tell them to do something seventeen times before they do it," Morgan told Buddy. "But not Archie. Once is all he needs."

Archie would lug a bag full of footballs onto the field, and, alone, he'd fire one after the next at the rubber tire. At different hours in the day—early morning, mid-afternoon, late in the evening—Morgan would drive by the field and see his quarterback throwing balls by himself. The coach soon realized he'd never come across anyone like this Archie Manning kid.

At the beginning of Archie's junior year—after hours spent on the track, in the weight room, and on the field with his rubber-tire receiver—Morgan was confident that Archie was going to be one of the state's top quarterbacks. But in the third game of the 1965 season, as Archie fought to gain a few extra yards on a run, a defender smashed into his left side just as Archie was falling to the ground. Archie's left arm snapped like a twig. His season ended then and there.

Buddy drove his son to the doctor to have the arm set. Concerned about Archie's mounting injuries—in eighth grade he'd broken his ankle, in ninth grade he'd broken his right arm, and now in eleventh grade he'd broken his left arm—Buddy wondered aloud if Archie should quit playing football. He asked, "Son, is it worth it?"

Archie turned to his dad and explained how much he loved the game, the camaraderie of being on a team, and the rush of testing himself against others. "Yes, Dad," Archie said. "It's well worth it." The rewards of playing football, to young Archie's way of thinking, outweighed the risks, no matter how high the risks.

In Drew, Archie's health was a topic of conversation from the soda-fountain counter in the five-and-dime store to the booths in the coffee shop. Archie was Drew's favorite son, and the locals worried that his next hit on the football field could be his last. Throughout Sunflower County he was now known as the "red-headed, freckle-faced boy with brittle bones."

For the remainder of his junior season, Archie stood next to his coach during practices and games, his arm in a cast. Archie learned as much as possible from Morgan, continuing to see the game through his coach's eyes, paying close attention to what Morgan was focusing on during plays. Archie also became the team's number one cheerleader. After Drew upset rival Cleveland 20–14 late in the season, Archie, outfitted in a thick winter coat, jumped around more than anyone else on the sideline.

Before his senior year, Archie had played in just a dozen high school football games, and none of those twelve games ended in a Drew victory. But Archie oozed athletic potential. In track, as a junior, he ran sprints and a 440-yard leg on the mile relay. In baseball he hit .425 and showed enough of a Major League arm at shortstop that a scout for the Braves wanted to sign him out of high school. And in basketball he averaged over 20 points a game.

Paul Pounds replaced Gerald Morgan as the Drew football coach before Archie's senior year. The new coach moved in to a house next door to the Mannings, and Buddy told him all about his son. Pounds was impressed. He believed if Archie could continue to gain muscle and weight, he had the natural tools to be a starting college quarterback in the Southeastern Conference.

"This might surprise you, but I think you're college material," Pounds told Archie. "I think you're good enough to get a scholarship." But Archie was a risk to college recruiters. Not only did he play in the backwater town of Drew, but he also had never led his team to a single victory. Plus, he couldn't stay on the field.

The summer before his senior year Archie worked as a bricklayer in Drew—hauling and laying bricks, concrete blocks, and stones—and the hard labor further solidified his upper body. At the team's first preseason practice he stood 6'2" and weighed 170 pounds. He felt like he was in the best shape of his life.

To help keep his quarterback healthy, Pounds didn't play Archie on defense, where during his junior year he had roamed the secondary as a defensive back. Drew had only twenty-five players on its roster—Archie was one of two boys who didn't play both ways—and the Eagles were considered an underdog in every game they played in 1967.

Drew opened the season at home. Pounds entrusted his quarterback to call the offensive plays, and the coach emphasized to Archie that he should use his feet as much as his arm. After the opening kickoff, Archie loped onto the field in his bowlegged gait.

Archie repeatedly called his favorite two plays: sprint-out to his left and sprint-out to his right. He flung tight spirals to his receivers down the field on some downs; he tucked the ball in his arm and ran on others, juking and faking out defenders as he threaded his way up the field. There was something seductive about the way Archie played. With his freewheeling style and improvisation, he floated across the field like jazz notes. His ability to evade tacklers was straight out of a Drew sandlot. It was only one game, but Archie had enchanted the home crowd like no one ever had in the history of Drew football. The Eagles handily won the game.

Midway through the season Tom Swayze, the Ole Miss baseball coach who also recruited football players, and Roy Stinnett, a graduate assistant on the Rebel football staff, drove to Grenada, Mississippi, the site of Drew's second game, to scout Manning.

"We went over to see him on a Monday night," Swayze told a reporter after his trip. "They'd postponed the game Friday and when we got there Grenada had Drew down 12–0. But before the half Archie ran and passed for two touchdowns and two extra points. We were apprehensive about his physical makeup. He weighed only about 160 pounds, and he'd had so many injures in previous years. We were concerned about his durability but we could see he had the prerequisites we were looking for—speed, quickness, balance, an adequate throwing arm, and he was a real driver. I already knew about his grade point average. It was a 94 or 95 in four years in high school."

On the last day of the 1966 season Drew played rival Cleveland. Before the game the seniors from both squads were asked to come to midfield for the coin toss. Twenty-eight boys from Cleveland marched to the referee; four players from Drew stepped forward. Yet with Archie leading the way, the Eagles won the game 18–14 to finish the season with a 5-5 record, the school's best in more than two decades. As soon as time ran out in the fourth quarter, the Drew fans surged onto the field, surrounding Archie, slapping him on his shoulder pads in congratulations. Nearly fifty years later some fans would say it was the greatest moment in the history of Drew football.

In Archie's final three years Drew went 7-21-2. Archie had played only one full season of high school football, but three schools—Ole Miss, Mississippi State, and Tulane—saw enough ability in him to put out feelers to Archie, sending low-level assistants to Drew to see if Archie would be interested in accepting a scholarship.

The mayor of Drew even got involved in Archie's recruitment. One winter afternoon Mayor William Williford—better known as Snake—called Archie with an odd request. "I need you," the mayor said. "Somebody over in Greenwood has stolen a car and he's kidnapped two policemen, and they're heading our way."

Archie told the mayor that he had a basketball game in a few hours.

"Don't worry," Williford replied, "this shouldn't take long."

Minutes later Snake, who had flown B-29 bombers in World War II and dropped explosives on mainland Japan, pulled up to the Manning house in a police cruiser. The mayor also served as the third "emergency" member of Drew's police force, and now he and Archie blazed down Highway 49 to the outskirts of town to wait for the kidnappers to arrive.

The two parked on the side of the highway. With a machine gun resting on his lap and words crackling on the police radio that updated the location of the kidnappers—"They've passed Ruleville"—Snake talked about Mississippi State. For half an hour, he detailed how special Starkville was and told Archie he could be the king of the campus and of the town if he committed to play quarterback for the Bulldogs. Finally, it hit Archie: Snake, a charmer, was putting on the hard sell for Mississippi State, where he had earned a degree from in the 1930s.

It was Archie's first experience with a zealous alum trying to win the heart and the signature of a recruit. Years later, he would tell this tale to two other high school quarterbacks who shared his last name, a warning about the category-five craziness of college football recruiting in the Deep South.

Mississippi State pursued Archie with the most fervor—in both football and basketball.

In the first five basketball games of his senior year, Archie looked like a Division I player. His textbook-perfect jump shot barely rustled the net from 20 feet, and his quick first step propelled his drives to the basket. He averaged about 30 points a game.

Mississippi State basketball coach Joe Dan Gold traveled to Drew to check out Archie. Only twenty-five-years-old, Gold already was a hoops legend in the Magnolia State: from 1960 to '63, as a 6'5" forward, he helped the Bulldogs win or share three SEC titles. He also had gained national attention when, in 1963, he shook the hand of Loyola player Jerry Harkness before their NCAA tournament game, the first time a Mississippi State basketball team had played against African-American players. The photograph of Gold and Harkness locking hands appeared in newspapers from New York to California.

Now Gold sat in the Drew gymnasium, his eyes trained on Archie. Just seconds into the game, Archie drained his first shot, filling him with confidence. *Oh man,* Archie thought, *I'm really going to show him something.* Archie believed, just as sure as he would be in church on Sunday, that he was about to author another stellar performance.

Then Archie unspooled his next shot—it clanked off the rim. Then he hoisted another brick, and another, and another. Frustrated, Archie started slapping the arms of opposing players after each miss. He picked up one foul, then two, then three. With four minutes left in the first half—and having scored only two points—Archie fouled out.

Dejected, Archie spoke to Gold after the game. Archie told the coach that he appreciated him flying all the way to Drew, but he didn't need to come back. That sorry performance of his had sealed a decision for Archie: he wasn't going to play basketball in college. The two shook hands—Archie, chin up, looked the coach in the eyes—and parted ways. Gold left the building thinking that Archie may be the politest, most considerate young man he'd ever met.

Though basketball was no longer in his future, Archie still considered signing with Mississippi State, the school his father quietly favored because their squad was a "farmers' team." For his recruiting visit to Starkville, Archie stepped onto a plane for the first time in his life. He was chaperoned around campus with other prospective recruits, every one of them in wide-eyed wonder. Riding in the van back to the Starkville airport after the visit, Archie sat with seven other high school players. All seven had pledged to play for State, but Archie didn't cave to the peer pressure. He still wanted to check out that other state school, in Oxford.

For as long as he could remember, Archie had been enamored with Ole Miss. He went to weekend dances in towns across the Delta to hear a band called the Gordian Knot, whose lead singer was Jim Weatherly, a former star quarterback for the Rebels.

Weatherly, who eventually wrote "Midnight Train to Georgia" for Gladys Knight and the Pips, was cool personified to teenagers in Drew. But there was more drawing Archie's eyes to Oxford: his athletic hero was former Ole Miss quarterback Charlie Conerly. After playing for the New York Giants from 1948 to '61, Conerly appeared in ads as the Marlboro Man. In Archie's imagination, as he listened to him lead the Giants on the radio, Conerly glowed in the dark. The thought of playing on the same college field as his idol was the stuff of Archie's boyhood reveries.

Roy Stinnett, the Rebels' graduate assistant who had watched Archie play in person earlier in the year, stayed in touch with the Manning family. More than any other coach, Stinnett simply liked the way Archie threw the ball, how it flew off his hand and how it could spin down the field with accuracy and power. Stinnett invited the Mannings to Oxford to see the campus.

Father and son arrived one December evening to watch an Ole Miss basketball game. Then they were escorted to the football offices. It was nearing ten p.m., and Archie figured they'd get a tour and then head back home. But then Archie, Buddy, and their escort turned a corner and there they were: the entire Rebel coaching staff, including head coach Johnny Vaught, smiling at the Mannings.

For several minutes, Vaught told Archie about Ole Miss, explaining how he could fit in and help the Rebels win football games. Archie hung on his every word, saying "yes sir" over and over as Vaught spoke. The Rebels were recruiting eight quarterbacks, but one of the assistant coaches told Archie and his dad that a few of those signal callers might get lost in the shuffle and wind up changing positions. Leaving the offices that night, Archie was virtually certain that he would play at Ole Miss.

But once he was home, doubt marched into his mind like an invading army. Archie kept thinking about those seven other quarterbacks Vaught was attempting to sign, seven either all-state or all-conference. Small-school Archie felt like a long shot, a country kid who perhaps didn't belong with the blue bloods at Ole Miss. He wondered if he should attend a school that would have less competition at quarterback. He didn't know what to do.

On an early December night, Buddy heard Archie crying in his bedroom. Concerned, Buddy walked to the doorway of the bedroom and asked, "What's wrong?"

Lying on his bed, Archie slowly sat up. He didn't want to talk, didn't want to unleash more pent-up emotion and discuss the swirling dilemma in his head. It wasn't in Archie's nature to burden others—he believed in solving his own problems, just as his dad did. But now, at this defining crossroads in his young life, he needed his father's help. He told his dad, "I don't know what to do. They've signed all those quarterbacks up there. I don't know if I can make it."

"Son, don't let that worry you," Buddy said. "They wouldn't want you at Ole Miss if they didn't think you could play. You're getting ready for the four most important years of your life. If you have made up your mind that's where you want to go, you shouldn't change it."

Deep down, Archie had wanted to go to Ole Miss. Just a few months earlier he had ridden a bus eighty miles to Oxford for High School Day. As the bus rolled along Highway 3, Archie memorized the names of the players printed in the Ole Miss football program, imagining how his own name would appear on its pages. His heart and his mind always favored Ole Miss, and now his father had told him precisely what he needed to hear, that he should trust his instincts and follow his gut to Oxford, no matter who was on the Rebel roster.

That validation from Buddy was all Archie needed to reach his final verdict.

———

On the first weekend in December, Archie phoned Roy Stinnett
and shared the news: he planned to sign with Ole Miss on December 10, the first day high school recruits could scribble their names
on national letters of intent. Stinnett was overjoyed. Like Archie,
he was from a small Delta town—Clarksdale—and he loved it
when Delta boys came to Oxford. It was Stinnett's experience
that players from this part of the country were tough-minded and
would do virtually anything to win. Archie, the coach believed,
was going to be the next big thing to rise from small-town Mississippi.

December 10 fell on a Saturday. That weekend Drew High
played in a basketball tournament in Clarksdale. Feeling liber-
ated, Archie dominated on the hardwood, controlling the ebb and
flow of the games with his expert dribbling, deft passing, and
long-range marksmanship. Drew won a game on Thursday, then
another Friday, and then yet another on Saturday morning. Archie
drew more fouls in these games than he had all season.

That evening Archie led his team to another win as Drew—the
smallest school in the field—won the tournament. Archie couldn't
remember the last time he had taken so many free throws. At the
trophy presentation Archie flashed a devilish smile at the referee
with the quick whistle: none other than Roy Stinnett.

Later that night Archie met with Stinnett and signed his letter.

For the first time, Archie experienced a perk of being an SEC
football player.

The note arrived in the Mannings' mailbox on December 14,
1966.

Dear Archie:

I would like to take this opportunity to tell you how happy we are that you have decided to attend the University of Mississippi and participate in our athletic program. We believe you to be an outstanding individual, anxious to excel, both in academics and athletics. . . . May I wish for you and your parents a most happy holiday season.

Sincerely yours,
John H. Vaught

The term "Ole Miss" dates back to before the Civil War. In the antebellum South, slaves often called the wife of the plantation owner the "Old Miss" (her daughters were known as "Young Misses"). The state university of Mississippi had an unmistakable link to slavery, and the school had felt under siege from civil rights groups for years when Archie signed his letter of intent.

At Drew, Archie had never played against African-American players, either in football or basketball. In his junior year, after looking at a potential matchup in the district tournament, it appeared that the Drew basketball team was going to face a team with black players. A few of the fathers of the Drew kids told their sons that, if they advanced, they would be forbidden to play. Archie asked his dad what he should do.

"When you started sports, the only thing I ever told you was whatever you go out for, don't quit," Buddy said. "Not playing in that game would be quitting, wouldn't it." Drew didn't advance to the tournament, but Archie had learned a valuable lesson from his father: on the fields of play—and in life—always be fair and just.

Archie had been one of the first white kids to welcome seven black children from a family named Carter when the school system at Drew was integrated in 1965. The oldest, Ruth, was Archie's classmate. He felt sorry for her, especially as other white kids threw spitballs at her and called her derogatory names. But Archie was one of the few at Drew High to talk to Ruth, to be seen with her. Archie didn't have strong feelings about African Americans—they were simply members of the community to him, just like the whites in town. But his heart silently ached when the scared-stiff Carters ate their school lunches on the gym steps while all the white kids were in the cafeteria. The Carter house in Drew was eventually shot up with bullets. No one was hurt, but it underscored the high risk of blacks attending a white school in the segregated South in those days.

Archie was a proud self-described member of the Old South, but he wasn't bigoted. He didn't, however, care for the "outside agitators" who traveled to Drew to help the local blacks register to vote. He described the long-haired college kids who volunteered to fight Jim Crow laws as "beatniks." And, like most locals, he wished that outsiders would keep to their own business and let Drew solve its own problems.

Archie pledged his commitment to Ole Miss at a critical moment. Mississippi was generally known for two things at the time: for producing the prettiest ladies in the land—in 1959 Magnolia State native Mary Ann Mobley was named Miss America; the following year another young woman from Mississippi, Lynda Lee Mead, was awarded the crown—and for its profound racial divides. In the summer of 1965 alone nearly forty black churches had been torched to the ground in Mississippi.

With much of Mississippi burning—and with so much of the nation looking at the state with scorn—Southerners were desperate for a hero. They wanted someone to remind them of their own greatness, someone whose triumphs could give them all validation, someone who would not just be admired but loved, someone they all could point to with pride and say, *Look at what he can do—and we can do—better than the rest of the nation.*

They didn't know it yet, but they were looking for Archie.

CHAPTER 4

=

The Redheaded Show-off

Philadelphia, Mississippi. Spring 1967.

The four cars rumbled south out of Drew on Highway 49, cruising through the flats of the Delta. It was a March weekend in 1967, and the Drew basketball team headed to Philadelphia, Mississippi, for the regional state playoffs.

The cavalcade snaked through the small towns of Greenwood and Kosciusko, traveling 130 miles until they pulled into Philadelphia, a town of seven thousand where three years earlier Ku Klux Klan members had murdered three civil rights activists. The barbaric act—a lynch mob had watched as the three were killed in a remote spot in the woods, and their bodies were buried in an earthen dam—was a touchstone moment in rallying nationwide support for the passage of the Voting Rights Act in 1965.

The boys from Drew knew the recent history of Philadelphia. After checking in to the Benwalt Hotel, where the players retrieved their mattresses from a storage closet, the team traveled a few miles outside Philadelphia to the Old Jolly Farm, the site where the bodies of the civil rights workers had been discarded and hidden under a red-clay dam. It was also where Cecil Ray Price, a deputy sheriff in Neshoba County and one of the mob's ringleaders, said to his fellow Klansmen, "You've struck a blow for the white man. Mississippi can be proud of you. You've let those agitating outsiders know where this state stands."

For Archie and the other kids, it was a chilling experience, seeing the place that had been the cauldron of so much hate. It also was a stark reminder of the racial unrest that still percolated in Mississippi. Just weeks earlier white supremacists had murdered Wharlest Jackson, a thirty-six-year-old NAACP leader, with a car bomb in Natchez, Mississippi.

Later that evening the Drew High basketball team returned to the Benwalt Hotel, located just feet away from the jail in which the three civil rights activists—James Chaney, Andrew Goodman, and Michael Schwerner—were held before they were slain. That night the sleep of many of the boys was visited by nightmares.

After winning their first game in the tournament, Paul Pounds, Drew's coach, took his boys to a movie at the local theater house. Pounds wanted his players to relax before their semifinal matchup with Philadelphia, a longtime state power in basketball. Pounds warned his players that the home crowd would be whipped into a boiling froth, and that fans standing on the sidelines of the court might try to interfere when the players were inbounding the ball. Pounds emphasized the need to be composed at all times, no matter the circumstances, and play heady basketball. Archie listened carefully to it all.

From the opening tip, Archie dominated the game. Dribbling

the ball up the court, he'd slash to the bucket and hit driving lay-ups or stop outside the key and put up long-range rainbows that barely stirred the net. From start to finish, he was oblivious to the screaming voices in the wooden bleachers. In one of the biggest upsets of the season, Drew won.

The locals were crestfallen. To protect the Drew players and coach from the upset Philadelphia fans, highway patrolmen escorted them on their walk from the gym back to the Benwalt Hotel. But the sight of the officers didn't stop Philadelphians from heckling the players through the car windows as they drove by. Some even tossed 7 Up bottles at the boys from Drew.

A young woman named Olivia Williams—a senior at Philadelphia—reared back and threw a bottle in the direction of Archie. Olivia couldn't remember the last time she was so upset with an opposing player who, in her eyes, was nothing more than a cocky redheaded hotshot.

The next day Olivia, a big sports fan, went with her dad to watch Drew play Leland High in the finals of the regional tournament. The winner would earn a spot in the state finals in Jackson.

Both teams froze the ball, simply holding it for the last shot at the end of each quarter. When Drew had possession, Archie dribbled around the court like a one-man showman, his long hair glistening in sweat as he dribbled behind his back and ran in circles. Olivia now thought he was *really* the biggest show-off she'd ever seen. Drew lost 4–2 when Leland's Peanut Horton made a late shot, and no one in the gymnasium was happier than Olivia Williams.

Olivia cheered loudly as the players walked off the court. Archie didn't cast a glance in her direction. But soon, Olivia Williams would command Archie's full attention.

———

Voted the class president at the start of the year, Archie had one more competition left in high school: the intellectual fight to become the class valedictorian.

Archie was pragmatic about protecting his grade-point average. He avoided subjects that he viewed as potential grade-busters—he stayed away from chemistry and physics—and enrolled in classes that required little homework, allowing him to spend as much time as he needed practicing football, basketball, baseball, and track. (He wound up earning fifteen letters at Drew.)

A classic overachiever, Archie was ultracompetitive about his grades. He never showed up for class unprepared—he considered not finishing his homework an Old Testament sin, a sentiment sternly reinforced by Buddy—and, when called on, he typically had the correct answer at the ready. It surprised none of his teachers or friends or his parents that, once the final grades were tallied, Archie had bested every other student at Drew and was named class valedictorian. That was, his mom told friends, Archie's greatest victory.

After graduation Archie pushed himself hard all summer. He worked for a local bricklayer, but carved out time to lift weights and throw passes to anyone he could convince to be on the receiving end of them. He still considered himself a genuine underdog—Johnny Vaught didn't even bother to visit Archie in Drew—and Archie knew the only thing he could control was his preparation. So under a tar-bubbling Mississippi sun he either laid bricks to increase his strength or threw passes on the football field across the street from his house.

In late July, Archie traveled to Jackson, Mississippi, for the annual Mississippi High School All-Star football game. Archie wasn't expecting to play more than a few series for the North squad, if at all: the starting quarterback, Bob White, was a high school all-American. White also had played for the coach of the North team, Bob Tyler, at Meridian High.

But early in the first quarter, a defender hit White in the knee. The quarterback, who also was heading to Oxford to play for Ole Miss, stayed on the ground, writhing in pain. Archie quickly loosened up on the sideline. Up until this moment, Archie— a country boy from Drew who hoped he wouldn't get cut from the Rebel freshman squad in a few weeks—didn't know how good he could be. He was about to find out.

Archie cantered onto the field. More than twelve thousand fans filled Memorial Stadium. Archie had never seen so many people in a grandstand before—heck, he'd never seen so many people in one *place* before—and his pulse quickened with excitement. Lining up behind center, he called out the signals. This was his moment of reckoning—could he play with these big-town guys who were all big-time recruits? He swallowed hard as the ball was hiked to him. But he fumbled the snap. In his first chance to prove he belonged on this field, he literally dropped the ball.

But Archie quickly settled down. He sprayed frozen-rope throws all over the field, fitting the ball through tight holes in the defense to complete passes. He was the most elusive player on either roster, able to avoid oncoming rushers with his now quicker feet, which suddenly seemed as light and lively as Fred Astaire's in the ballroom. He threw four touchdown passes to wide receiver George Ranager—who had committed to Bear Bryant at Alabama—and he ran for another score. Subbing for the injured White, Archie led the North team to a 65–33 win over the South squad and earned MVP honors.

The score more than doubled the old record for most points in the game, set in 1954 when the South beat the North 21–20. Archie completed 13 of 25 passes for 227 yards. In a span of about two hours, he transformed himself from an overmatched small-town player who fumbled his first snap to a young man who looked like the best player on the field.

Wobble Davidson watched from the grandstands. Davidson, Ole Miss's freshman coach, didn't know much about this Manning kid until this afternoon, but now he liked what he saw. He decided that once Archie arrived in Oxford, he would give him a red jersey to wear. This was significant: the starters on the freshman team wore red jerseys, the second teamers donned blue, and the third were outfitted in white. Archie may have been the biggest sleeper of the eight quarterbacks in his recruiting class, but Davidson's eyes told him that he deserved the first shot at the starting position.

As Archie walked toward the locker room, he felt like a new player. Confidence coursed through him like electricity. And now, for the first time, his dreams began to materialize more clearly, stretching further into the future than ever before. Maybe the game wouldn't be too big for him at Ole Miss. Maybe he had what it took to make it in college after all.

Olivia Williams, who had driven from Philadelphia with friends to watch the game, couldn't believe that this showboating boy from Drew had won MVP honors. Worse, she learned that he would be attending Ole Miss, where she was enrolling in a few weeks.

If she ever bumped into him in Oxford, my, how she planned to give him a piece of her mind.

CHAPTER 5

───

The Cerebral Signal Caller

Oxford, Mississippi. Summer 1967.

Their boy was leaving.

The fresh-faced eighteen-year-old, lanky and scarecrow thin, packed his clothes into a pair of suitcases. He had accomplished so much in Sunflower County—he was a sports hero to little kids in Drew, a favorite of his Sunday school instructors, and a dream student to his high school teachers—but now it was time for him to leave home. Archie was excited and nervous—excited about the possibilities that lay ahead, nervous about venturing into the unknown.

Before Buddy drove Archie to Oxford to begin the rest of his life, the father sat his son down for one final talk. Buddy had a parting piece of advice he wanted to hand off to Archie, and Buddy hoped that his son would carry it with him for the rest of his life. "I don't care how successful you are in football and baseball," Buddy said. "I want you to be a nice guy."

Archie nodded his head and replied, "Yes, sir."

Buddy's words swirled in Archie's head the entire eighty-mile drive to Oxford. *Be a nice guy.* They stayed with the son as he hugged his father goodbye and watched him drive away and disappear into the Delta.

On August 1, 1967, a few days after Buddy returned from Oxford, a letter arrived in the mailbox at the Manning house. It was from Jay Boland, the basketball coach at Drew who had mentored Archie for three years. Boland, overcome with pride, felt moved to tell the Mannings that the best was yet to come for their son.

"Mr. and Mrs. Manning, you certainly deserve most of the credit for Archie's success," the typed note read. "Archie, you always remember that. The headaches and turmoil you all went through must have been tremendous. Mrs. Manning, I think you will remember me telling you that there would be disappointments. I say, 'Congratulations' from the bottom of my heart to a most deserving family. Archie, the 'All American' name is not beyond reach. May the Lord bless and keep you. Very Truly Yours, Coach Boland."

During the first football practices in the sticky heat of August, the Ole Miss coaches noticed something different about Archie. Once the final whistle blew and the sweat-soaked players retreated to the air-conditioned cool of the locker room and the showers, Archie always lingered behind. He'd grab a receiver and, with his right knee on the ground, throw one pass after the next to him for a solid thirty minutes. Small streams of perspiration would flow from underneath his helmet and dribble down his face, but the

6'3" spindly kid who weighed all of 170 pounds was determined to strengthen his arm.

Archie also impressed the coaches with his ability to throw harder while running to his left than other right-handed quarterbacks did when moving to their right. Archie was more natural out of the pocket than in it, his accuracy better when his legs were churning as opposed to being set. Those were two of the freakiest things the Ole Miss offensive coaches had ever seen—no other quarterback in Oxford had ever possessed those characteristics—and the staff began calculating how to use Archie's unique gifts to their advantage.

Freshman coach Wobble Davidson ran his players like he was training them to become Navy SEALs. But he was testing their mettle, gauging who had desire and fight and who wanted to be on the varsity the most. There were only so many spots available on the varsity roster, and it was Davidson's mandate to thin the herd. So he ran his boys up and down the field, and then he ran them some more. In the heavy late-summer heat the pounds dropped off Archie's frame.

But at every whistle that signaled another sprint, Archie ran like his spot on the team depended on him finishing first. He was named the starter at quarterback for the freshman squad in their season opener against the LSU junior varsity team in Oxford. Archie confided to a few buddies on the team before the game that he was nervous and unsure if he belonged.

Right away he played like a quarterback who had no confidence. He overthrew open receivers and misread his blockers on running plays. He played safety on defense, and on one play he gambled and was completely outclassed by a Tiger receiver, who scored a touchdown. Davidson was furious with Archie. On the sideline the coach—at the top of his lungs—excoriated his player, telling Archie that he was a lost cause out there on the field. The final humiliation of the day for Archie was that he played with an oversized helmet, and whenever he dove to tackle an LSU player— or when a Tiger defender drove him into the ground when he was playing quarterback—his helmet painfully dug into the bridge of his nose. By halftime Archie had suffered a cut and his face was a bloody mess.

The Tigers beat the Rebels 28–0. After the game the coaches let the Ole Miss freshmen go home for the weekend. Davidson asked all the players to shine a spotlight on their souls and ask themselves if they really wanted to commit themselves to playing college football in the SEC.

Archie returned to Drew. He never contemplated quitting, but he wasn't anxious to return to Oxford either. On Sunday afternoon, when the time arrived for Archie to head back to school, his dad asked, "You ready to go?"

Archie thought about it for a moment. His worn-out body was telling him he wasn't ready to go, but his spirit was still willing— barely. Finally he told Buddy, "I guess so."

It was the last time in his college career that Archie would ever hesitate when it came to anything related to football.

She cast her charms over Archie their freshman year at Ole Miss. He was strolling across campus with a mutual friend named Jim Poole when she drove up beside them in her new white Ford LTD. Olivia Williams took one look at Archie and immediately remembered that he was that cocky, red-haired football and basketball player from Drew.

"Where you heading, Jim?" Olivia asked.

"The drugstore."

"Get in, I'll drive you."

"Both of us?"

"Sure."

Jim introduced Archie to Olivia. "Oh, I know who *you* are," she said. "You're the one who beat Philadelphia."

Tall, thin, and possessing a wide and sweet smile that made men weak in the knees, Olivia was a classic Southerner, a softly pretty Scarlett O'Hara come to life. She grew up in Philadelphia, the daughter of the town's wealthiest man, Cooper Williams. Olivia's father had played football at Ole Miss—he was a walk-on—and after he graduated he flourished in business. He owned a Standard Oil distributorship, a cotton gin, and a family country store named Williams Brothers, which had been featured in *National Geographic* in 1939 and was cited for selling more types of items—groceries, needles, overalls, farm equipment, collared shirts, horse collars—than any other general store in America.

In the male-dominated universe of Philadelphia in the 1940s, Olivia's mother—a calm, serene woman named Frances Williams—was a mold-breaker. She became the town's first licensed female pilot and was an all-state basketball player in high school. Olivia's brother was a junior on the Rebel basketball team. Sports had been central to Olivia all her life, and she could discuss athletics the way most sorority girls at Ole Miss talked about makeup.

Olivia rarely wore the same dress twice. Starting at age thirteen, she drove a new car practically every year. She could sweet-talk her father into buying her anything, usually without hesitation. At Philadelphia High she never acted like her upper-class status made her better than anyone else, and she was voted Most Polite. But it wasn't her wealth that captivated Archie; it was that smile, those soft brown eyes, and her magnetic personality. She was enthralling. Archie was taken with her immediately.

Archie hoped to meet Olivia Williams again. A sports fanatic, she would watch carefully this boy from Drew throughout the autumn, keeping her distance yet increasing her interest.

Seven days after losing to LSU, the Ole Miss freshman team played Alabama, the measuring-stick program of the SEC. Archie stood out. From his safety position on defense, he intercepted three passes. He anticipated where the Crimson Tide quarterback was going to throw the ball before it flew from his hand—Archie read the quarterback's eyes—and his interceptions were the key plays in Ole Miss's 21–2 victory.

The next week against Vanderbilt, Archie again started at quarterback. Wild and playing like he had no script, he'd take off on a scramble against the Commodores, juke a few defenders, run circles in the backfield, then stop in his tracks, square his shoulders, and fire a completion down the field through a zone defense. Vanderbilt was touted by many reporters to have its best freshman class in history, but Archie was a force of nature out there on the field, running and passing for a total of eight touchdowns in the Rebels' 80–8 win, the most points the Ole Miss freshmen had ever scored. Johnny Vaught, watching from the sideline, couldn't take his eyes off Archie, Vaught's mind raced with possibilities. This was the most exciting young player he had ever seen.

The final game of the freshman season was against rival Mississippi State, Buddy's favorite team. Archie was again the best player on the field, improvising and running around in the backfield before flicking the ball to a receiver for a completion. When the Bulldog defense was about to pin him down, he used his 4.7 40 speed to escape from harm's way. It was arresting to watch— Vaught was falling fast for Archie—and the Ole Miss freshman team handily beat its rival. Buddy had driven to Oxford from

Drew for the game, and he beamed as he viewed the action. He never verbalized his feelings to Archie, but Buddy had raved about his son to the Ole Miss coaches, telling them how proud he was.

In four games on the freshman team Archie completed 30 of 55 passes for 7 TDs. He also intercepted 4 passes as a defensive back. After the season he lifted weights and gobbled down fattening foods—he especially loved banana cream pudding—and took every weight-gain supplement he could find. By March he'd gained 20 pounds, and his weight was up to 180 when spring practice began.

Playing against the older players for the first time in spring ball, Archie continued to grow as a quarterback. He had spent hundreds of hours studying the playbook over the winter, and now he knew the nuances of the offense almost as intimately as did the coaching staff. But it was what Archie did when plays broke down that convinced Vaught he had a once-in-a-generation quarterback on his Ole Miss roster. Three defenders could have Archie in their sights, and yet, somehow, he would spin, twist, juke, and break free.

Vaught also marveled at how quickly Archie could read defenses and instantaneously come up with ways to exploit their weaknesses. Soon the coach was so confident of his cerebral young quarterback that he allowed Archie to call about 95 percent of the plays, something Vaught had never allowed a sophomore quarterback to do. Archie had an uncanny ability to foretell—even at this stage of his young football life—what plays would work against a certain defense and in a given situation. And when Vaught would make a play call from the sideline, Archie could usually guess what it was going to be—based on the down, distance, and field position—before it was spoken into his ear. On the field, Archie was the ultimate extension of his coach.

By the end of spring practice Archie had come on so strong

that Vaught decided that in the fall he would start a true sophomore at quarterback for the first time since 1949. Vaught told
friends, "I've got a boy who's going to be better than all of them."
Vaught, who began coaching at Ole Miss in '47, even began telling reporters that Archie could be the best player he'd ever been
around. For now, Vaught reminded the reporters, that assessment
was off the record.

Late in the fall of his freshman year, Archie joined the Sigma Nu
fraternity with several of his teammates. One evening Sigma Nu
had a "swap" dance with the Delta Gamma sorority, where Olivia
Williams was a pledge. Archie, who hadn't seen Olivia since she
had given him a ride a few months earlier, asked her to dance. She
accepted his invitation. Afterward they talked about the one subject they both knew intimately: football.

Archie was as quiet as Olivia was talkative. He hung on her
every word—*be a nice guy,* his dad had said—as she chatted the
night away. Olivia was shocked to realize that Archie was actually
an introvert. She apologized for thinking he was an egotistical,
conceited athlete at Drew. Minute by minute, their rapport grew.

It didn't take Archie long to summon the courage to ask Olivia
for a date. Almost immediately Olivia called her father in Philadelphia.

"Hey, Daddy, guess who I'm going out with tonight?"

"Who?"

"Remember that show-off from Drew that beat us?"

"Archie Manning?"

"Yes. It looks like he might be Ole Miss's next varsity quarterback."

Her father couldn't contain his excitement. "When are you
gonna bring him home for dinner so we can approve?"

With no money to spare, Archie took Olivia to the campus library for their first date. That night they disappeared into each other's eyes. Olivia talked on and on, and Archie breathed in her every syllable. Walking out of the library that night, they were aglow in the blush of happiness. They would never be the same.

The quarterback had found his dark-eyed, 5'11" Southern belle.

Archie finished his classes in the spring and returned home to Drew for the summer of 1968. Vaught had given Archie a list of drills—labeled "quarterback basics"—to work on during the two months he was away from campus.

Vaught was a football fundamentalist. He believed that a player could reach his potential only after mastering the basics. And so he wrote in precise detail exactly what Archie had to do to become an elite quarterback.

On passing, Vaught instructed: "Grip the ball with fingers overlapping the laces slightly behind the middle of the ball. Grip firm but not hard, remember, fingers and not the palm should grip the ball. If you can push the index finger of your hand between your palm and the ball, you have the proper grip.

"You can control the ball with your fingers but not with the palm. When delivering the ball, the quarterback's action of transferring weight from back foot to front foot, leading with the front foot, and developing the follow through with the arm should be a rhythmical, fluid motion. Prior to the weight transfer, get the ball above the head by extending the throwing arm. The left hand can only guide the ball up part of the way. If you attempt to let the left hand guide the ball all of the way up, it will destroy the rhythm.

"After getting the ball up, attempt to coordinate the weight transfer and the 'darting technique' of throwing the ball. By attempting to throw the ball like you throw a dart, you emphasize finger control. The fingers are the last parts of the body to touch the ball. The fingers release the ball from the little finger to the index finger. Rotate the wrist away from the body. The index finger is the last finger to touch the ball and it is with this finger that you put RPMs on the ball.

"The sequence: Stand tall and balanced; ball high; step with the left foot and point with the left arm; dart the ball—put RPMs with fingers; follow through with right foot.

"Three common faults the passer must recognize. 1. Ball going high to target—Indicates early release by fingers. 2. Ball going low to target—Indicates late release by fingers. 3. Ball wobbly— Indicates inward rotation of wrist instead of outward rotation which allows finger control."

Archie read and reread these instructions. The words may as well have been engraved in the two stone tablets on Mount Sinai, the way they became absolute truths to Archie.

One day he would pass these etched-in-stone-worthy instructions down to his quarterback sons.

That summer, when he wasn't trying to master the art of throwing a football, Archie worked for a bricklayer again. From early in the morning until late in the afternoon, Archie laid bricks at Drew City Hall, which was nicknamed the Alamo because it didn't have any windows. Once the day's work was finished, Archie went home and lifted weights. Then he'd head outside and run circles around the high school track. His internal motor rarely stopped revving.

But then one afternoon, not long after Vaught had let it slip to a reporter that Archie would be his starting quarterback in the fall, a load of bricks fell on Archie's ankle. It swelled to the size of a baseball. He went to the town doctor, who wrapped it in a bandage.

That evening Archie hobbled gingerly into his house. When Buddy saw his boy and his ballooned ankle, he turned serious and concerned. Buddy knew that Archie was tabbed to become the first sophomore to start at quarterback at Ole Miss in twenty-two years, and he didn't want a freak injury to jeopardize his ability to play.

"What happened?" Buddy asked. "What'd you do? Are you all right?"

Buddy phoned Ole Miss wide-receivers coach Bob Tyler, who the next day chaperoned Archie to a clinic in Memphis for X-rays. The ankle wasn't broken; Archie would be healthy for preseason camp.

A group of cigarette-smoking, pen-wielding reporters arrived on the campus of Ole Miss a few weeks before the opening kickoff of the 1968 season. The SEC reporters bombarded Vaught with questions about the red-haired, freckle-faced sophomore he was planning to start at quarterback. Vaught told them that Archie Manning was going to be one of the best to ever play in Oxford. The skeptical writers thought Vaught was taking a big bite into the apple of hyperbole.

"How do you compare him with Joe Namath?" an Alabama writer asked.

Vaught refused to take the bait and make a comparison, then moved on to the next question. But deep down, he wanted to say that Archie was going to be even better than Namath.

Entering his twenty-second SEC season, Vaught tried to suppress his glowing feelings about Archie, but he couldn't help himself. In the preseason he confided to a Memphis reporter. "At this point Manning is ahead of any quarterback we've ever had," Vaught said. "Everything Manning does shows he is an athlete. He's a fine basketball player and a good defensive back. He has all the qualifications. He's a good runner, has good speed, and has the brains, vision, and leadership. . . . Manning is real strong on the option. He can size up the situation and act accordingly."

Vaught noted to reporters during their preseason swing through Oxford that Archie had hurt his foot while doing construction work in Drew over the summer. At first, Vaught said, the team thought it was broken, but it turned out to be only a bruise. Archie stayed off it about a week. "Everything is fine now, thank goodness," Vaught said.

Vaught explained that he had given his team a facelift. He had thirty-five sophomores on his varsity team and ten new starters on offense. He was going to play a freewheeling style of offense. He didn't say it, but the reason he was changing his approach from a three-yards-and-a-cloud-of-dust offense to a more vertical, pass-heavy style of football was because of Archie. "We are in the process of making a complete change in the variety of our offense," Vaught told reporters. "We will play a more diversified brand of football—and I do mean wide-open football. We will be lighter, faster, and hungrier."

On September 2—three weeks from the season opener against Memphis—Vaught gushed as though holding a royal flush as he spoke to reporters about Manning. "I'm finding it fun to coach again," he said. "It's been a long time."

On September 8, a reporter asked Vaught how he picked Manning, a kid whose high school team only won seven games in his three years playing on the varsity. "You had to consider what Manning had to go with—a team from a small town playing bigger teams," Vaught said. "The kid has athletic ability, the good arm, the movements. He was a great prep basketball player and that helped too. Every report we got was good—on his attitude, his ambition, his academics. I saw more ability in those freshman games he played. He's tall, he's fast. I'll say again, he has more ability than any sophomore I've coached and he's got good sense to go with it."

Archie tried not to read what his coach was saying about him, but he was aware of Vaught's great expectations. Before the first start of his career, on a warm summer afternoon in Oxford, Archie sat quietly in front of his locker reading the game program. Next to Archie was offensive lineman Skipper Jernigan, a fellow sophomore who also was making his first start on the varsity. Jernigan thumbed through the program when he stopped on a page that listed the biographical details of Memphis linebacker Joe Rushing.

"Look at this, Archie," Jernigan said, pointing to his program. "It says Joe Rushing is twenty-five years old. He's a Vietnam veteran, and he's married and has four children. He's going to be twenty-six in October. Do you realize that he was in the second grade when you and I were born?"

Not exactly the pep talk Archie needed. For several seconds he stared wide-eyed at the photo of Joe Rushing in the program. At that moment Jernigan didn't know if he'd ever seen a more nervous quarterback in his football life.

Minutes later Archie ran onto the field with his teammates, his heart pounding. Normally even-keeled in the most heated of moments, Archie's mouth grew dry when he looked up into the seats at Hemingway Stadium and saw some 30,000 in attendance. Vaught had riled up the fan base with his preseason comments about Archie, and now the fans were anxious to be seduced and dazzled by this youngster's play on the field. The pressure was on.

Archie struggled. In the first half he guided the Ole Miss offense—which featured seven sophomore starters—to only two first downs. Heading into the locker room for the fifteen-minute halftime break, the Rebels trailed 7–0. Worse, when Archie looked around, he saw that the defensive starters were bent over and gasping for air, bone-tired. The offensive players had barely broken a sweat.

Vaught told Archie to calm down, to not press, to not even think, to just play. Then early in the third quarter, it happened: the Manning magic show, for the first time in front of the Ole Miss crowd, officially debuted. Archie burst into the open field for a 44-yard run. He passed for one touchdown, then another. He capped the game by scoring on a quarterback sneak. Ole Miss won 21–7, and as Archie walked off the home field the crowd thundered its approval at their new star. Archie was named the SEC Back of the Week.

Five weeks later Ole Miss traveled to Baton Rouge to play eighth-ranked LSU, which was riding the wave of a six-game winning streak. Archie had led the Rebels to a 4-2 record, including wins over Alabama on October 5 (10–8) and Southern Miss on October 19 (21–13). In the three months since preseason practice began, he had grown increasingly close to Vaught. Archie told his coach how he used to listen to Ole Miss games on the radio when the Rebels were led by quarterback Jake Gibbs, and Vaught would regale Archie with stories about Gibbs and what it was like to coach against the likes of Alabama's Bear Bryant and Georgia Tech's Bobby Dodd.

Archie mentioned that he'd heard the Ole Miss–LSU game in 1959 and had his heart broken by Billy Cannon's punt return, and Vaught detailed what it was like to be there in person on that rainy night in the Bayou. Archie soaked in all the history, rapt. He could sit and listen for hours to his coach replay old games from memory, letting Vaught's words paint the pictures of long-ago touchdowns.

Five days before Vaught and his Rebels visited LSU, the coach took a few of his quarterbacks on a car ride across that campus. Vaught wanted his quarterbacks to visualize what it would be like to run onto the field in Death Valley in front of 69,000 screaming fans. "Boys, we're going to Tiger Stadium," Vaught said from behind the wheel. "We're going to play LSU. This is what college football is all about."

On the eve of the game, Ole Miss flew to Baton Rouge on two planes—the starters on one plane, the backups and equipment on the other. The second plane was delayed, so after the first plane landed, the players waited in the Baton Rouge airport. When a few Tiger fans spotted the Rebels, they immediately looked for Ole Miss's starting quarterback.

"Wheh's AWWW-che Mannin," one said in a thick Cajun accent. "Wheh's dat Ole Miss quawdeback, AWWWW-che Mannin?"

The next day Buddy listened to the game on the radio in his living room. He could close his eyes and imagine he was in Tiger Stadium with his son. Puffing away on one Chesterfield after the next, a constant string of smoke drifting from his lips, Buddy was a bundle of nerves and nicotine as LSU jumped to a 17–3 lead in the second quarter. Despite the fact that the Ole Miss team was undermanned, with three minutes to play in the fourth quarter, the Tiger lead was only 24–20 The Rebels took over possession at their own 24-yard line. As Archie jogged onto the field, the crowd was in full throat. The stadium literally shook.

Archie was a portrait of confidence as he spoke to his team in the huddle, telling them that this was their moment, their time, and—repeating what his coach had told him earlier in the week—that this was what college football was all about. Willing to take chances, Archie slung two passes into double coverage, each time fitting the ball into the hands of his receivers. He kept plays alive by running around in the backfield, stiff-arming defenders, then flicking passes downfield for completions.

During practices leading up to the game, Vaught had installed a sprint-out, run-pass option play for Archie, and the LSU defense couldn't stop it. With 45 seconds to play, Archie had moved the Rebels to LSU's 9-yard line. On second down Archie took the snap, ran to his left, then unleashed a pass to the left flat, but Tiger defensive back Craig Burns tipped the ball. For a moment, it appeared that LSU would intercept the pass and end the game. But the ball caromed into the arms of Ole Miss tailback Steve Hindman, who fell into the end zone. In living rooms across the state of Mississippi, where fans gathered to listen to the games in front of their radios, the Ole Miss faithful leaped out of their chairs. The Rebels won 27–24, and more mythology was added to the growing Manning legend.

Archie had broken single-game school records for pass attempts (40), completions (24), passing yards (345), and total offensive yards (362). He threw for two touchdowns and ran for one—a performance that earned Archie the SEC Back of the Week award and UPI's Sectional Player of the Week honors. After watching Archie's historical performance against LSU, the New Orleans Saints chief scout, Henry Lee Parker, said, "I'll take him right now."

Back in Drew, Buddy couldn't have been more proud. Listening to his son's heroics had transported him from the problems in his life, which were becoming more serious by the day.

Two weeks after engineering the comeback in Baton Rouge, Archie and the Rebels rode three buses into the hills of Tennessee to play the Volunteers on November 16 in Knoxville. Vaught instructed his quarterback to stay in the pocket in this game, to drop straight back and beat the defense with his right arm.

A swirling wind blew hard in Neyland Stadium, and it caused Manning's passes to flutter and wobble. He threw six interceptions in the 31–0 loss. After the game Vol linebacker Steve Kiner told reporters that this Archie kid was the most overrated quarterback he'd ever seen. "It's not so tough defending against Manning," Kiner said. "He'll tell you what he is going to do with his eyes. He looks where he's going to throw or send a runner."

It was the worst game of Archie's life. Years later, one of his sons dug through the Tennessee archives and discovered the film of that game. The son copied the film onto a videotape and mailed it to his father with a note. It read, "Dad, you were awful."

In 1968 there were only nine bowl games. Ole Miss was invited to play in the Liberty Bowl in Memphis against Virginia Tech.

It was a raw and blustery December afternoon in the River City. Archie put on a sweatshirt underneath his shoulder pads for warm-ups, but it hindered his throwing motion, so he took it off. Yet when he jogged out onto the field minutes before kickoff, he was struck with one thought: *I'm going to freeze to death*.

Olivia Williams hadn't missed a game all season. She and Archie had been inseparable, except for one argument they had following the Ole Miss–Mississippi State game, which had ended in a 17–17 tie, on November 30, two weeks after the loss to Tennessee. Olivia was continually impressed with Archie's ability to forget about what happened on the football field the minute he left the stadium—he could compartmentalize his life like no other young man she had ever met—but after tying the despised Bulldogs, Archie still felt the frustration wash over him when he talked to Olivia after the game.

Archie had been scheduled to have dinner with Olivia's family in Philadelphia that evening, but Olivia didn't appreciate Archie's frame of mind as they spoke. The two had a testy exchange and agreed that they would go their separate ways that night—Archie to Drew, Olivia to Philadelphia. The spat didn't last long, however; they made up a few days later, ending the last serious fight of their lives.

Now in Memphis, Olivia and her girlfriends hatched a plan: to stay warm during the Liberty Bowl, they would go shopping for a few hours and then return to the stadium near the end of the fourth quarter. They would greet Archie and the other players outside the locker room, and none of the players would know that they missed the game, which in the South was about as big of a deal as missing a Sunday sermon.

Archie's parents made the one-hundred-mile drive from Drew. To stay warm in the frigid stadium, Buddy pulled out a bottle of Jack Daniel's. Keeping his eyes on Archie down on the field, he took a few nips of the brown liquid. Buddy had suffered a mild stroke five years earlier. There weren't any obvious lingering effects, but he didn't have as much energy as he once did. In his younger days Buddy enjoyed hunting and, some nights, playing poker with his buddies. But since the stroke he just didn't have the stamina to go duck hunting or to stay up for late-night card games anymore. But nothing was going to stop him from seeing his son play in his first bowl game. Buddy told his friends that watching his kid play filled him with a kind of joy—so powerful yet indescribable—that he'd never experienced before.

Being in Memphis brought back happy memories for Archie. His older sister, Pam, had allergies growing up, requiring her to see a specialist doctor in Memphis. Archie would tag along with Pam and his mom, Sis, as they drove north on Highway 61. Little Archie counted down the miles until they reached the outskirts of the big city, where Sis would stop the car at a doughnut shop. Drew didn't have one, so getting fresh, warm doughnuts made the trip even more special for Archie.

After they visited the doctor's office, Sis would lead her kids to the Peabody Hotel, which was famous for its ducks in the lobby fountain. Back in the 1930s the general manager of the hotel, Frank Schutt, went on a hunting trip in Arkansas. When he returned to the hotel with a friend, they both were full of Jack Daniel's—and liquid courage. They thought it would be a hoot to place a few of their live duck decoys in the pristine Peabody fountain. A tradition was born. Little Archie always looked forward to seeing the Peabody ducks.

Buddy also took Archie to Memphis to watch basketball games. Father and son were far from close—Buddy kept his emotions to himself and he could be very demanding, especially when it came to Archie finishing the food on his plate—but the hours of sitting courtside at a college basketball game bonded the two like almost nothing else could. Archie, like most boys, was desperate for his father's approval, and maybe, his friends later wondered, that was why he pushed himself so hard, why he viewed every practice and workout session like it was the most important of his life. Archie always tried to please his father even though he handed out praise less often than a blue moon rose over Drew.

In spite of the chilly weather, 42,206 fans filled Memphis's Memorial Stadium, the largest crowd in the ten-year history of the Liberty Bowl. (The crowd ate 20,000 hot dogs, also a record, depleting the entire supply by the third quarter.) The curiosity about the red-haired quarterback from Drew was beginning to spike throughout the South. Buddy and Sis shivered in the December cold as Virginia Tech raced to a second-quarter 17–0 lead.

But then the curtain rose again on the Manning magic show. Following a failed onside kick by the Hokies, Archie led Ole Miss on a 51-yard drive that ended in a 21-yard touchdown pass to Hank Shows. Minutes later Archie threw a picture-perfect pass to Leon Felts for a 23-yard touchdown. Even in the cold, Archie's play was so fluid, his sense of anticipation so keen, it was as if he knew where the defenders—including a young Virginia Tech safety named Frank Beamer, who would become the head coach at Tech in 1987—were going to run even before they moved their legs.

On the first play of the second half, Ole Miss running back Steve Hindman sprinted 79 yards for a touchdown. For the rest of the game, Archie bled the clock with running plays and high-percentage passes. Ole Miss won 34–17.

After the final whistle blew, Archie met Olivia outside the locker room. She couldn't tell a fib to her boyfriend and keep a straight face, so she confessed that she and her girlfriends had spent the afternoon in the warmth of department stores, shopping and spending her father's money. Archie couldn't blame her; one of the things he hated most in life was the cold.

Archie signed a few autographs—the crowds waiting for him after games were steadily growing—and then he spoke to his parents. Buddy was silently proud of his only son. Archie had dazzled the entire crowd with his play, but no one was more impressed than Buddy, who could still remember throwing a ball around with his boy in their front yard in Drew when little Archie was barely out of diapers.

What memories they were—memories to last a lifetime.

This was the last game Buddy Manning would ever see his son play.

CHAPTER 6

A Storm Gathers

Drew. Summer 1969.

They were alone together, the father and his son, cruising along Highway 3 through the Mississippi countryside. In early August of 1969, Archie had just finished a summer-school session at Ole Miss and Buddy picked him up to come home. Archie planned to spend about two weeks in Drew before returning to Oxford for the start of fall practice.

What a pair they were, blazing through the backwoods on this summer afternoon. The father appeared so happy for his son, and for good reason. With each passing week of Archie's sophomore year, the frontiers of what was possible had expanded for Archie. What was unthinkable one week—setting, for instance, a school record for most yards in a game—became thinkable the next. On the field Archie had displayed long, sustained moments of grace, the kind that had never before been seen on the football fields in the Magnolia State. This caused Archie's popularity to spread across the South as if he were being blown by the wind. Yet he retained the small-town values of humility and gratitude that Buddy had taught him, and that filled Buddy with even more pride.

Buddy didn't tell his son that he loved him—it wasn't in his makeup to reveal the bedrock of his emotions—but Archie understood that his dad was his second-biggest fan, just behind his mom, who had attended every game in every sport that he had played since Archie could throw a ball. Buddy, at 5'6", had been a standout offensive lineman at Drew when he was a teenager, and now he was in awe of the athleticism of his son. He never imagined his boy would become the Ole Miss starting quarterback, much less an emerging folk hero.

But Buddy wasn't just proud of Archie's growing football achievements; he reveled in knowing that Archie was making his own way in the world, narrating his own compelling story, maturing into a man of substance. Archie was on the path to a college degree, and that was Buddy's top goal for his son.

And yet . . .

There were storm clouds gathering in Buddy's eyes that Archie couldn't see—that no one could see. Buddy was a workaholic; he had rarely seen the opening minutes of Archie's high school games because Buddy felt obligated to stay late at the shop. Buddy's job as manager of the farm machinery dealership in Drew had always seemed his top priority.

After Archie left home for school, Buddy's business deteriorated. More than ever, Buddy worried that he couldn't collect overdue payments for the farm equipment he loaned out. His customers—many of whom were his friends—weren't paying their bills, which in turn made it hard for Buddy to cover his family's expenses. Buddy just didn't have it in him to press his friends for payments, because he saw that the entire farming community in Drew was struggling. He didn't want to play the role of the bill collector and keep food from family dining tables.

Buddy also wasn't feeling well. The stroke of five years earlier had robbed him of much of his strength. Buddy never believed in doctors—he refused to go to the hospital until five days after his stroke—and so he had no interest in seeking medical treatment now. He didn't suffer any slurred speech from the stroke and he could walk without a hitch, but the family noticed that Buddy seemed a few beats slower, his movements more labored. He was only fifty-nine, but he was a worn-down fifty-nine. The internal fire that once flamed his passion for life—he loved to read poetry and was something of a biblical scholar—had been reduced to a few fading embers.

But even after the stroke, even with the stresses of his job mounting, Buddy almost always showed up at Archie's high school football games. Though before the games he'd tell his son, "I don't know if I'll be able to make it tonight," Archie would look up in the third quarter and see his dad standing by himself away from the crowd, his eyes locked onto his son's every move. Archie, immediately, would feel relieved, as if somehow everything would be okay now that his dad was at the stadium.

Buddy never wanted to show favoritism to Archie over his older sister, Pam, so he rarely congratulated his boy on his athletic accomplishments. Archie understood that his dad was only protecting Pam, and he never questioned his father about his reticence. Archie inherited his dad's low-key personality—their emotions rarely swung too high or too low—and they usually avoided discussing their feelings.

But the time away from home had made Archie more appreciative of his father. He valued how Buddy played with him when he was a boy, that he taught him the fundamentals of football, basketball, and baseball. Looking back, he savored how Buddy would sit with him and listen to those Ole Miss games during his childhood. Buddy was the reason Archie loved sports, and now, driving from Oxford to Drew on this summer afternoon, the two enjoyed a nice father-son moment as they talked of old games and old times. Buddy appeared to be happy.

That night, after returning to Drew, Archie, Buddy, and Sis drove to nearby Indianola, Mississippi, for an Ole Miss alumni gathering. The keynote speaker was Billy Mustin, a Rebel football coach and former player. Mustin knew Archie well; he and his wife oversaw the football dorm on the Ole Miss campus. After his speech, Mustin walked over to the table where the Mannings were seated. Looking at Archie and speaking loudly enough for his parents to hear, Mustin said, "I hope my son grows up to be like you." But Buddy didn't react; his face remained expressionless.

It was odd, Archie later thought, that his dad wasn't moved by that comment.

The next morning, on August 16, 1969, a hard wind stirred the cotton in the Mississippi Delta. Hurricane Camille, a category-five storm with winds that reached 185 mph, churned through the Gulf of Mexico and approached the Mississippi shoreline. In the coming hours Camille would rip apart much of the Magnolia State, leaving death and destruction in its wake. More than 150 in Mississippi alone would lose their lives to Camille, and century-old towns would be wiped from the landscape.

Life in Drew went on. Rain fell from a blue-gray sky, the first hint of the approaching hurricane. In the afternoon the Manning family attended a wedding—without Buddy. He wanted to stay home alone, but before Archie walked out the door, he told his son to come back after the reception so they could "cook steaks" and spend time together, just the two of them. As Archie left, his dad said, "See you back at the house."

Buddy recently had had a will drawn up. He had seen death creeping toward his older sister, who had been an invalid for several years. He witnessed the burden she had become to her family, how she was now a shell of what she had been. Nothing in life terrified Buddy more than the thought of becoming like her. But on this late morning he appeared to be in fine spirits.

After the wedding a few of Archie's friends asked him to go to a watering hole in nearby Cleveland. There they would have a few beers and talk about Archie's upcoming season at Ole Miss, the games against Bear Bryant's Alabama squad and other SEC heavyweights. But Archie didn't want to while away the afternoon drinking and dreaming; he wanted to see his dad. "I want to go on home," he said. "I'll hang around there this afternoon and catch up with you guys tonight."

Archie left his mother and sister at the reception and drove home alone, eager to spend time and have a steak with his dad. He walked into their little wooden house on Third Street and turned down the hallway toward the first-floor bathroom beyond his parents' bedroom.

Out of the corner of his eye, Archie noticed his father lying on his bed, his legs hanging over the end, his feet on the floor. Archie kept moving toward the bathroom, taking several steps. But something didn't seem right. It was so quiet in the house, too quiet. Deathly quiet.

He turned back.

CHAPTER 7

―――
―――

Why Now?

Drew. Summer 1969.

First he saw the shotgun on the floor. Then the stick that was used to leverage and activate the trigger.

The images registered like a series of still frames, ones that would be burned into Archie's mind for the rest of his life. He lifted his eyes to the bed and—oh dear God no—there was a big blood spot on his chest. Buddy's face was up, eyes closed, mouth open. He was perfectly still. Blood was spreading out beneath his body.

Archie ran to the phone and called the family doctor. "I think Buddy's dead," he stammered into the phone, then begged him to come quickly. He then called Louie Campbell, a family friend who frequently hunted with his dad. "Louie," Archie said, "you need to find Sis and Pam right away and get them down to your house. Whatever you do, don't bring them here."

Then, with his beloved father motionless on the bed from the self-inflicted gunshot, Archie began cleaning the room, working against the clock. He knew Sis and Pam would be home soon, so he needed to act fast. In the Delta, this was a son's duty—to spare his mamma and sister as much trauma as he could.

Tears streamed down his cheeks as he mopped up the blood that was splattered across the room. Even before the doctor arrived, Archie stood over his father's body and cleaned him up as best he could. As emotionally crippling as this was, Archie believed that his father had planned it this way, for his boy to find him before his wife and daughter could lay eyes on his lifeless body. So Archie took it as his responsibility to prevent Sis and Pam from witnessing this horror, this bloody end that his father had scripted.

Archie talked to the police. He watched as his father's body was carried out of his bedroom and placed into the back of an ambulance. He then burned Buddy's mattress and the bedroom linens.

In the summer of 1969 Archie was twenty years old. Now, in a matter of minutes, he was forced to become a man. Now every major decision that would be made in the Manning household from this day forward would involve Archie.

Except one: the son's desire to quit playing football.

Down in Gulfport, Mississippi, the waves from Camille continued to batter the shoreline. A barge that was ripped loose from its moorings washed ashore. On the hull there were two words that stretched twenty-five feet. Whoever wrote them didn't know of the searing pain that now seized Archie, but the author made clear his feelings about the quarterback from Drew. The words read:

ARCHIE BABY!

———

One hundred and thirty miles away from Drew in Philadelphia, the Williams family was preparing for the hurricane when the phone rang. Outside a hard rain continued to fall from the foreboding Southern sky when Louie Campbell, Buddy's good friend whom Archie had called earlier in the day in a panic, broke the news: Buddy was gone.

Olivia was devastated, plain heartbroken for her boyfriend.

Buddy had left instructions about where to find his important papers, such as his will. But he didn't leave a note explaining his final decision.

Archie would never precisely know why his father chose to end his life—the question would dog him for decades—but he speculated that his father believed that his health was eroding and he feared he would soon become a strain on his loved ones.

Olivia and her family drove to Drew for the funeral. After laying Buddy to rest, Archie, Sis, and Pam hosted a lunch at the Manning's home. Archie rose to his feet and delivered a few words, blinking back the tears and staying composed while expressing what his dad meant to him. Looking at Archie as he spoke, Olivia was in awe of her boyfriend's strength. He was so eloquent, as he opened his heart and let his feelings pour forth.

But later, once he was alone with his girlfriend, Archie's emotional walls finally crumbled. He felt like his soul had been ripped out of him. It hurt Archie that his dad never told him he loved him, and now Archie would never hear those three tender words flow from his dad's lips.

The tears dripped out as he explained how his dad would never get to see him play another football game. Archie believed with all his heart that he was about to be the architect of a special season starting in less than a month, that he was finally about to arrive as an athlete, and now his dad wouldn't get to enjoy any of that. *Why now?* Archie kept asking. *Why now?*

Archie told Olivia and others that Buddy had worked so hard in his life, and yet he had so little to show for it. It didn't seem fair. Archie was only a few years away from turning pro. Then he'd be able to ease his family's financial strain. No, Archie said, life just wasn't fair.

But if Archie ever had kids, he would tell them every day that he loved them. Even if a thousand miles separated him from his kids, he would make sure that they knew they were cherished and adored, the most important of everything in the world to him. They would never wonder about their dad's love.

Archie made a decision: he was going to quit school, return home, and get a job coaching. He would become the man of the house and provide for his mother and sister. This was the way things were done in Drew when fathers passed away.

Archie shared his decision with his mother. He told her that his football career was over, and that he was moving back home. Sis reacted sharply: never would she allow that. Never. Archie needed to pursue his own dreams, whatever they may be, and not pick up the pieces of his father's shattered life. She told Archie he was going to write his own story, and it was going to be grand and sweeping. She wouldn't hear any more talk of her son dropping out of school. He would return to Ole Miss and fulfill his own destiny. The decision was firm and final.

Days later, Archie drove to Oxford. He lost himself in football, burying his grief. Every game he would play like he was trying to prove something. Every game he would run around the field like he was chasing a ghost—and running from a haunted memory.

CHAPTER 8

—
—

The Birth of a Folk Hero

Oxford. Fall 1969.

The joke started to be told throughout the South about two months after the funeral. It began with a man in Tupelo who was about to jump off a bridge.

"Wait," said a friend. "Think about your family and your religion."

"Don't have any family," the man said, "and I don't believe in religion."

"Well," his friend said desperately, "then think about Archie."

"Archie who?"

"Jump, you S.O.B., jump."

At first, Archie's teammates at Ole Miss feared he would never return to school. Days after Buddy's suicide the scuttlebutt on the team was that Archie had given up football. He was going to stay in Drew, start working a nine-to-five job, and take care of his family. As players sat in their dorm rooms and contemplated football without Archie, they agreed that the team would have virtually no chance of winning the SEC if Archie remained in Drew.

But the rumors were false.

When Archie arrived at Ole Miss for the start of football practice in the late summer of 1969, he was shrouded in a fog of grief. His sadness would sometimes come in slow drips; other times it smashed at him like a tidal wave. His teammates didn't know what to say to Archie; most of them had never dealt with the loss of a parent, much less one who ended his life by his own hands. But his teammates could see in Archie's eyes—once so bright but now glazed over in confusion—that he missed his father dearly.

Archie also felt guilty. One of Buddy's favorite pastimes was hunting. His dad loved to take his 12-gauge shotgun—the same one he would raise to his chest—and tramp through the wilds of Mississippi in search of game. But Archie didn't like to hunt, so he rarely tagged along. Now Archie wondered: *If I had gone hunting, would I have known Buddy better? Would I have known that something was wrong? Could I have prevented this?* The questions haunted his sleep and tormented Archie's waking hours.

During two-a-day practices in preseason camp Archie didn't recall the things he did with his dad—like playing catch in the yard—but focused on the games his dad missed and those moments when he seemed so distant and unreachable. And he pondered how his dad would never get a chance to see him score another touchdown, or sit in the front row at his wedding, or be present at the birth of his children, or attend any of his grandchildren's games. There was so much Buddy was going to miss. And for what? Why was he gone? Why did he do it? Archie would never truly know.

Archie's teammates saw a different person when he returned. He was more determined to be a leader, to do everything—from practicing to studying to lifting weights—the proper way, as if his dad was watching him twenty-four hours a day, seven days a week. He rarely opened his heart to his teammates—the pain was too great—but before the season, after another grueling practice session under the blazing Mississippi sun, he told defensive end George Lotterhos, "It's time for me to man up."

And that was what Buddy's son did.

In the summer of 1969 change in America was in the air. President Nixon declared he was withdrawing 25,000 troops from Vietnam. Nearly 400,000 tie-dyed souls descended on a farm in Woodstock, New York, to see the likes of Jimi Hendrix and Janis Joplin at a music festival. And ABC announced it would launch a grand experiment by televising its first-ever prime-time SEC college football game on October 4, 1969, when Ole Miss played Alabama at Legion Field in Birmingham.

The Crimson Tide had won three national titles in the 1960s ('61, '64, and '65) and was the nation's premier program; the Rebels were overmatched at nearly every position. Vaught was so worried about the historic contest in prime time that he implemented a vanilla, power-I running formation for the Rebels game against Kentucky, played seven days before the Alabama kickoff. Vaught didn't want to show Alabama scouts any of the offensive plays he planned to unleash against the Crimson Tide. But the plan backfired: Kentucky upset Ole Miss 10–9, a loss that Vaught later called the worst coaching performance of his career.

In the days leading up to the nationally televised game Vaught was as secretive as ever. He closed practices and barred his players from speaking to the media. Vaught always was suspicious of spies—once, when he saw a small plane circling the practice field, he called the FAA and had the plane grounded; the pilot turned out to be a faculty member—and he had several campus cops with walkie-talkies patrol the perimeter of the Ole Miss practice area. A player once joked that if Vaught thought God was peeking down on his players, he'd put a roof over the practice field.

Ole Miss was ranked number 20 in the AP poll when the team traveled to Birmingham to face number 15 Alabama. The game didn't start until nearly nine p.m. Central time. Roone Arledge, the executive director of ABC sports who in a year would enter into a risky venture known as *Monday Night Football,* wanted the kickoff to be earlier, but he ran into a formidable obstacle: Lawrence Welk. Every Saturday night at 8:30 Eastern time the big-band leader hosted *The Lawrence Welk Show,* featuring the wholesome entertainment of his orchestra. The one-hour show was a ratings boon: it routinely finished second among all of ABC's programming in the Nielsen ratings. Arledge asked Welk to move his show into an earlier time slot, but Welk, a TV icon, refused.

So at 8:30 Central time on the first Saturday night in October the starters for the Rebels and the Crimson Tide were announced, one by one, live in front of the cameras. The national anthem followed. It was nearly 8:50 when Archie trotted onto the dimly lit grass at Legion Field for Ole Miss's opening possession.

Sitting in the stands was fifteen-year-old David Cutcliffe, a native of Birmingham. A football junkie, Cutcliffe dreamed of playing quarterback in the NFL. On many afternoons he would walk into a pasture near his house on the edge of town and, alone, throw a football at the branches of a tree. He would imagine that New York Giants linebacker Sam Huff was charging at him, and Cutcliffe would give himself only a few seconds to get rid of the ball as he avoided the make-believe rush. Once he threw it at a branch, he would retrieve the ball and repeat the game for hours on end. One day Cutcliffe—who in a few years would become a student manager for Bear Bryant at Alabama—hoped to become a coach.

Now Cutcliffe focused his eyes on Archie, who under the lights was a sight to behold. Sprinting to his left or his right on designed rollouts, he slung passes all over the field with surgical precision. When he didn't see an open receiver, he tucked the ball under his arm and blazed up the field. He was a blur in a blue jersey, spinning and faking out defenders, breaking tackles, and, a few times, throwing the ball just before he was brought down, connecting with a receiver for a long completion. It once again looked like he was playing in the sandlot, improvising as he went along. For television viewers across the country, it was riveting theater.

The freckle-faced quarterback was so spectacular that, with Ole Miss leading 32–27 late in the fourth quarter, ABC play-by-play announcer Chris Schenkel became momentarily thunderstruck; he had exhausted his wellspring of adjectives to describe Archie and fell silent. With a curious nation watching, the Rebel junior completed 33 of 52 passes for 436 yards and 2 touchdowns. He ran 15 times for 104 yards and another 3 touchdowns. Bear Bryant, on the sideline, was so infuriated by Archie that he told his defensive coordinator Ken Donahue that he was fired—three times. (The Bear eventually cooled down, and Donahue remained on Bryant's staff until 1982.)

Before October 4, 1969, no player in a major college game had ever thrown for 300 yards and run for 100, and now Archie set school records for pass attempts, completions, yards, and total offense. In living rooms across the country, thousands and thousands of football fans were being seduced by the wild and wonderful play of Elisha Archibald Manning the third.

With just under four minutes to play in the fourth quarter, as the clock was approaching midnight local time, Alabama faced fourth and goal on the Ole Miss 14-yard line. Alabama still trailed 32–27. Bryant called a time-out.

Scott Hunter, the Alabama quarterback, jogged to the sideline, where Bryant was puffing furiously on a Chesterfield cigarette, its red-orange ember glowing in the night. "What do you want to do?" Hunter asked his coach.

There was confusion on the Alabama sideline. The coaches in the press box were still trying to determine the play call when the referee yelled to Bryant, "The commercial is over. It's time to play ball."

Bryant, the Chesterfield still dangling from his mouth, pushed Hunter onto the field. He yelled to his quarterback, "Run the best you got!"

In the huddle Hunter took a deep breath, his mind racing for a play. Finally he shouted to his teammates, "Fire Red Right, Max Protect, Fifty-Six Comeback In." Hunter expected a blitz, so the play call instructed halfback Johnny Musso to stay in the backfield as a blocker. The "Fifty-Six Comeback In" meant that Hunter would try to hit wide receiver George Ranager on a comeback pattern in the middle of the field.

Archie knew Ranager well; the receiver was a big reason the coaches at Ole Miss fell in love with him. Archie had thrown four touchdown passes to Ranager in the 1967 Mississippi High School All-Star game, and now Ranager's old teammate watched helplessly from the Ole Miss sideline.

The ball was snapped to Hunter. The Rebels blitzed a linebacker, who was stopped in his tracks by Musso. Hunter, with time to throw, rifled the ball to Ranager, who caught it at the 1-yard line and pushed into the end zone. Across the field Archie could only shake his head. After Hunter's pass fell incomplete on the attempted two-point conversion, Alabama clung to a 33–32 lead.

With time running out, Archie led the Rebel offense down the field. But then the Rebels turned the ball over on downs. The Ole Miss defense stiffened, forcing an Alabama punt, which was downed by Ranager at the Rebel 5-yard line. Only seconds remained. Archie completed a 15-yard pass to Riley Myers. Then he tossed a 7-yard strike to split end Floyd Franks, who set single-game records for catches (13) and yards (191). Franks was dragged to the ground. The wide receiver popped to his feet and pleaded for a time-out, but the referee merely stared at Franks as the seconds ticked away. Ole Miss was out of time-outs. The clock expired. The game was over.

The television cameras immediately shifted to Archie. His helmet off, he looked through the black night at the white lights of the scoreboard, which read: Alabama 33, Ole Miss 32. Tears welled in his eyes and spilled down his cheeks. The nation saw this spontaneous flow of emotion—raw and real—and in an instant a folk hero was born. In defeat, Archie really had won.

Archie found Hunter and shook his hand. Archie tried to talk, but he was overcome. He had just set an SEC record for most total yards in a game, with 540—a record that would stand for more than four decades—and now he couldn't put to words what he was feeling.

He was sure of one thing, though.

He wished his dad could have seen him on this night.

Up in the television booth, as Archie wandered around the field in a daze, the announcers tried to put the moment in perspective. Chris Schenkel breathlessly said into his microphone that this was "the most exciting game I've ever seen in twenty years of broadcasting." Bud Wilkinson, the former Oklahoma coach who won three national titles with the Sooners, was the color analyst. He added, "This game is an all-time TV epic."

In the Alabama locker room Bryant, puffing on another cig, growled to reporters in his bass-thumping voice, "I've never seen a game like it, not with us, anyway."

Back at the team's Birmingham hotel at two a.m., Vaught couldn't sleep. He told a friend, "I've never had a team give everything they possibly had into one football game. That's what we did and we were one point short."

That night the Bear was asked about Archie. Bryant, incapable of hyperbole, offered the finest compliment he could articulate. He said Archie was better than the best quarterback he'd ever had at Alabama. "He dominates a game better than Namath did," he said.

From local barbershops in Birmingham to diners in New York City to dusty tents in Vietnam—where Archie's exploits had been heard over the Armed Forces Network—the topic of the game dominated conversations the following day. A total of twenty-five NCAA, Ole Miss, and Alabama records had fallen at Legion Field. The first national broadcast of an SEC game had been a smashing success, and it ushered in a new era in college football—the game was ready for prime time.

Overnight, Archie became a household name. He received more than five thousand pieces of fan mail the following week. High school students across the country who had tuned in to the game applied to Ole Miss in record numbers; many of those who were accepted later told school officials that Archie was the reason they decided to attend Ole Miss. After seeing him play against Alabama, those students wanted to be at the school Archie called home.

The outlines of a legend were beginning to form. After the Alabama game, church buses took detours to pass the home in Drew where Archie grew up. Strangers began calling the house in the dead of night, wanting to talk to Archie. And people from across the nation traveled to the Mannings' front door in Drew, wondering if Archie was home, hoping for an autograph and wishing to shake the hand of this fine young man.

Archie is at school, Sis would politely tell the strangers. She would then shut the door, pride swelling inside her.

After Buddy's death Sis began working as a legal secretary to pay the bills, and life could be hard for her. But the success that her boy was having filled her heart with a joy that made her most difficult days bearable, made the pain a little more tolerable, the memory of that terrible day a little less stinging.

But Sis's son was no longer just hers, and she knew that now. Part of Archie now belonged to an admiring sports nation.

A week after the nationally televised game against Alabama, Ole Miss faced Georgia, the sixth-ranked team in the nation. Playing in 100-degree heat in Jackson—the Rebels had two home games in Mississippi's capital city that season—Archie dropped back to pass on the game's second play. But the ball was deflected and intercepted by Bulldog end David McKnight, who ran 34 yards for the touchdown. Forty-four seconds had ticked off the clock.

Later in the first quarter Manning called his favorite play—the run-pass option. From the Ole Miss 27-yard line, he took the snap and rolled to his right. No one was open, so he turned and ran back to his left. With several Georgia players chasing him, Archie retreated 22 yards to his own 5-yard line. Just before he was slammed to the ground, he launched the ball downfield. The Rebels' Floyd Franks snatched the ball at midfield for a 23-yard gain. The crowd roared. Ten plays later Manning threw a 4-yard touchdown pass to Jim Poole. The score was tied at 7.

With five minutes left in the first half, Archie drifted back in the pocket to pass. Georgia defensive lineman Steve Greer crushed him, smashing his head into the grass. For Archie, everything went dark.

He lay on the grass for several minutes. He wouldn't remember walking off the field and into the locker room, where Rebel trainers found a trough full of ice and Coke bottles. The trainers quickly removed the bottles and helped Archie climb into the icy trough. He remained there for several minutes.

Georgia led 14–13 at halftime. Archie, in a whirling daze, sat in the ice-cold trough as Vaught tried to talk to him, but the words didn't register. For a few minutes, Archie felt like he was in a dreamlike haze, with everyone's movements happening in slow motion. He blinked his eyes repeatedly, trying to gather his wits as his teammates walked back onto the field to begin the second half. Finally, in the third quarter, Archie told the trainers that he was awake and alert.

In the opening minutes of the second half Georgia kicked a field goal to take a 17–13 lead. But then, with seven minutes remaining in the third quarter, a murmur began to ripple through the crowd. It emanated from above the portal to the Ole Miss locker room. Soon thousands in the stands were pointing in that direction: there was Archie jogging out of the locker room with a towel over his head. The crowd noise rose a decibel, then another, then boomed like thunder. Governor John Bell Williams, who was just returning to his box seat, smiled and waved to the fans, believing the cheering was for him.

Archie was on the way. Seeing him return, the Ole Miss players were reborn. "We are going to win this game," safety Danny Hooker said to a teammate. "The man is back."

Archie emerged from the ice-cold trough and once again was red-hot on the field. He led one touchdown drive in the third quarter, and in the fourth he threw a 43-yard bomb to Riley Myers for another score. Ole Miss won 25–17. Georgia coach Vince Dooley told reporters in the losing locker room, "I'm not sure I've seen a quarterback who is better." Then, in near disbelief, Dooley added, "We pressured him, had him trapped four or five times, and he got out of it and kept drives alive with great plays. He improvised back there, got away from us and hit receivers who had been milling around downfield for two or three minutes. Once we had him on the one-yard line for what should have been a 20-yard loss, and he got away and hit a receiver up about at the 50. He was completely the difference."

The next day, at the hotel where the team had stayed in Jackson, the words on a towering sign read:

ARCHIE SLEPT HERE

A surname was no longer needed to identify the red-haired Ole Miss quarterback. Like Elvis, he had become a one-name wonder. The mythology was growing.

Three weeks later, the Rebels faced another undefeated team: LSU.

Jimmy Bryan, a reporter for the *Birmingham News,* watched the action from the press box at Memorial Stadium in Jackson. He was so moved by Archie, who orchestrated another comeback victory, that he reworded a classic 1924 sports story from Grantland Rice for his piece.

"On a gray, windy November day, Mississippi's one horseman rode again," Bryan wrote. "His name is Archie Manning and what that brilliant junior quarterback did was bounce Louisiana State from college football's undefeated ranks in another of those TV suspense thrillers, 26–23. Manning took charge of the battlefield after Ole Miss spotted LSU a 23–12 lead early in the third quarter and the long-legged redhead brought it in with running and passing. Magnificent Archie scored three Ole Miss touchdowns, passed for the other and ran a two-point conversion to personally slay [coach] Charlie McClendon's talented Bengals."

The LSU coach was asked after the game about Archie, who at one point completed ten consecutive passes. "He just may be the best there ever was," McClendon said.

Shortly after Archie and Ole Miss defeated the Tigers, a New Orleans attorney named Frank J. Polozola filed a suit in the federal district court seeking an injunction to prevent Manning from "further harassment" of the LSU team. Polozola was joking, but the point was clear: it was going to take something extraordinary to slow down number 18 this fall.

During this first autumn without his father in his life, football filled a psychological cavity for Archie—one that had been hollowed out the moment he found Buddy in a pool of his own blood. Archie lost himself as much as he could in the game, hoping football would replace the burning pain of the suicide. Yet the spirit of his father still loomed over everything the son did.

Archie's teammates believed he was channeling his inner pain and pouring it into football. They saw him studying the playbook longer than anyone on the roster—his bedroom lamplight always seemed to be on—and he was as focused as the coaching staff during practices. A few of his teammates joked that Archie appeared to have a more intimate understanding of the plays and where everyone was supposed to move once the ball was snapped than even the offensive coaches.

Advance, never retreat—that was how Archie dealt with his grief. He still thought of his dad every day, and how he wished

Buddy could see him now: see how he'd become popular from New York to North Dakota to New Mexico, how he'd guided the Rebels to victories over nationally ranked teams, how he was still earning high grades in class. But Archie never let himself sink too far into that dark hole of wondering what might have been if Buddy were still alive.

Danny Hooker, who was a senior and Archie's close friend, often told his quarterback how much he admired him, especially how he was able to cope with his debilitating grief, maintain good grades, and play so well. It required a level of concentration and compartmentalization that amazed his teammates. "You will always be my hero," Hooker told Archie. "It's not because you're a great football player, Archie. It's because you're a better person."

Archie opened up to only a few people—a couple of friends, Olivia, his mother and sister—and in those rare instances when he did unchain his emotions and speak from his broken heart, it was as if the tragedy had occurred not months but minutes ago. He didn't run from his pain or try to hide it; he simply chose not to dwell on its devastating effects or to be paralyzed by them. Always look forward, he told a friend, because you never know what's coming at you next in life.

The red-and-blue buttons bloomed like springtime flowers across the Ole Miss campus and for miles beyond. Inscribed "Archie" and "Archie's Army" and "Keep Calm, Trust Archie," the buttons were worn by virtually every man, woman, and child in Oxford. Bumper stickers with the same messages were affixed to seemingly every other car within a fifty-mile radius of Archie's frat house. In the course of a few weeks, Archie had become a conquering hero in the Magnolia State. He was now public property— *one of ours,* they liked to say—and to show their love and devotion to college football's newest star, the locals wore the buttons like fine jewelry and placed the bumper stickers on their cars as if they were supporting Archie for President. Even Mississippi governor John Bell Williams sported an "Archie's Army" button.

Archie was asked why he thought he was known only by his first name and not his last. "The only thing I can figure out is that Archie is a different name," he told a reporter. "Maybe if it were Bill or something none of this would have started. I don't mind too much because I've always wanted to be an athlete. The only thing that worries me is how my teammates feel. If they keep joking about it, then it's all right with me."

Archie was so idolized that even fans of Southern Mississippi and Mississippi State wrote letters of admiration to him. The sweetheart notes arrived by the bundle at the Ole Miss football offices. At the start of the season Archie received forty letters a week, and the flow of typed and handwritten notes grew each day. In October athletic department secretary Jean Burt was enlisted to help Archie with the correspondence.

By November, Archie, who tried to answer every missive, fell four hundred letters behind. The notes were postmarked from as far away as South America, Alaska, and Maine. A young man from Gholson, Mississippi, wrote, "My uncle had a little baby the other day and he said it looked just like you." A ten-year-old from Alabama—who said he was the president of the Manning Fan Club in the Yellowhammer State—asked for advice about how to keep girls from joining the club. And an eight-year-old girl from Greenville, Mississippi, wrote, "I am your greatest fan besides your mother."

The deluge of love letters made it clear: Archie Manning was as famous as any football player had ever been in the history of the South. From juke joints to feed stores to classrooms across the region, he was hailed as a hero, their hero. It was a status he would retain for nearly three decades—until a boy named Peyton came along.

Before the start of the 1969 season, forty-five sportswriters had traveled across the Southeastern Conference, stopping at every school to speak with coaches and key returning players. The preseason press tour rarely generated news that was remembered once the calendar flipped to November—but rarely did a player speak with the candor and bravado of Volunteer linebacker Steve Kiner.

A senior all-American, Kiner was asked what he thought about Ole Miss, a team that Tennessee had dismantled in 1968 by the score of 31–0. The writer said, "How about Ole Miss? They look like they have the horses this year."

"*Everybody* says Ole Miss has got the horses," Kiner replied. "Well, I think they have mules." After the blowout, Kiner had told reporters that Manning wasn't hard to defend because he telegraphed every throw with his eyes.

Archie had read Kiner's critique. Instead of dismissing it as a verbal jab, he told his teammates that he appreciated it, because it gave him something specific to work on in the off-season. So throughout the spring and summer, whenever Archie was scrimmaging, he wouldn't shift his eyes to his primary receiver until the precise moment he felt the player would break into the open. That became a constant for Archie, a habitual trait he would use with great effect for the rest of his football career.

Now, in the days before the November 15 kickoff in Jackson, Mississippi, against Tennessee, Kiner's "mules" comment was resuscitated and reprinted in newspapers throughout the South, riling the Ole Miss fan base into a frenzy. Fans in Tennessee—tired of the media attention being showered on Archie—started wearing their own buttons, which read "Archie Who?"

The Ole Miss campus was electric before the game against the undefeated Vols, ranked number 3 in the country and on the verge of clinching an Orange Bowl berth. The *Daily Mississippian,* the student newspaper, promoted the sale of "Crush the Big Orange" bumper stickers for a dime. It took one day to sell two thousand.

Five nights before kickoff a student pep rally featured the introduction of the Rebel players. After the rally the campus fell quiet for a few hours. But at 10:30 several hundred young men, feeling frisky and full of game-day adrenaline, proceeded to go on a panty raid. "The campus exploded," the *Mississippian* reported. Twenty-two male students were apprehended.

That night, after the large-scale panty raid, a crowd of four thousand gathered and marched to the athletic dorm. The throng then walked to the coliseum for a bonfire. At three a.m. university officials served soft drinks to restore calm. Hours later a mule meandered onto campus and bore the battle cry "Squeeze the Orange" on its left rump. Some students literally counted down the minutes until Archie ran onto the field.

Always looking to gain any advantage he could, Vaught tried to exploit the hullabaloo between the schools. On Wednesday, November 12, three days before kickoff, the Ole Miss players were on the practice field when a small plane roared across the blue sky above. The coach didn't lift his gaze as the plane buzzed overhead— the surest indication that Vaught had paid the pilot to help him pull off a motivational trick.

On first pass the pilot dropped leaflets over the field with the phrase "Archie Who." On the second pass he dropped more; these read "Archie Mud" and "Wreck the Mules" and "The Voles are No. 1." Either Kiner or coach Doug Dickey supposedly signed all of the leaflets. But on the third pass the pilot, unable to continue the ruse a moment longer, cut his motor and yelled, "Go get 'em, Rebels! To hell with Tennessee!" The players, looking to the heavens, whooped and hollered.

By Friday the Ole Miss campus sizzled with anticipation. Thousands of fans proudly affixed a button to their chest that read "You Know Damn Well Who." The Rebel players were no longer looking to the heavens. They were looking at their star quarterback.

On the night before the game, lying in his bed in the team hotel in Jackson, Archie had a dream. He was on the Memorial Stadium field and nothing was going right. He couldn't control his passes, and every time he tried to run he stumbled to the ground. His play was so atrocious that Ole Miss fans ripped off their buttons and chucked them onto the field like rocks.

Archie stirred awake. The nightmare represented his worst fears coming true. But he didn't view the dream as just his imagination running wild; this was a reminder to never stop working and never take anything for granted. The key to all that he accomplished had been his work ethic—that was the fuel that powered his engine—and Archie was happy that this nightmare had revealed what could happen if he ever changed his approach to the game.

It was as if his dad were once again whispering in his ear.

The sun rose into an overcast sky over Jackson on the Saturday morning of the game. The temperature hovered in the fifties. As kickoff approached, it remained a steel-gray afternoon, the cold sky thick with an underbelly of clouds. It was the kind of football weather that Johnny Vaught loved: raw and foreboding, conditions that he believed were ideal for a game that would be decided by a battle of brute force.

In sports books around the nation Tennessee was favored from 6.5 points to 11. Vaught had referenced this to his team repeatedly throughout the week, and now, in the locker room, he told his boys that it was finally time to exact revenge on the Vols—time to show the nation that Ole Miss was an elite team.

No individual had more to prove than Archie. He had played the worst game of his life against Tennessee twelve months earlier, throwing 6 interceptions in the 31-point loss. Worse, Steve Kiner had publicly called him out. Archie never responded in the media to Kiner's comments; that wasn't his style. Archie told his friends he planned to get back at Kiner where it really mattered—on the field—by not doing what he'd done in the past: stare down his receivers.

Ole Miss won the opening coin toss and elected to receive. Archie and Vaught had spent the week plotting their plan: the Rebels offense would attack the heart of the Vol defense, running between the tackles. Nothing broke the spirit of a team quicker than ramming the ball straight through its defense. This would be something of a surprise attack: the Vols were expecting Archie to be the centerpiece of the offense.

One play after the next, Archie handed the ball off to a running back. On each carry, a back slammed into the line for a positive run. Nine times during the opening drive the Rebels ran the ball, and nine times Tennessee's defensive line was knocked back on its heels. As quarterback Archie wanted to throw the ball, but as play caller, Archie wanted to do what was best for the team, and now that meant dialing up bruising running plays in the huddle.

Archie threw only two passes in the game's first drive—a 13-yard strike to Riley Myers and a 38-yard completion to Floyd Franks. The final play was a 1-yard quarterback sneak for a touchdown. Less than five minutes into the first quarter, Ole Miss led 7–0.

On the sideline Archie implored his teammates to give more—more effort, more energy—and to score more points. Archie never appeared satisfied when the game clock was running, and that was one reason why his teammates felt so much affection for him. Now he was as animated as many of them ever remembered, walking up and down the bench, a liquid glimmer of intensity flickering in his eyes, exhorting everyone to keep pushing, pushing, pushing.

The Ole Miss defense forced a punt. Archie then hit Jim Poole for a 17-yard pass completion, which set up another touchdown. A few minutes later, Archie tucked the ball into his chest on a quarterback keeper, broke a tackle, and gained 11 yards around the left end. Then, on third and goal from the 5, he floated a perfect pass to Riley Myers for a touchdown. Less than thirteen minutes into the first quarter, the Rebels were up 21–0.

With the crowd roaring, the Ole Miss players started taunting their rivals. Between plays some yelled, "Where's Kiner?" Another said, "How do you like them mules?" Archie kept quiet; it just wasn't in his DNA to boast.

(But it was in Olivia's. Years later she would playfully remind a former Tennessee offensive lineman named Phillip Fulmer of this day when, sitting in the Mannings' living room as the Vols head coach, Fulmer offered their middle son a college scholarship.)

The final was Ole Miss 38, Tennessee 0. Manning, who finished 9 of 18 for 159 yards, was named the SEC Back of the Week for his play calling as much as his production. Even Kiner would admit that Archie's mind was as responsible for winning the game as his body. The Jackson Massacre, as the game became known, was a critical turning point for Archie. It was the day that he unofficially became the most cerebral quarterback in college football.

After the fans had dispersed into the Jackson night, in the quiet of the locker room, Archie looked over at Skipper Jernigan, his close friend on the offensive line. Out of the blue, in a voice barely louder than a whisper, Archie said, "I sure wish my dad was around to see this."

Lamont Wilson, a postal clerk in Magnolia, Mississippi, was struck with Archie fever. A Rebel fan, he was so emotionally touched by Archie's play in the Tennessee victory that he hastily wrote a ditty about his favorite player set to the tune of Johnny Cash's "Folsom Prison Blues." He called it "The Ballad of Archie Who."

> *The ball is on the fifty,*
> *The down is third and ten,*
> *He runs it down the sidelines;*
> *Yes, Archie takes it in.*
>
> *He plays for the Ole Miss Rebels,*
> *Archie Manning is his name,*
> *The best dadburned quarterback*
> *To ever play the game. . . .*

A guitar-twanging group called the Rebel Rousers recorded the song on the Hotty Toddy label. They had no idea what they were about to tap into. The vinyl record sold out throughout Mississippi, Alabama, Georgia, and Tennessee; more than 35,000 copies were purchased at $1.50 each. The song seemingly ran on an end-less loop on record players in dorm rooms in Oxford.

Country music stations played the record as often as six times a day. Now that he had a song written about him, quarterback Archie Manning was a full-fledged folk hero.

CHAPTER 9

=====

The Best I Ever Saw

Oxford. Winter 1969.

His name wasn't only sung in ballads on the radio. It was printed on paper cups, T-shirts, and coffee mugs and emblazoned on license plates. It was crafted from chicken wire stuffed with napkins in basketball arenas and baseball stadiums. It was seared onto dashboard figurines and appeared on countless numbers of buttons and banners. The letters usually just spelled "Archie," but sometimes there were multiple words: "Archie's Army," "Archie of Drew," even "Broadway Archie."

The machine of fame was cranking and humming on all cylinders. Determined not to enter its maw, Archie continually reminded his friends that he was still just a kid from Drew, that nothing had changed about him. But even his teammates looked at him differently now, as if he had transformed from a shy Peter Parker into a superhero, as if what he did on the football field against Bear Bryant and Alabama had altered the core of who he was.

Archie didn't understand his emerging fame—and he certainly wasn't comfortable with it. He didn't allow his mother or Olivia to wear an Archie button on game day or place an "Archie from Drew" bumper sticker on their cars. At frat parties and in the dorms his teammates serenaded Archie with a rendition of the ballad, which caused him to blush profusely and politely ask them to stop. Archie was loved everywhere he went—folks who had never met him felt like they had known him for years, because on television he looked like the quintessential boy next door—but it was hard for him to deal with strangers who approached him with arms extended. He had outgrown much of his childhood shyness, but not all of it.

Archie was forced to learn how to act as a public figure. When he walked into a restaurant in Oxford, all eyes turned to him, fingers pointed, and hushed voices uttered, *Oh my gosh, there's Archie.* No matter how he was feeling, Archie kept a smile on his face—he wore it like a mask—and always exuded optimism, even if the team had lost the previous Saturday. Vaught told Archie that he needed to be a quarterback every day of the week, every hour of the day. This meant Archie needed to act like a leader, and a major aspect of leadership was to let everyone know—through words and actions—that the best was yet to come for Ole Miss football.

There was one thing, however, that annoyed Archie. If he was introduced to someone who clearly knew that he was the starting quarterback for the Rebels, it would grate on him if the stranger responded by saying, *Archie Who?* The stranger would typically laugh like he or she was the most clever person in Mississippi, but in reality Archie heard that one literally hundreds of times.

But when Archie grew irritated, a voice would fill his head: *I want you to be a nice guy.* The words his dad counseled before

Archie left for Ole Miss would come back to him. And just like that, Archie the nice guy would reemerge, the kind persona and the country-friendly smile would be back. And Buddy's boy would just say, *I'm Archie Manning. Pleasure to meet you.*

Archie was an early riser, just like his father. In the Manning world one hour of work in the morning was worth two or more in the afternoon. Archie liked to get up in the early-morning darkness, alone, to do some of his best thinking. When he wanted company before the sun rose, Archie softly knocked on the dorm-room door of Skipper Jernigan.

Archie would peek his head inside. "You up?" Archie would whisper to his friend.

"Yeah," Jernigan would reply, wiping the sleep from his eyes.

"Let's go get a cup of coffee at the bait shop."

Then, as the sun awoke and glowed like a campfire over the eastern horizon, the two would drive to the off-campus store that sold fishing supplies, sundries, and coffee. Sipping from their mugs, Archie and Jernigan broached every subject imaginable: school, football, love, dreams, and even their fathers.

During these quiet talks, Archie would open up about Buddy, sharing how profoundly he missed his old man and how he couldn't understand why he had taken that gun to his chest. Jernigan said he wished he had the answers.

Archie had rarely asked his friend to go on these early-morning coffee runs when his father was alive, but now they had become frequent sunrise companions. Jernigan eventually realized that just listening—perhaps the simplest thing he could do for his friend—was helping Archie grieve.

———

At the end of the 1969 regular season, Sugar Bowl officials invited Ole Miss (7-3) to play third-ranked Arkansas (9-1) in New Orleans on New Year's Day. The Rebels had beaten Mississippi State 48–22 on Thanksgiving afternoon—Archie had rushed for 109 yards and thrown for 212—and reporters across the country already were touting Archie as a Heisman Trophy candidate for the next season.

Midway through the first quarter of the Sugar Bowl at Tulane Stadium, Archie took a snap and immediately ran to his left on his signature sprint-out play—the most exciting in the Ole Miss playbook. Fans never knew what was going to happen during his sprint-outs—and often, neither did Archie—and the thrill of possibility arose like an ocean wave throughout the crowd whenever Archie took off on a mad sprint with the ball. This was Archie at his most creative.

Archie didn't even have a quarterback coach. He practiced his sprint-outs in the winter and early spring with Jake Gibbs, the former Ole Miss quarterback in the late '50s and '60s. Gibbs had also been the punter on the '59 Rebel team and had booted the ball to LSU's Billy Cannon on Halloween night, resulting in the 89-yard return for the touchdown that had brought little Archie to tears as he listened over the radio in his living room in Drew. Gibbs, who had been one of the last players to have a shot at tackling Cannon, went on to become a platoon catcher for the New York Yankees from 1962 to '71, where he earned the nickname "Dead-Eye" for his ability to hit. Gibbs returned to Oxford in his off-seasons to mentor Archie.

Hour after hour, they practiced the sprint-out maneuver. For Archie, it was a scheme born out of necessity; playing behind an average offensive line, Archie didn't have time to drop back and wait for a receiver to come open down the field. Instead, he would usually receive the snap, take a few steps back, then bolt to either his right or left to avoid the rushing defensive linemen. Archie never trained to be a drop-back passer.

So, early in the Sugar Bowl in his first game in the city that would later define his life, Archie sprinted to his left. Not seeing any open receivers and with several defenders collapsing on him, Archie twisted out of a tackle, retreated 15 yards, then ran back to his right. Just as two players were poised to wrap their arms around Archie, he flung a pass into the right flat to Buddy Jones, who caught the ball for a 9-yard gain—the most spectacular 9-yard gain of the entire bowl season.

Later Archie received the snap and ran to his right. Stopping suddenly, he planted his feet and lofted a 45-yard rainbow into the outstretched arms of Vernon Studdard. The completion gained 57 yards. Even the red-clad Razorbacks fans in the crowd of 80,096 *ooooohhhed* and *aaaaahhhed* at the throw.

A few plays later Archie again darted to his left. While in a full sprint he unleashed a pass that flew into the middle of the field, where he hit Preston Carpenter in stride for a 15-yard gain. Then, on fourth and 1 from the Razorback 18, Archie sprinted to his right, broke a tackle, cut up the field, shed two more tackles, and plowed into the end zone. This was only one drive, but it revealed Archie at the height of his football powers. He displayed it all— the strength of his arm, his throwing touch and accuracy, his quickness, his powerful legs, his agility, and his uncanny knack for delivering when the play design broke down.

Ole Miss won 27–22. Archie, who passed for 273 yards and scored two touchdowns, accepted the Miller-Digby Trophy as the game's MVP. Despite having two sons who would one day play quarterback in the SEC, Archie would be the only Manning to ever play in a Sugar Bowl.

Up in the stands, Henry Lee Parker, the director of player personnel for the New Orleans Saints, was bewitched by the virtuoso performance of Manning, who would be named the SEC player of the year and finish fourth in the Heisman balloting. That night Parker called Archie "the best quarterback prospect I ever saw."

Late in the evening on January 1, as a cold wind whipped through the open press box at Tulane Stadium, the newspaper writers pounded the keys of manual typewriters, writing stories that detailed the exploits of Archie. Several thousand Mississippi fans lingered outside the stadium, their joyous screams still audible to the reporters on deadline.

Ole Miss sports information director Billy Gates paced through the press box, his face a portrait of concern. "What's the matter, Billy?" a writer asked. "Ole Miss did win, didn't they? You should be celebrating."

"Hell," Gates replied. "If Archie doesn't win the Heisman Trophy next year I'll lose my job."

At the end of the season Archie was invited to the Washington Touchdown Club in the nation's capital. He had won the Walter Camp Memorial Award, given to the outstanding college football quarterback, and he would be feted at a black-tie banquet by some of the country's brightest luminaries in D.C.

At dinner Archie sat between Supreme Court Justice William Douglas—who then held the record for most written opinions in Supreme Court history—and former Justice Tom Clark. It was a dizzying evening for Archie, but he still found a way, when the spotlight was trained on him, to turn on his Mississippi charm. He was still the fire-haired kid from the farming town of Drew.

"Well, young man," Justice Clark said to Archie, waving from the dais to the crowd of 2,500, "I guess you're used to crowds like this."

"No, Mr. Justice," Archie replied. "Why, there are more people here tonight than live in my hometown of Drew."

Eight months after finding his father on his bed, Archie had set twenty-seven school and conference records as a junior. He believed his final season in Oxford would be his best. Maybe, he thought, he could lead Ole Miss to the national championship. Perhaps he could even become the first Rebel to win the Heisman Trophy.

A few months later, in March, Ole Miss held its spring game. The officials were Butch Lambert Sr. and Butch Lambert Jr. They weren't allowed to call Rebel games during the season because they were Ole Miss alums—and certifiable Archie Manning fanatics.

Archie served as team captain for his squad, and Dennis Coleman, a defensive player, was captain of the other team. Archie and Coleman walked to midfield for the opening coin toss.

Big Butch Lambert reached into his pocket, but he didn't have a coin. "I'll tell you what," he said. "I'll just pick a number between one and ten. All right, I got the number. Dennis, you pick first."

"I pick six," Coleman said.

"That ain't it," Lambert replied. He then turned to Archie. "Archie, you win. Whatcha wanna do?"

In early 1970 virtually every college football fan in the South—some officials included—rooted for Buddy's freckle-faced boy.

CHAPTER 10

=====

The Fear of Failing

Oxford. Summer 1970.

They were in young love—the flush, the anxiety, the excitement of it all—and they both knew it. So Archie did what every well-mannered young man born and raised in the genteel South was taught: he asked her father for permission to marry his daughter.

Cooper Williams, father of Olivia, was a fixture in Philadelphia, located 130 miles southeast of Drew. In 1907 he opened the Williams Brothers general store, located at 10360 County Road 375. Most days Cooper Williams remained behind the large wooden counter and operated the gleaming silver, extra-sharp bacon slicer and cheese cutter. He knew most of the customers by first name and welcomed the poor and wealthy, black and white, as if they were kin. He allowed families who endured hard times to buy food and materials on credit. No matter what anyone needed—barbed wire, clothing, groceries, snuff, farm implements, boots, plow lines—they could find it at the Williams Brothers general store, which locals swore sold the best hoop cheese in the South.

Olivia's father loved Ole Miss football. Following the team was his favorite hobby, and he never missed a Rebel home game. "I don't hunt, I don't fish, I don't play golf," he told Archie when he was dating his daughter. "I just go to football games."

After receiving Cooper's blessing in the summer before the start of his senior year, Archie dropped to a knee and asked for Olivia's hand in marriage. *Yes,* she exclaimed, melting into a puddle of joyful tears, throwing her arms around him.

Archie had just made the most important play call of his life. And as usual, it worked.

In late summer 1970, Archie fever swept the nation. His boyish face beamed on several national magazine covers, a Tom Sawyer in a football uniform with haunting blue eyes. Even though he was only twenty-one, five writers offered to pen his biography (he declined). Businesses wanted a part of the Manning mania: a fast-food chain offered Archie Burgers, a few businesses sold Archie dolls and Archie T-shirts, and a company in Memphis attempted to manufacture life-size Archie balloons. The public wanted a piece of him too: so many requests for Archie's autograph flooded into the Ole Miss athletic department that the school had to fashion a rubber stamp of his signature and assign a special secretary to "sign" his name on pieces of paper.

"I've never seen anything like it," said Ole Miss coach Johnny Vaught, entering his twenty-fourth season as head coach at Mississippi. "I guess it's the times, the desire to glorify athletes, like the Namath thing. Thank goodness Archie is a smart man, a sensible man, and he hasn't let any of it go to his head. Why, I don't think he even thinks about it."

Archie was desperate to remain one of the boys, to blend in to the background like a normal college kid. When he attended the annual Roaring '20s party at his Sigma Nu fraternity, Archie poked fun at himself by donning an "Archie Who?" button. He knew the quickest way to win over skeptical teammates was to laugh at the absurdity of his celebrity, and more often than not Archie—a closet comedian—was the butt of his own jokes. His teammates adored this aspect of his personality, and it strengthened their connection to their quarterback.

The night of the Roaring '20s party Archie sang with the band, rode around on the shoulders of teammate Jim Poole, then hoisted Poole onto his own shoulders and carried around the offensive lineman like a bale of cotton. Archie was having fun, letting down his guard. Years later Archie would remind his own sons of the importance of enjoying good times with their teammates away from the field, which was one of the many traits of Archie's leadership.

In the preseason Vaught continued to be amazed by Manning. The coach believed he was the best athlete who had ever played for him. Archie's weight was up to 205—he had spent two months during the summer toiling again for a bricklayer in Drew, earning spending money for the fall and honoring a promise that he had made to his dad to work when he was home from school—and he was as strong as he'd ever been. He had been unofficially timed in the 100-yard dash at 10.2 seconds. And he now knew the intricacies of Vaught's offense almost as well as the coach himself.

As a sophomore Archie had called his own plays 40 percent of the time. But now, as a senior, he would come up with 95 percent of the play calls. Vaught was so confident in his quarterback that he didn't even flinch when Archie dismissed his instructions on what to run, which was often. If Archie didn't like his coach's play call, he looked into the eyes of his teammates in the huddle and said, "OK, guys, we're going in a different direction. Here's what we're going to do."

Vaught believed that Archie was better prepared than any quarterback he had ever coached. He was borderline obsessive about studying every opposing team's defenses. Vaught enjoyed watching Archie walk to the line of scrimmage. Before taking the snap, Archie would quickly inspect the defensive alignment. If there was a weakness, Archie would spot it, shout the command for a new play, and exploit that area on the field that the defense had left most vulnerable. In his junior season Archie had changed 30 percent of the plays at the line.

"He has a great football mind," Vaught said of Archie. "I have now reached the point with Archie that anything he wants to do from any place on the field at any time is all right with me."

Every summer Vaught wrote a letter to his players, reminding them what was important.

Have a daily work schedule planned and start training by the 1st of August. The first thing you should do is reach your playing weight. You can lose weight by exercising and by pushing away from the table. Run distances up to a mile for your wind, short sprints of 25 yards (and gut them out) for toughness, and calisthenics and grass drills for quickness, agility and control of your body. A well-conditioned squad will not be bothered by injuries. Remember, running is the secret.

Above all else, there is no substitute for desire, for spirit and morale. To be a winning team, we must be a hungry team. We must want to win more than the teams we encounter this fall, and I can assure you they'll be hungry. Be ready to start practice here September 1 at top speed. And remember—every football Saturday is the most important date on our schedule, with no exceptions and no reservations. Until proved otherwise, we're No. 1. We want no one moving up at our expense.

On the eve of his final season in Oxford, Archie met with reporters. His most powerful motivation, he said, was his fear of failing, a trait that he would one day pass on like genetic code to his sons. "I have confidence in myself, but I can't help thinking what would happen if I didn't do it this season," Archie said. "Man, if the roof fell in, that would be sad."

During the preseason practice period, fans throughout the South mailed cakes and cookies to Archie, which arrived by the box-load at the football players' dormitory. Archie happily gave his treats away to his offensive linemen, whom he thanked repeatedly for their hard work. On off days, Archie and his O-line buddies liked to drive to Memphis and go to the Rendezvous restaurant for barbecue. They always had the same waiter, a rabid Ole Miss fan who refused to accept any money from Archie and his teammates. But the trips to Memphis weren't really about the slow-cooked slabs of ribs to Archie; he simply wanted to spend time with his teammates away from football.

The Rebels opened the 1970 season by defeating Memphis (47–13) and Kentucky (20–17). The victories set up the most anticipated matchup of the early college football season: Alabama was coming to Jackson.

In the days before the game against the seventeenth-ranked Crimson Tide, Archie spent a lot of time in bed. He pulled his groin muscle against Kentucky and didn't run all week in practice. He slept with a heating pad. "I don't know if I'll be able to run full speed," he said. "But I think I'll be all right. I've been throwing as well as I ever have."

Archie spent nearly every free minute he had analyzing the Alabama defense, watching film and studying the tendencies of each Crimson Tide defender. He was so engrossed with Alabama—a team that, since 1910, had a 20-1-1 record against Ole Miss—that one day he skipped class to spend time alone in the film room. As the date of the game drew near, Archie began filling his class notebook with more X's and O's than actual class notes, his mind unable to focus on professors, with Bear Bryant looming on the calendar. On Thursday, Archie was so caught up in thinking about the Tide that he almost forgot Olivia's birthday. But he rallied late in the day, scrambling to hand-deliver a dozen roses.

"I've never seen him like this," Olivia said. "Even before the Tennessee game last year he wasn't this fired up. Why, I think he wants to hurt somebody, and that's not like Archie."

All week long the game had been a water-cooler topic in offices around the nation. President Nixon was aboard the U.S.S. *Saratoga* when a few sailors asked about the college football scene. "Well, Texas looks pretty good," the president said. "But watch out for Mississippi and that . . . ah . . . ah . . . ah. That Archie Manning."

Blaylock's Drug Store, which sat across the street from the antebellum courthouse in Oxford, sold hundreds of "Archie for Heisman" buttons. In the student union in Tuscaloosa a group of Alabama students peddled their own buttons that read "Wreck the Rebel Rabble." And Bear Bryant hung pictures of Manning in the Crimson Tide locker room, reminding his players that Manning "beats you in so many ways" and that there wasn't a better quarterback in the nation. During practice Bryant assigned three scout-team freshmen to play the role of Manning, but Bryant understood that no one in college football could come close to running, passing, and thinking like the Ole Miss signal caller.

Archie viewed the game as the continuation of last year's heartbreaking loss. When the final whistle had blown in Birmingham twelve months earlier, the Rebels were driving down the field for what they were certain would be the winning score. Archie told his teammates that they had merely run out of time last fall, but now they had a second chance at Bryant and the Tide.

On game day the Memorial Stadium home crowd of 46,000 fans—the marquee matchup had been sold out for six months—thundered as the seventh-ranked Ole Miss Rebel players ran onto the field. A team captain, Archie walked to midfield for the opening coin toss. He shook hands with Tide quarterback Scott Hunter, who wasn't in uniform. Three days earlier during practice in Tuscaloosa a guard pulled the wrong way on a running play and smashed into Hunter's right shoulder. Bryant was sitting on a folding chair up in a viewing tower—he felt under the weather and so he wasn't pacing around the field as usual—and Bryant's heart sank at the sight of his quarterback writhing in pain on the ground. The next day Bryant's worst fears were confirmed: Hunter's right shoulder, his throwing shoulder, was separated. This meant Hunter, who in the NFL would replace Bart Starr as the starting quarterback of the Green Bay Packers in 1971, wouldn't get to play in Round 2 against Archie.

But Hunter was one of Manning's biggest fans. After the nationally televised game at Legion Field, Hunter received hundreds of letters from admirers around the nation. Late in the following week he opened a piece of mail postmarked Oxford, Mississippi. Though he was emotionally crushed by the loss, Manning had sent a handwritten note to Hunter, congratulating his rival quarterback on winning the game and playing with such poise. Archie ended the missive by stating, "One of these days when we're older, we need to get together and 'toast' to this game for old time's sake." As Hunter read the note, he was overwhelmed with one thought: Archie Manning may be the classiest college football player he'd ever met.

Now the two quarterbacks shook hands at midfield. Alabama, 2-0, would receive the opening kickoff from the 2-0 Rebels.

The ABC cameras rolled as Hunter's backup, Neb Hayden, threw an interception less than one minute into the game. Manning then unleashed a 7-yard dart to Randy Reed for a touchdown and a 7–0 lead. Less than 200 seconds had ticked off the clock.

The Rebel defense quickly forced another punt. Archie and the Ole Miss offense, playing fast, drove 47 yards with relative ease. The final play was a 1-yard touchdown plunge by Archie. Minutes into the game, the Rebels held a 14–0 lead. The Ole Miss fans frantically waved their Stars and Bars flags.

Despite his groin injury, Manning ran the option to near perfection for a stretch in the third quarter. He'd pitch the ball to a running back just before Alabama defenders swarmed him, and he'd cut up the field with the ball when the Tide players covered the back. Other times he'd act like he was going to run the option and then, at the last possible moment, take a few steps back and fire the ball down the field. Bear Bryant, nursing a head cold, glowered onto the field and shook his head as Manning led a long third-quarter touchdown drive. No one in the stadium was happier than Bryant that Manning would soon be graduating.

Ole Miss won 48–23. Manning's stat line wasn't impressive—he completed 10 of 24 passes for 157 yards and three touchdowns and ran nine times for 46 yards and two touchdowns—but he was playing at half speed. Standing in front of his locker after the game, sipping Coke from its classic glass bottle, Archie was quick to do what he always did during his postgame comments: he deflected the attention away from himself. "The defense won this game," he said. "They gave us all the breaks and we took it in."

Archie had never been a quote machine, and reporters covering Ole Miss knew that the best way to gather information for a story about Manning was to get others to talk about him. Following the victory over Alabama—a win that players in the Rebel locker room believed stamped them as the number one team in the nation—reporters sought Vaught. The coach was normally low-key, but now he was effusive in his praise. "Archie Manning has the best football mind I've ever been associated with," Vaught told reporters.

Vaught made it clear that he wasn't just talking about players; he was also referring to every coach who had been by his side during his thirty-five years as a football coach. Vaught believed with all his heart that his deep thinker of a quarterback was going to carry the Rebels to the national title.

CHAPTER 11

====

What Might Have Been

Oxford. Autumn 1970.

On October 17 the front page of the sports section in the *Meridian Star* featured a photo of Archie sitting in the Ole Miss locker room and pulling up his socks. That afternoon the Rebels, now ranked number four in the nation, faced Southern Miss, a team they dismantled 69–7 the year before. The caption of the photograph posed what seemed a legitimate question: "Archie Manning . . . Is This One Worth Suiting Up For?"

In the opening minutes of the game it appeared that Archie's day would be short and successful. He threw a deep, high-arching spiral that landed in the arms of a streaking Floyd Franks for a 51-yard touchdown. It looked like a varsity team playing a junior varsity squad. The lambs had entered the slaughterhouse.

But then, as quickly as lightning flashes, the tenor of the game dramatically changed. For the rest of the muggy afternoon in Oxford it was as if Southern Miss had fifteen players on the field at all times. Archie, who could barely run due to his sore groin, attempted a school record 56 passes—and was brutally slammed to the ground over and over and over, at least twenty times total. He completed 30 of his throws for 341 yards.

By the fourth quarter, with the Rebels trailing Southern Miss by two touchdowns, blood was spattered on Archie's uniform. He was so battered that Vaught sent backup quarterback Shug Chumbler onto the field to replace Archie in the final minute of the game—an act of mercy from the coach. But Archie wouldn't leave the lineup. "Hell no, I'm not quitting," he told Chumbler and pushed him back toward the Ole Miss bench.

At the final whistle Vaught ambled off the sideline, devastated by the 30–14 loss to Southern Miss. As he neared the middle of the field, Vaught felt more run-down than usual after an emotional defeat.

Two Southern players hoisted their portly coach, P. W. "Bear" Underwood, atop their shoulder pads. But just before they reached Vaught, Underwood tumbled to the ground like Humpty Dumpty falling off the wall. "Hell, Bear," Vaught said, mustering a smile. "You couldn't expect two miracles in one day."

It would be the last time Vaught would ever be on the field as Archie Manning's football coach.

Three days after losing to Southern Miss, Vaught had supper in the athletic-dorm cafeteria around six p.m. When he rose from the table, his face looked pale and he shuffled his feet like he had concrete blocks tied to each ankle. Vaught's labored walk caught the eye of assistant coach Billy Mustin, who also was Vaught's frequent hunting partner. "Coach, you're tripping over everything," Mustin said.

Vaught didn't pay attention to Mustin as he continued to his office, where he watched film of the Rebels' next opponent, Vanderbilt. Vaught planned to analyze the Commodores with his assistants until nine p.m., but was overcome by a wave of nausea. "Boys, I'm sick," he said. "I've got to go home."

Vaught ambled to his car and drove five miles to his house, where he immediately collapsed into his bed. But at ten p.m. he turned to his wife, Johnsie, lying next to him, and said, "There's something wrong with me."

Johnsie quickly popped up. Her husband never complained about his health. "How do you feel?" she asked.

"My arms are aching and I have a nauseous feeling in my chest," Vaught said.

Johnsie picked up the phone and dialed the Ole Miss team doctor, who rushed to the house. The doctor gave Vaught a nitroglycerin tablet and then drove him to the Oxford-Lafayette County Hospital. The initial diagnosis was a heart-circulation problem.

During the next few days Vaught went in and out of the hospital. But on Sunday, November 1—a week and a half after feeling the first tightness in his chest—Vaught was ferried by ambulance to the intensive care unit at Methodist Hospital in Memphis. He had suffered a heart attack.

The Ole Miss players were crestfallen, especially Archie. Vaught had spent more time with Archie since his father died than virtually anyone else, and Vaught had become a paternal figure in Archie's life. Together, Vaught and Archie had hoped to accomplish so much this fall—winning the SEC, the national title, a Heisman—but now, in a span of only a few days, those aspirations had been extinguished. Vaught was in a hospital room with a weak heart, and Archie was left to once again ponder the unfairness of life.

But Archie made a vow to his friends after he learned of

Vaught's sickness: he would never take anything for granted, and he would savor the smell-the-magnolias moments in life whenever they arose. Vaught had often said that Archie was the most observant football player he'd ever known. Now the coach admitted that he needed to amend that statement: Archie was the most observant *person* he'd ever known.

She graced the front page of the *Daily Mississippian* on Monday, November 2, 1970. Wearing a white turtleneck, her dark tresses falling to her shoulders, she smiled demurely from the black-and-white page. The top headline on the paper read "Archie for Heisman—pages 7 & 8." But the lead story on page 1, strategically positioned above the fold, was topped with the headline "Voting Is Tomorrow: Olivia Lacks Opponent." Now Archie wasn't the only one who was afforded first-name-only status in the university newspaper; his fiancée also had campus-celebrity standing.

The story of the upcoming homecoming election began, "Olivia Williams, a 21-year-old Elementary Education major from Philadelphia, remains as the only candidate to have qualified for the crown of Homecoming Queen 1970. There have been no rumored write-in candidates."

No one dared to run against Olivia, because she may have been the one person on campus who was more popular than her fiancée. In the October 12 issue of *Sports Illustrated* that year the first feature story listed on the table of contents was "Archie's War with Alabama." Yet beside it appeared a small photo not of Archie but of an Ole Miss sorority girl named Olivia Williams. Then, once the story on Archie began on page 14, a larger version of that photo of Olivia dominated the layout, as if the editors of

SI knew what Archie had figured out shortly after he met his future bride—Olivia had the magical ability to make *him* look better whenever she stood next to him.

Olivia appeared on the cover of the homecoming-game program for the November 7 contest against the University of Houston. Smile aflame, she wore a white blouse under a light jacket and held an Ole Miss Rebel flag. She was a vision of Southern beauty. The photo did nothing to diminish the widely held belief across the nation that the most gorgeous coeds in America lived amid the gently rolling hills of the Ole Miss campus.

On page 4 of the one-dollar program was a photograph of Archie. Mississippi was ranked number sixteen nationally with a record of 5-1, and the Houston Cougars were the only team that had beaten Ole Miss in each of Manning's first two years as a Rebel starter. Now, to atone for that and especially because it was an important day for his bride-to-be, Archie wanted to perform well. At halftime Olivia would be crowned the 1970 homecoming queen of Ole Miss.

During the week, like all weeks in Oxford, Archie called home to Drew several times to speak with his mother, Sis. A dutiful son, Archie kept his mamma abreast of the latest in his life, and he always wanted to know how his older sister, Pam, was faring. Hearing his mother's voice had a soothing effect on Archie—the conversations were always a comforting port amid the storms in his life—and the talks connected him to his past in a way that nothing else could. He still missed his dad desperately—he often mentioned Buddy to his friends—and speaking to his mom made some of the good memories of Buddy come alive.

Archie always called collect. He would dial "0" on a rotary phone and say to the operator, "This is Archie Manning." But one time the operator didn't buy it. She thought she was being conned.

"I bet you feel really big for saying that," she replied.

Archie wanted to unload on the operator—he immediately felt like saying, *Aw, cut it, baby!*—but instead he held his tongue and simply repeated his name and again asked to be connected. As usual, Archie acted exactly as Buddy had taught him.

In the third quarter against Houston, in front of 36,535—the largest crowd to ever watch a football game at Hemingway Stadium—Archie faked a quick pass and rolled to his right with Ole Miss leading 14–7 and driving for another score. But just as Archie released his pass, two Cougar defenders drilled Archie and drove him into the ground. Archie stuck out his left arm to break his fall, but his left forearm bent grotesquely. After the play was over, Archie continued to roll around on the grass in obvious pain.

Archie writhed in agony. He couldn't get up. His teammates surrounded him and were startled by the pained look on his face. Olivia, the newly crowned homecoming queen, put both hands to her mouth as she watched in horror from the grandstands.

Interim coach Frank Kinard ran onto the field. Archie was clutching his left arm and grimacing. "I hurt my arm, Coach, and I don't think I can stay in the game," he told Kinard. The way the arm was bent to a near L-shape it was clear to everyone on the field that it was broken, along with the dreams of the Ole Miss faithful.

Archie was helped to his feet. Trainers and teammates guided him to the sideline. The arm was wrapped in ice and bandages. Then, with his number 18 uniform still on, Archie was driven eighty-five miles to Baptist Hospital in Memphis—not far from Methodist Hospital, where Vaught was recovering from his heart attack.

Archie had broken the radius bone in his left forearm—the same arm he fractured in the eleventh grade. He eventually was taken to surgery, where a temporary cast was removed. It didn't get tossed into the trash can, however; a nurse kept it as a souvenir. When the operation was over, the surgeon threw away his gloves. Later those were retrieved as well by a member of the medical team, who believed the gloves could one day carry historical significance.

Archie recovered at Baptist Hospital, the nation's largest private hospital, for eight days. Security guards stood sentinel outside his room, protecting Archie like he was a sitting president. Of course, to many people in Mississippi, Archie was more important. The hospital staff was accustomed to dealing with celebrity patients because Elvis was a frequenter visitor at Baptist, but the staff had never seen anything like the Archie-mania that was now in their midst.

In one day Archie received 1,500 pieces of mail from wellwishers and concerned fans. Stanford quarterback Jim Plunkett, his main competition for the Heisman Trophy, sent a telegram expressing his hope for a speedy recovery, as did dozens of other players from across the nation. There was so much mail that it had to be brought in large sacks to Archie, who tried to read every word but simply did not have enough hours in each day.

Dozens of people tried to sneak into Archie's eighth-floor room in the hope of glimpsing the star quarterback and securing an autograph. One young man, after being turned away by the security guards, returned to the hospital dressed in pajamas, a bathrobe, and slippers. Looking just like another patient, he quietly walked past nurses and dozing guards and entered Archie's room. He saw Archie in bed, his left arm strung up, elevated straight toward the ceiling, and an Ole Miss flag hanging behind his bed. Security was quickly called and the autograph seeker was escorted out. Another patient, a ninety-four-year-old woman, begged to be let in for an autograph, and Archie obliged.

Thousands of people called the hospital asking to speak with Archie. The eighth-floor secretary, Mrs. L. Franklin, screened all his calls, including one from a man who said he was phoning from South America. Another caller swore he was Archie's coach. Franklin dutifully jotted down all the phone numbers and handed them to Archie.

Reporters, unable to breach the wall of security around Manning, instead visited Methodist hospital and interviewed Vaught. "Archie Manning is the greatest college football quarterback I have ever seen," Vaught said from his hospital bed. "Archie can do more things on the field than anyone I've ever seen." Vaught lobbied as vociferously as he could for Heisman voters to award Manning the trophy. He wasn't alone: an advertising agency in Memphis mailed a brochure to prospective voters called "Heis-Manning."

Alone in his hospital room, Archie once again was forced to confront the fragility of life. That had become a running theme for him, the lesson of how things could be taken away so fast. He wasn't consumed by why-me pity; rather, he told his friends that he accepted that much in life was out of his hands, that the best he could do was focus on the things he could control. That was his mantra—one of the key life lessons he would eventually pass on to his progeny.

Archie was released from the hospital in time to attend "the Egg Bowl" against the Mississippi State Bulldogs on November 26, a rivalry that stretched back to 1901. In '26 Ole Miss ended a thirteen-game losing streak against the Bulldogs, and Rebel fans poured onto the field in Starkville. They tried to rip down the goalposts in celebration, but Mississippi State fans intervened and a fight broke out. The two schools then agreed that, to prevent future brawls and future students from trying to tear down goalposts, the winning team would be awarded a brass trophy in the shape of a football. Back then the footballs were similar to egg-shaped rugby balls, and in 1979 sportswriter Tom Patterson gave the game its nickname.

On a gray Thanksgiving afternoon in Oxford, Archie paced the sideline like an expectant father as he watched his teammates play against the Bulldogs, the school that had been his dad's favorite. For only the second time since World War II, Mississippi State beat the tenth-ranked Rebels. The final was 19–14. "This is the worst day I have ever spent in my life," Manning told teammates on the sideline. "I feel so helpless."

Doctors initially said Archie wouldn't play again in 1970, but he returned to the field on December 5 against LSU. The start of the game had been pushed back a few hours to accommodate a national television audience—TV executives now understood that this Manning kid was ratings gold. Archie wore a protective plastic sleeve on his left arm. He looked like an injured player, and he was. The bulky contraption on his left arm made it difficult for him to run in that direction. Not only was his quickness gone, but he also struggled to complete passes. LSU won 61–7.

The final college game of Archie's career was the Gator Bowl against Auburn. With the plastic sleeve still on his left arm, Archie completed 19 of 28 passes for 180 yards and ran 11 times for 95 yards. Archie's favorite professional quarterback to watch on Sundays was the Minnesota Vikings' Fran Tarkenton—he loved the way that Tarkenton darted around the field like he was running from the law and also that Tarkenton was a native of Georgia, an "ol' Southern boy" like himself. Archie tried to replicate Tarkenton on some plays in the Gator Bowl, but with the cast on his arm Archie couldn't run like he did when he was healthy. Auburn and its future Heisman Trophy–winning quarterback Pat

Sullivan topped the Rebels 35–28 in the highest-scoring game in the bowl's history at the time.

"That old hospital bed never got off my back," Archie said afterward.

No one was more disappointed with the events of the season than Vaught, who had watched the game on television. He was finally allowed to leave the hospital in Memphis but in a few years was forced to retire from the sidelines, the job too taxing on his weak heart. His final game was in 1973.

On doctor's orders, Vaught walked for one hour every day around his 160-acre farm outside Oxford. In the twilight of his life he would hunt turkey and duck, fish, play golf, and think about what might have been with Archie.

"We went into 1970 with such high hopes," Vaught said. "But life is full of misfortunes. Now we can only wonder what might have been had Archie been whole all year."

Vaught predicted that Archie would set professional football on fire and become the prototype for future NFL quarterbacks. "I look for him to revolutionize the professional game," Vaught said. "I think it's fairly obvious the defense has caught up to the offense. The passing pocket has got to move. And Archie is going to do it in an exciting way. Fran Tarkenton caused a stir with his scrambling but, compared to Archie, he has just scratched the surface."

Agents and attorneys from around the country sent Archie letters, each explaining why they were best suited to negotiate his first NFL contract. Archie stuffed the correspondence in a box and slid it underneath his bed. He had too much going on in his life before the draft to concern himself with hiring representation.

One agent was particularly aggressive. Herb Rudoy, a promi-

nent agent from Chicago, flew to Drew to talk to Archie. When
Rudoy arrived early for his appointment at the Manning house,
Archie had stepped out and wasn't scheduled to return for a few
hours. Sis insisted that Rudoy wait inside. The minutes passed.
Rudoy, growing impatient, finally stood up to leave. But Sis, like
any good Southern host, wouldn't let him leave empty-handed:
she gave him a mason jar of homemade pickle relish and a con-
tainer of homemade peach preserves.

When Sis told her son that she didn't let that fine man from
Chicago leave empty-handed, Archie couldn't stop imagining
Rudoy returning to the Windy City and being asked if he had the
paperwork in his bag that said Manning was now his client.

Archie then pictured the big-city agent lifting the two mason
jars high in the air, telling everyone in his white-shoe firm that he
didn't snag a new client, but, well, he did have some down-home
goodies from the Mannings of Drew, Mississippi.

CHAPTER 12

A Married Man
Becomes a Saint

Philadelphia, Mississippi. Winter 1971.

In the Deep South, it was the equivalent of a union between two historic royal families, the biggest social event anyone could remember in Philadelphia.

A few days before Archie and Olivia formally stepped up to the altar and said their "I do's," a full-page picture of Olivia appeared in the local paper, the *Neshoba County Democrat,* with the wedding announcement that read: "Friends and Family Are Invited Through the Medium of the Press." What precisely constituted a friend was open to interpretation, and so hundreds of folks who had never met Archie or Olivia—but still considered the couple to be their "friends"—descended upon Philadelphia on January 21, 1971, a Thursday night, to crash the most-talked-about wedding in years in Mississippi.

Governor John Bell Williams was so caught up in the marriage hubbub that he told a session of the legislature that he planned to "scalp" his invitation. He was only half joking. On the morning of the event, the governor dispatched several state highway patrolmen to Philadelphia to make sure that order would be upheld.

Archie spent the morning of his wedding day attending to important personal business. Though scores of sports agents from around the nation had reached out to him, Archie was only comfortable with one person handling his affairs—Frank Crosthwait, a friend of the Manning family for years who was an attorney in nearby Indianola. It was Crosthwait who had arranged for Archie and Buddy to visit Ole Miss and the Rebel coaches when Archie was in high school, and it was Crosthwait who had helped Archie navigate those hard, hazy days in the aftermath of Buddy's suicide.

Archie wanted an agent he could trust implicitly—someone whose word was his bond—and Crosthwait had repeatedly proven to Archie that he would stand tall and true when it mattered most. So on the morning of his nuptials, Archie met with Crosthwait for two hours in a motel in Meridian. Archie and Crosthwait had so much in common—Crosthwait was a redhead who had quarterbacked Drew High to its last league championship, in 1953—that they could speak in a language that practically only they understood. Conventional wisdom among NFL general managers and scouts was that Archie would be the second player picked in the draft, behind Stanford's Jim Plunkett, who had beaten out Archie for the Heisman Trophy. And now Archie felt good that he had a smooth-talking country lawyer in his corner.

The wedding was scheduled to begin at 6:30 p.m. at the First Baptist Church in downtown Philadelphia. Archie and his groomsmen had stayed in Meridian, and on the way to church the groomsmen stopped for a few cold ones at Ed's Beer Joint. A highway patrolman had been assigned to chaperone Archie's buddies, and after waiting outside the honky-tonk for about an hour, he entered the bar and told the wedding party it was time to go. The patrolman's number one order came from the bride: *Don't let anyone in the wedding be late!* The patrolman led the wedding party toward the church.

Hours before the ceremony hundreds of guests and curious spectators milled about on the church lawn. Once the doors swung open, the stampede was on; people didn't even wait to be escorted by the ushers. Many couldn't find a seat, including several reporters, some from as far away as Memphis. The Memphis *Press-Scimitar* covered the event like it was a football game, with a written story and numerous photos spread across several pages.

The governor sent two plainclothes officers to guard the bride and groom. After Archie and Olivia said their vows and the groom sweetly kissed the bride, the newlyweds reversed course down the aisle and out the church, hand in hand and as incandescent as a pair of shooting stars. During the ceremony even more people had gathered in front of the church, and the throng went wild at the sight of Archie and his beautiful new wife. The entire police force of Philadelphia monitored the crowd, and many of the officers cheered along with everyone else as Archie and Olivia waved and moved to their awaiting limousine.

The country club was too small for the occasion, so the couple was driven to the National Guard Armory, the only place in Philadelphia large enough to accommodate the reception of the magnitude that Olivia's parents were hosting. The vast armory was a shoulder-to-shoulder mass. Souvenir-hounds stole tablecloths, flowers, and even silverware—anything that proved they had attended the union of the South's favorite football son and his bride who looked like a New York City fashion model. When Sis saw people swiping bottles of champagne off the tables and taking them to their cars, she told Olivia's father.

"They're taking the champagne," she said.

But Cooper Williams was too happy to be bothered, even if the bottles were disappearing by the caseload. "Aw, let 'em," he said.

The next day the freshly married couple jetted to Acapulco for their honeymoon. Archie and Olivia stayed at a resort where they had their own private swimming pool. But the fair-skinned Archie had too much fun in the sun: he suffered the worst sunburn of his life. On the flight home he couldn't bear to wear shoes; his fried feet were red as tomatoes.

When Archie gingerly walked off the plane back in the United States, it was January 27. Shuffling and wincing, he looked nothing like a franchise quarterback. The NFL draft was less than twenty-four hours away.

The New Orleans Saints thoroughly researched and vetted Archie. They spoke to his college and high school coaches, his friends in Drew and in Oxford. They contacted several coaches whose teams had played against Archie, asking them about his strengths and weaknesses. They watched hours and hours of game tapes, analyzing virtually every snap he had taken as the starting quarterback at Ole Miss.

They liked everything they heard and saw. The Saints graded players in several categories on a scale of 1 to 9, with 9 being the best. The card on Manning overflowed with 9's. It read:

- Character—9
- Quickness, Agility and Balance—9
- Competitiveness and Aggressiveness—9
- Mental Alertness—9
- Strength and Explosion—9
- Ability to Throw Short—9
- Ability to Throw Long—8

- Ability to Time a Pass—9
- Delivery—9
- Quickness of Delivery—9
- Ability to Scramble—9
- Courage—9
- Quickness to Set Up—6
- Determination to Stay in the Pocket—6
- Poise—9

The debate about whom to draft didn't last long in the Saints' headquarters. The team needed a quarterback—veteran Billy Kilmer threw nearly three times as many interceptions (17) as touchdowns (6) in the team's 2-11-1 season in 1970—and Archie could do something better than any available quarterback in the upcoming draft: he could scramble.

This was crucial, the Saints' brass knew, because the team's offensive line was as porous as any in the NFL. Their quarterback in 1971 would need to move his feet to keep the Saints in games. He would have to run to give his receivers time to get open downfield, and he'd have to run for first downs.

He would, basically, have to run for his life.

On Thursday morning, January 28, Archie was summoned to the Ole Miss sports information office. That morning the NFL draft, which was held at the Belmont Plaza Hotel in New York City, had kicked off. The New England Patriots had just picked Stanford quarterback Jim Plunkett with the number one overall selection. Archie liked Plunkett—he remembered the Heisman winner's show of class by sending Archie a get-well note as he recovered from his broken arm in the Memphis hospital—but that didn't mean that Archie believed Plunkett was the superior quarterback.

Archie would never say he was better than Plunkett—it wasn't in his character to boast or, in Buddy's words, "shine your ass"—but Archie was no longer the shy kid from Drew who questioned his own abilities. He had flourished as a starter at Ole Miss for three years, slaying traditional giants like Alabama and Arkansas, and now he was as confident of his own abilities as ever. He was only twenty-one, but he already had a lot of emotional miles on his personal odometer. He was an old young man.

Archie was handed a telephone by a sports information publicist at 9:06 a.m. Central time. His cheeks red and his skin peeling from his honeymoon, he put the receiver to his ear. A representative of the New Orleans Saints informed Archie that the team had just selected him with the number two overall pick in the 1971 NFL draft.

"Yes, sir; thank you, sir," Archie said as he conversed with John Mecom, the team's owner. Also on the other end of the line were the Saints' general manager, Vic Schwenk, and the team's director of player personnel, Henry Lee Parker.

"Archie, good to have you with us," Mecom said. "I think we have a great future—you with us and us with you."

The chat lasted five minutes. Mecom invited Archie to fly to New Orleans for a press conference the next night, but Archie respectfully declined because he had to attend class; he was taking eighteen hours this semester. Plus, he and Olivia were moving in to their first apartment as husband and wife, and he had floors to scrub, furniture to put in place and a mountain of dishes to unpack and clean.

But Archie—always Southern as grits—was ecstatic that he would play pro ball in the South. He hadn't spent much time in the Big Easy, but it was only a five-hour drive from Drew, which meant Sis and Pam would be able to attend his games. This was important to Archie, because ever since he played Little League baseball, Sis was always in the crowd for his games, no matter the weather or her other obligations. Archie had been her top priority; her support was unrelenting and unwavering. For Archie, it was comforting just knowing she was there, and now he was over-the-moon happy that she would be able to share his NFL experience. Archie promised himself that if he had children he would try to emulate his mom and be a fixture in the crowd at their games. He knew exactly how much it meant.

After the conference call with the New Orleans front-office officials ended, a photographer from the Associated Press snapped a picture of the newest Saint. Archie then grabbed his book bag and was about to hustle to class, where the topic that morning was slated to be the military draft. But before Archie reached the door, the phone in the Ole Miss offices jingled again—and again, and again, and again. Reporters wanted to talk to Archie, who obliged them all. He was asked about what it felt like to be drafted, how his left arm was healing, and who his agent was.

Archie missed his class and then missed another at eleven a.m. He fielded twenty calls. At one point he asked Larry Liddell, the assistant sports information director, "Why don't you call Sis the first chance you get?"

Archie hadn't seen his mom since his wedding. Once on the phone, Sis asked her son what he'd been doing since he returned from Acapulco. "I guess I spent the day before the draft differently than most of the other guys," Archie said into the receiver. "I was unloading dishes, scrubbing the bathroom floor, and things like that. This moving is something else. . . . By the way, did you get my grades in the mail for last semester? Oh, you did. Well, don't worry about that INC. It stands for incomplete. I didn't turn in a book report. What about the other grades, a B and three C's, I guess? Two B's and two C's . . . well, now that's all right."

Archie wasn't overly concerned with his grades. He was now

officially a professional football player. Soon he would sign a contract that would bring more wealth to his family than he ever imagined as a boy growing up in Drew. He still dreamed of Buddy, and oh how he longed for his dad to be by his side on this day, at this crowning hour of his life, when he was the second player picked in the draft. His dad would have been mighty proud, Archie told his friends. Mighty proud indeed.

Archie knew he could have eased Buddy's financial burden. But the past was the past. There was no point in dwelling on that now. Because at this moment, Archie's future was brimming with promise. There was so much he hoped to achieve in the NFL.

The next morning Olivia read a newspaper column about her husband being selected by the Saints. Ten words in the story would haunt Olivia for years: "Archie Manning," the columnist wrote, "is going to the cesspool of the NFL."

Two weeks after the draft, on February 6, Archie drove to Memphis for the Mid-South All Sports Awards Banquet. The Memphis Jaycees were to present Archie with an award at a dinner at the Holiday Inn in Rivermont. The scheduled keynote speaker was George Blanda.

Two months earlier Blanda, at age forty-three, had become the oldest quarterback ever to play in the AFC championship game when he relieved Oakland's starting signal caller, Daryle Lamonica, against the Colts. Blanda threw for 217 yards and two touchdowns in the 27–21 loss to Baltimore. (He also booted a 48-yard field goal and two extra points.) Blanda would play five more years for the Raiders and would retire in 1976 after twenty-six seasons, the most in NFL history. On this night in Memphis he had some kernels of knowledge to share with the callow quarterback sitting next to him on the stage.

"You're 0 for 0 up there when you start in the pros," Blanda said from the dais, looking directly at Manning, dressed in a red, white, and blue striped shirt. "You've got to have your teammates respect you. Once you gain that respect, then one half of the battle is over. I believe you'll do just that. And, I hope I'll be playing against you for another ten years."

Blanda was a natural speaker, as his words cast a spell over the crowd. A native of Pennsylvania, he shared an anecdote about being recruited to Kentucky by Paul "Bear" Bryant. "I didn't have the best scholastic average when I was trying to get into Kentucky," Blanda said. "So Coach Bryant said he would get the dean to give me a special test with just one question. Since I was from Pennsylvania, the question was, 'What is the capital of Pennsylvania?'

"I thought about it for a while. I knew it was in the eastern part of the state. I said Hershey, because I'd been eating a lot of those candy bars. Really the answer should have been Harrisburg. So the dean said, 'Well, Hershey is only thirteen miles from Harrisburg. Thirteen from one hundred is eighty-seven. You passed!"

The crowd erupted in laughter. So did Manning, who was quickly learning about the power of storytelling. Then the graying Blanda looked directly at Archie again. "When you're a star player, youngsters emulate you," he said. "During your career, if you can lead just one, two, or three in the right direction, that's a reward money can't buy."

A reporter cornered Manning after the event and asked him about Blanda. "I don't think I have enjoyed talking to anyone more," Archie said. "He has a tremendous outlook. He loves every part of the game of football, even the hard work and the practice. It's easy to see why he is so well thought of."

Blanda had struck a deep chord within Archie. The old quarterback offered the kid QB the kind of wisdom on this night that Buddy might have given his son.

CHAPTER 13

"I'll Always Be from Drew"

Drew. Winter 1971.

From neighboring states and all across Mississippi they came—the faithful and the curious, the young and the old. Jamming into cars and buses, they traveled on secondary roads through the black dirt Delta flats. Through the windows they saw fleeting images of shanties, abandoned farms with rusted machinery, and towns gasping for life. They passed the infamous Parchman Farm state prison and finally were greeted by a billboard that read "Welcome to Drew, Home of Archie." No last name was needed.

It was February 27, 1971, Archie Manning Day in Drew. Thousands of his most devoted fans made the trip from Memphis, Jackson, Oxford, and dozens of small towns throughout Mississippi and the region. Archie had become a hero to the entire South, an acclaimed, swashbuckling football star who filled everyone in the area with pride. And now, before he would begin the next chapter of his football life with the Saints, they turned out in droves to let him know just how much they admired him.

Archie had given the people of the Delta a reason to be proud again. If nearby Parchman Farm was symbolic of the institutions of the dark days that spawned the civil rights movement in the South—the Freedom Riders had been released from Parchman only a decade earlier—Archie had become a symbol for all that was grand and glorious about his home state. A self-made young man, Archie had become a larger-than-life icon of the rising new South. Archie carried not just the hopes and dreams of his family; fans throughout Mississippi, Louisiana, Alabama, and Georgia—a.k.a. Archie's Army—lived through him and felt redeemed because of him. This was the magic of the original Manning quarterback.

The day in Drew represented the culmination of all that Archie had accomplished so far on the playing fields. At first Archie didn't want to be feted in his town, but the mayor of Drew, Snake Williford, had been insistent. Before the celebration, Archie was asked what he'd like as a gift from the town elders. "A Lincoln," he sheepishly replied, never believing he would ever be handed the keys to a shiny new car.

Drew was dressed up like never before for Archie's Day, as the event became known. On Main Street all twenty storefront windows featured displays and collages of Archie's life. The store windows were adorned with bunting and told Archie's story, illustrated in chronological order, beginning with yellowed baby pictures at the drugstore. A window at Planter's Bank housed several of Archie's old trophies, including a tiny cup he won in a Cub Scout fishing rodeo in 1959 and another trophy he earned for winning a junior Ping-Pong tournament in 1962.

Scores of cars searched for the Manning house, which local

volunteers were happy to point out. Upon entering the town, lo-cals told the drivers to go right at the second light, then travel two blocks, where they'd find the Manning residence on the left. It was impossible to miss on this morning, because a large crowd stood in the front yard. Hundreds wanted to glimpse the man of the hour.

One of the admirers was Mike Edmonds, a former teammate of Archie's at Drew. "I was a guard and we had about twenty-four boys on the squad," he said. "All of us played full-time. Every-body on the team liked Archie, and we knew he could do every-thing a quarterback should, so I wasn't much surprised at what he did at Ole Miss. He's a fine one."

Before a parade began, Sis sat in her living room and visited with several friends from Oxford and other Delta towns. The walls of the house were covered with pictures of Archie. There was a photo of four-year-old Archie dancing with his older sister, Pam. In another, President Nixon was declaring himself an Archie fan. Sis told her friends that she never let the commotion about her son affect her; she swore that nothing really had changed in her life other than Archie was now known around the world. By all accounts she appeared as relaxed and poised as ever. Like her son, she rarely grew flustered.

In the back of the house, not far from where he had found his dad, Archie sat on a bed next to Olivia, who was listening to Ar-chie explain to a few friends how he chose football over basketball several years before even though he had been an all-state basket-ball star at Drew. "I'd been averaging about 30 points," he said. "And Joe Dan Gold [then the Mississippi State coach] came to see me. I had a terrible game. Everytime I missed I slapped somebody. I fouled out before the half. Then I made up my mind and I told Joe Dan, 'Thanks, but I am going out for football.'"

By noon the population of Drew had swelled from two thousand to twelve thousand. On this pleasant, blue-sky winter afternoon the parade started at two p.m. Several high school bands
marched and played music. A drill team performed, and a few
clowns walked the short parade route and interacted with the
crowd. A friend of Archie's drove the old car he had in high school,
with "007" emblazoned on it in honor of James Bond. (In high
school Archie had his Plymouth painted burnt orange and royal
blue, his school's colors. The police never had reason to stop him,
according to Police Chief J. D. Fleming.)

The dignitaries were ferried down Main Street. The grand
marshal was Johnny Vaught, who rode in the back of a convertible with his wife, Johnsie. Vaught was wearing a new mod hair-
piece and looked twenty years younger; Archie couldn't control
his laughter when he saw his freshly sodded old coach.

Dizzy Dean, the Hall of Fame baseball pitcher, smiled at the
crowd. A native of Lucas, Arkansas, who now lived in nearby
Bond, Mississippi, Dean identified with Manning's ascendance
from a small Southern town. Dean, who saw part of himself in
Archie—as did so many others, which was one of Archie's
appeals—felt drawn to the festivities.

More household names rolled down Main Street. Former Ole
Miss quarterback Charlie Conerly, Archie's boyhood hero, greeted
the crowd. Saints coach J. D. Roberts, U.S. senator James O. East-
land, Mississippi attorney general A. F. Summer, and Governor
John Bell Williams also waved to Archie's followers. Never before
had so much star power visited Drew, and never again would it.

Then Archie appeared. Dressed in a red, white, and blue collared shirt, he rode in the back of a green Cadillac convertible like
Caesar entering Rome. Olivia and Sis were by his side. Archie
looked out at the swarm of people and saw all types: farmers in

overalls, businessmen in silk suits, women in sundresses, kids in T-shirts. Every slice of the wide economic spectrum of the day was represented in the crowd, but the Archie buttons they wore on their chests unified their standing. Even black children at the parade carried the Rebel flag in support of Ole Miss and Manning.

As Archie rode through town along the parade route, memories of his youth flashed in his mind like snapshots. There was the barbershop, where the children of Drew would hang out and listen to the elders speak about life beyond the confines of the city limits. Drew was quintessential small-town America, a place where kids walked everywhere, where everyone knew one another's business, and where curfew was measured by the hour the streetlamps flickered to life.

Archie and his buddies never felt parental pressure to excel at sports; they played only because they loved it. At pee-wee football games parents never argued with coaches and officials; at baseball games everyone in the stands viewed the umpire's decisions as gospel. There was a wholesomeness to sports in Drew, and it fueled the passions of Archie and his childhood buddies, many of whom stood on Main Street on this day and waved admiration at their longtime friend sitting atop the rear seat of the Caddie convertible.

After the parade the crowd of ten thousand gathered at Maxwell Memorial Field at Drew High, just across the street from the Manning house. Standing on a makeshift wooden stage and speaking into a microphone, the governor and Dizzy Dean praised Manning for his dazzling play on the field and his strong-as-oak character off the field. "I'm glad to welcome the hero age back again," Governor Williams said, his voice booming through the bright afternoon sunshine. "Archie Manning is giving this generation of Americans a hero to look up to."

Archie then stepped forward and began to tell the story of his rise from a tiny Delta town to a national star. He spoke about how he received, as a young boy in Drew, encouragement from his family and friends and community. "It is my sincere belief that the system which worked for that boy from Drew will work for anyone who has the desire to attain his goals in life," Archie said. "And I want to say that I know America is the greatest country in the world, Mississippi the best state. And Drew has got to be the number one hometown anywhere."

Archie concluded his speech by saying, "I'll always be from Drew."

The crowd erupted in cheers. Archie and Olivia were handed the keys to a new white Lincoln Continental Mark II, which was hitched to a red ski boat. The Lincoln was worth more than $9,000 and was financed by contributions from deep-pocketed fans from across America; the boat was a gift from a firm in Florida headed by Archie admirers. Gazing at his new car, Archie joked, "I'm sure you people from Drew know that this is a long way from that old orange Plymouth I used to drive."

Archie took a moment to talk to Money Lockett from Clarksdale, Mississippi. She was in a station wagon and living in an iron lung. After Archie approached, she explained that she was his biggest fan and she had typed letters to monks in the Far Pacific asking them to remember Archie in their prayers. The monks wrote back and agreed to pray for Archie. Lockett then said she sent the monks a bumper sticker: *Archie is a Saint.*

Archie listened intently to Lockett. All day long he heard people express their devotion to him, one after the next, and he was overwhelmed by all the fanfare and anecdotes of how he had brought them so much joy. Yet there still remained a lingering sadness—an emptiness. Just across the street from where he was now being celebrated was the house in which he had found his father only two years earlier. It was a pain that time would never completely wipe away.

Later that evening, as the last blush of sunlight filled the Mississippi sky, Archie and Olivia drove away in their new car. Just like that, the adored young man from Drew was off again.

CHAPTER 14

———
———

The Beat-up Quarterback

New Orleans. Summer-Autumn 1971.

He drove down a street in New Orleans, sitting behind the wheel of his red Corvette, another new car that had been given to him. Archie was twenty-two years old, wealthy beyond his imagination in the fall of 1971, and now he was motoring through his new city as the starting quarterback for the New Orleans Saints. Life was good as he approached a stop sign in his sports car that was as shiny as a polished apple.

In August, Archie signed a contract that was more lucrative than what the Patriots had given the number one overall pick, Jim Plunkett. Frank Crosthwait, the Mannings' longtime family friend who acted as Archie's agent, had outwitted the Saints front office by playing the role of a country-bumpkin lawyer during contract negotiations. Crosthwait hit the jackpot for his client: Archie signed a five-year, $410,000 contract—at the time the richest rookie deal in NFL history.

One of the first things Archie wanted to do with his money was to buy his mom a new house in Drew. But Sis insisted that she would never move from the three-bedroom, one-bath home where she had raised her two children. "No, this is our house," she told Archie. "I don't need a new house. I need this one." But Sis finally allowed Archie to brick the front of the house, her only concession to her son's newfound wealth.

Archie instantly became the face of the franchise. A Chevrolet dealership signed him to an endorsement contract and handed him the keys to the Corvette, which had a hood that Archie swore stretched on for a country mile. Early in the autumn of 1971, only days after Archie had played in his first NFL game, he was behind the wheel of his new car when . . . *smash!* Archie rammed into the back of a car at a stop sign. He failed to properly judge just how long his hood actually was—his first *really* bad read as the Saints quarterback.

The driver of the car that had been hit popped out of the driver's seat. Angered, he marched toward Archie.

The irate driver looked at Archie up and down, examining him closely. Suddenly, the man's face softened. "Hey, Arch!" he yelled. The man returned to his car. As he drove away, he screamed, "Go Saints!"

Standing in front of his car, Archie began to fall in love with the fans in his new city.

But would the people of New Orleans—in good days and bad, in sickness and in health—continue to love him back?

In Archie's rookie season, on one of the first mornings of training camp, held in Hattiesburg, Mississippi, Archie spotted the team's living legend sitting in a wheelbarrow. He didn't look like a football player, with a belly so big it looked as if he had swallowed a medicine ball. But in the summer of 1971, kicker Tom Dempsey was the franchise's most notable player—damning testimony on the state of the Saints.

The previous fall, on November 8, 1970, New Orleans trailed Detroit 17–16 with only two seconds remaining in the fourth quarter on a chilly afternoon at Tulane Stadium. The Saints had the ball on their own 37-yard line and it was fourth down. In a private booth high above the stadium, New Orleans assistant coach Don Heinrich radioed down to head coach J. D. Roberts: "Might as well kick it," Heinrich said.

Roberts, who had replaced Tom Fears only five days earlier, sent the punt team onto the field. Frantically, Heinrich yelled into his intercom, "No, no, kick a field goal."

Roused from the bench, Tom Dempsey trotted onto the field. Born without toes on his right foot, Dempsey wore a modified black shoe with a flattened toe surface. At the time the goalposts were even with the goal line, making this a 63-yard attempt. The longest field goal in history was a 56-yarder kicked by Baltimore's Bert Rechichar in 1953. But now Dempsey—using a straight-on, toe-first style—swung his leg like a giant pendulum and booted the ball. It sailed end over end through the cold sky, tumbling through the Tulane Stadium uprights with a few feet to spare. The minuscule crowd leaped to its feet in disbelief. The Saints won 19–17, their second and final victory of the 1970 season.

Dempsey spent the off-season enjoying the fruits—and desserts—of his accomplishment on the banquet tour. Archie figured he weighed at least 300 pounds as he lounged in that wheelbarrow. Archie wasn't the least bit surprised that Dempsey, a few weeks later, was cut before the Saints' first game in 1971.

There was another distressing sight at the 1971 training camp: Archie saw Sam Holden, a rookie offensive lineman, standing around with a hamstring injury. When the draft was unfolding months earlier, Archie realized that Dan Dierdorf, a consensus all-American tackle at Michigan, was still available when it was time for the Saints to make their second-round selection. But then New Orleans picked Holden, who had played at Grambling State.

After the selection was made Archie looked at Olivia. "Wow, this guy must be really good," he said. "They picked him ahead of Dierdorf."

The intention was that Holden would become Archie's blind-side protector for the next decade. But then Archie started to watch Holden run around a track in Hattiesburg, and Archie wasn't impressed with his speed or agility. The more Archie looked at Holden, the more he believed Holden's lap times could have been measured with a sundial. Archie nicknamed him Sudden Sam.

Holden played in nine games in 1971 but didn't start. The Saints coaches gave him every chance to flourish the following preseason, but in a game against Pittsburgh, the Steelers' L. C. Greenwood beat Sudden Sam repeatedly and greeted Archie in the backfield with bone-jarring hits just as Archie was completing his seven-step drop.

Sudden Sam never played a down in another regular-season NFL game. Dierdorf was voted to six Pro Bowls, was named first-time All-Pro five times, and was on the NFL's 1970s All-Decade team.

After the Saints' final preseason game of 1971, J. D. Roberts named Archie the starting quarterback. Archie wasn't sure if he was ready. In his home debut in the preseason two weeks earlier, a Kansas City Chiefs defender hurled him into a concrete sideline dugout at Tulane Stadium as Archie scrambled out-of-bounds. Archie injured the arch of his foot; it hurt to walk.

More disturbing than the injury was how it happened: it came on a busted play. The Saints players for years were notorious for missing assignments and not executing what was called in the huddle, and nothing was more frustrating to Archie the perfectionist than undisciplined play. But Archie was now the show horse of the franchise, and if he was upright, he was going to play. The only way to combat broken plays was to do what he did best: improvise and run like hell.

In his first regular season start on September 19 against the Los Angeles Rams and its famed Fearsome Foursome defensive line led by Deacon Jones and Merlin Olsen, Archie kept the Saints in the game by extending plays with his feet. With four seconds remaining in the fourth quarter, the Saints trailed 20–17 and had the ball on the Rams' 1-yard line. Archie called a time-out.

He ran to the sideline. "We're going for it," J. D. Roberts said.

Roberts conferred with Ken Shipp, the team's offensive coordinator. Roberts and Shipp, a pair of deliberative thinkers, bounced ideas back and forth. A referee finally approached. "C'mon, men, let's play!"

Archie loped back onto the field, looking back at the bench, waiting for the play call. When he reached the huddle he peered back again, but the coaches still hadn't made a decision. A wide receiver asked Archie, "What are we going to do?"

"I don't know," the rookie quarterback said. "They never told me."

Fearing a delay-of-game penalty, Archie reached back to his college days for his favorite play call: a sprint-out to the left and option to run or pass. Archie took the snap, outran the Fearsome Foursome to the left, and dove into the end zone. The Saints' new kicker, Skip Butler, split the uprights on the extra point and New Orleans won 24–20.

That evening Archie, Olivia, and several of the players and

their wives went to the French Quarter. They enjoyed a long, lei-
surely dinner at the Rib Room and toasted their upset victory.
Those players believed it would be the first of many celebrations.
For at least one night, led by their red-haired, sharp-jawed rookie
quarterback, the Saints were marching.

Archie and Olivia began to sink their roots into the Crescent
City. They moved in to a penthouse apartment in Metairie, a sub-
urb in Jefferson Parish where the Saints trained. They visited art
galleries and enjoyed the music scene. They became regulars at
Drago's—the spot where the charbroiled oyster was claimed to
have been invented—and they couldn't get enough of the barbecued shrimp at Pascal's Manale restaurant. They were young and
curious, and now a new world of culture and cuisine was opening
up to them. Who knows, they wondered, maybe they could spend
their lives in this vivacious city where so much seemed possible.

The best times in New Orleans were after victories, when Archie and Olivia would often head to Manale. During the week
they'd have to wait in line for ninety minutes to get in just like
everyone else. But on a Sunday night after he guided the Saints to
a win, Archie and his guests would be waved right in—one of the
perks of being the toast of the Big Easy.

It just didn't happen very often.

CHAPTER 15

===

Archie One and Archie Two

New Orleans. Autumn 1981.

The boos cascaded from every section in the New Orleans Superdome—not counting those sections that were silently empty—hurled like sharpened spears by thousands of fans with brown paper bags covering their heads. After Archie threw yet another interception in what was surely going to be yet another loss for the Saints during the NFL's 1981 season—Archie's eleventh—the boos reverberated like rolling thunder for nearly a minute. Archie, who had been described by former Saints coach Hank Stram as a "franchise player without a franchise," was the object of everyone's disgust.

Olivia Manning, pregnant with their third child, had taken her two young boys to the game earlier in the afternoon. Cooper was seven and Peyton was five. Olivia had quit sitting with the other players' wives and girlfriends because of the verbal abuse that was directed at them during the losses—and there were a lot of losses.

In Archie's first ten seasons with the Saints, they had a 41-102-3 record. In 1980 the Aints, as they were dismissively called, finished 1-15, an ignominious record of NFL futility in the era of the 16-game schedule. Now, a year later, the woebegone franchise floundered once again and was about to lose another game. The Aints would finish 4-12 and dwell in the NFC West cellar.

Hoping to blend into the crowd, Olivia had moved to more inconspicuous seats with her father and the boys for this game. A Southern lady to her well-mannered core, she tried to hold her tongue and ignore the thousands of voices who were chastising and yelling at her husband in the bluest of language, but sometimes she just couldn't help herself. During an earlier game a fan near her screamed, "Manning stinks, get him outta there! He stinks!"

Olivia, turning to the man, summoned all the charm she could muster. In her soft, sweet-as-honey drawl, she said as politely as possible, "Please don't say that. He's my husband."

The man looked at Olivia for a moment. Then, shrugging his shoulders, he replied, "You have my sympathies, lady, but I don't care. He still stinks."

Olivia continually was mystified by the anger of the fans. There were times when Archie would be standing on the sideline talking to coaches when, suddenly, a torrent of expletives would fly from the crowd at her husband. Confused, Olivia wouldn't know why people were in such a lather until she'd look up at the jumbo screen on the Superdome scoreboard. Archie had an endorsement deal with Royal Oldsmobile, and when his smiling face would appear in an advertisement on the big screen, the fans would holler and fuss like Archie was personally leading a crusade to ban Mardi Gras.

Now, on this autumn afternoon in 1981, it was happening again. "You suck, Manning!" they screamed. "You're awful!"

Down on the field Archie was running for his life, terrorized, scrambling from sideline to sideline. He was sacked several times, and on other plays he was slammed to the ground like a rag doll after throwing the ball away. By the third quarter he was wheezing in pain. But the fans showed no mercy for their quarterback.

In full throat, they called him every foul name Olivia had ever heard—and some she hadn't—and finally she cracked. She'd had enough. She was going to tell every soul in that building what a kind and wonderful and caring man Archie was, what a doting father he was, what a loving husband he was, and how much he had overcome in his life just to be on this field and giving everything he could for his adopted city. They just needed a little education, and then they would stop booing. She was sure of it.

"You suck, Manning!"

Olivia rose to her feet, ready to calmly articulate her latest defense of the love of her life. She turned to her husband's haters and she was about to speak when . . .

Two high-pitched voices sounded familiar. Very familiar. She looked down and the sight took her breath away: Cooper and Peyton, with crumpled bags over their heads that they had picked up off the ground, were leading the chorus of boos.

"Boo," the Manning boys yelled. "Boo, Archie! Boo!"

Cooper arrived on March 6, 1974, about two and a half months after Archie's third season in the NFL. Cooper weighed 12 pounds and 3 ounces, and was 22 inches long. "I don't know whether the weight is an NFL record," Archie said, "but maybe Cooper and I can go in as a package deal when my contract is up for negotiation."

"I weighed eight and a half pounds and was twenty-three inches long and I was all arms and legs," Archie said. "But this li'l dude is big. You can spot him in the nursery a hundred yards away." Olivia spent several days in the hospital recovering from the childbirth. One night Dick Brennan, the owner of Commander's Palace in New Orleans, sent a six-course dinner to Olivia's room. Archie dressed up for the feast, donning a coat and tie. As they ate, the new parents sipped some of the finest wine in New Orleans—courtesy of Mr. Brennan. Olivia felt so good she didn't even take any pain medication that night.

Archie fell hard and fast for his first son. Cooper was born in the off-season, so Archie had hours of free time on his hands—one of the many perks of being a professional athlete. He loved putting Cooper in a stroller and pushing him through their leafy Uptown New Orleans neighborhood. Archie proudly showed off Cooper to anyone they passed on the sidewalk. By the time Cooper was two years old, Archie was carrying him into the Superdome on Saturday mornings before Sunday games. After Archie watched film of the upcoming opponent and took part in a quick walk-through practice in which formations and plays were reviewed, he and Cooper often played with other fathers and their sons. The Saints even put out a spread of doughnuts and milk for the kids.

Two years after Cooper arrived, Olivia was pregnant again. Not finding out the sex of the child before birth, the Mannings picked a name that would work for a boy or a girl—though both of them believed it would be a girl. Archie thought back to his childhood, to those halcyon Friday nights spent with his uncle, the Mississippi farmer who grew cotton and soybeans and raised cattle. The uncle had as much fun as Archie did when they drove to small towns across the Delta following the Drew High football team and afterward enjoyed late-night breakfasts at a diner in Cleveland. Those were some of Archie's richest memories as well. Just mentioning his uncle's name brought back images of family and football in Archie's mind. The uncle would die a bachelor, but now after Olivia gave birth to a baby boy on March 24, 1976, his first name would live on in the nephew he never met: Peyton Williams Manning.

Their family expanding, Archie and Olivia briefly discussed buying a bigger house in the suburbs of New Orleans, but Olivia eventually told her husband, "There are a million suburbs, but there's only one Uptown." In the Manning household, Olivia's words were law when it came to living arrangements. They stayed in their neighborhood and bought a quaint camelback cottage on Seventh Street.

Peyton and Cooper shared an upstairs bedroom. As soon as Peyton was old enough to walk, the brothers turned the bedroom into a mini–athletic arena. They wrestled. They played indoor tennis with a pillow-soft ball. They shot a tiny basketball at a miniature hoop. And whenever one of them had a football in his hands, a game of some sort immediately was on. No matter what hour of the day or night, no matter what room they were in, no matter if only one of them felt like playing. Anytime was playtime.

In the downstairs living room, on a sprawling rectangular carpet, Archie often played a game he called "knee football" with his boys. After practice Archie would stroll through the front door. If he dropped to his knees on the carpet, it meant the game was on. Little Cooper and Peyton would try to take down Archie, who would be holding a miniature football. If the boys had the ball, they would try to run around or over Archie. Other times, little Peyton would attempt passes to Cooper, throwing the ball over Archie's outstretched arms. No matter how tired Archie was from practice, the father would play his boys one-on-two.

Archie later put up a basketball goal in the driveway. The games were often two-on-two: Archie and Peyton against Olivia and

Cooper. The boys attacked the hoop with extreme competitive-ness, as if all the cookies on the block were to be awarded to the winner. As the kids aged, Peyton and Cooper would play their dad one-on-one in games to 20. Archie would let them keep the score close, but the father always emerged victorious—even as his kid would grab at his body and hack his arms to prevent his un-corking the potential clinching shot.

The yard on Seventh Street was small, so Archie and the boys would trek across the road to an empty field to toss a football or play a pickup game with others. Archie often acted as a commis-sioner for the games; he would come home from practice, head across the street, and organize two teams of neighborhood kids. He would be worn-out from his hours at the Saints' facility—his workday usually started at the crack of dawn with film study—but the sight of his kids would energize him, as if his boys always gave him a second wind.

Sometimes Archie would grab his camcorder and lug it outside to film the action. He would pretend that he was a cameraman for a nationally televised game, and the boys happily played along with the make-believe. One time Archie had the boys run in front of the camera and state their name, age, and favorite player.

First up was Cooper. "Cooper Manning. Six years old. My fa-vorite player is Roger Staubach. And I really like the San Diego Chargers."

Then Peyton stepped forward. Before uttering a word, he flashed a dimpled smile, like he knew it was time to perform be-cause the tape was rolling. Then he said, "Peyton Manning. Age four. And my favorite team is Wes Chandler."

Everyone in earshot laughed at Peyton, who immediately balled his hand into a fist and started swinging through the air. At only four, he already despised the idea that he had come up short at something. "You need an attitude adjustment," Archie frequently told Peyton. But when Archie playfully pushed Peyton too hard, the boy would find a way to retaliate against his father.

During a Thanksgiving football game when Peyton was six, he was tackled hard by a defender, which Archie recorded on video-tape. Immediately, Peyton wanted to quit, but Archie wouldn't let him, employing the directive taught to him by his own father. Peyton was furious. Crying, Peyton ran up to the camera, snarled at his dad, and yelled, "I'm going to tell Mom what her Christmas present is!"

Like Archie when he was a kid, Peyton searched for perfection as a child. When he was five he played in a coach-pitch baseball league. His team lost every game by about a dozen runs, but the coach always told the boys that the contests ended in a tie. "He thinks we're stupid," Peyton said to his parents. "It was not a tie."

In Little League baseball Peyton was so focused on winning that he became a little dictator around his teammates, telling them what they needed to do better. Concerned that Peyton was about to lose his friends, Archie and Olivia sat Peyton down and told him he needed to ease up on his teammates. "Hey, everybody is not like you," Archie said. "Everybody does not like baseball as much as you do. Some kids just show up. They are not going to take extra batting practice. They are not going to work on the double play."

Peyton listened to his dad intently; there was one thing that was unquestionably obvious about the boy—Archie was his hero. When Peyton was three, Archie had the video camera rolling when Peyton was asked what he wanted to be when he grew up.

"A quata-back," Peyton said.

Then Peyton was pressed to name his favorite quarterback. He responded in a split second:

"My dad," he said.

Around the Saints practice facility, Cooper and Peyton were

known as Archie One and Archie Two. After Saturday walk-through practices at the Superdome, the boys usually trailed behind their dad, politely answering questions from Archie's teammates with "yes sir" and "no sir"—demonstrating Mississippi manners that Olivia had taught them. When Archie was in meetings, Cooper and Peyton would go on scavenger hunts in the locker room searching for wads of leftover tape. They rolled the pieces into a ball and then they would bolt onto the Superdome field and play one-on-one football, their laughter echoing up, up, and up into the rafters of the empty stadium. For Archie, it was a welcome sound compared to the boos that all too often filled the dome. When the boys weren't tackling each other, they threw the tape ball back and forth—Peyton's first passes in an NFL stadium. After the walk-throughs, Archie would take the boys to Domilise's in the French Quarter for messy po' boy sandwiches and tall mugs of Barq's root beer.

On Sundays after home games, Olivia would guide little Cooper and Peyton into the locker room to see Archie. Cooper often wandered away; if he spotted a player from the opposing team he liked, such as Pittsburgh wide receiver Lynn Swann, he would march up to him and start peppering him with questions: *What's it like to play for the Steelers? Why are you a wide receiver? Do you know my dad?*

Other times after games Cooper and Peyton would dart onto the Superdome field. The stadium lights would be out, and in the dark Cooper and Peyton would play catch and try to tackle each other. Sometimes Archie would join them—his happiest time on game days.

In the summers, before training camp began, Archie enjoyed jogging along the streets of the Big Easy, up and down St. Charles

Avenue, past some of the South's most famous mansions on that equally famous tree-lined and canopied landmark. Archie had been a public figure for years, but now in New Orleans he could blend into the crowd—or so it seemed, because people tended to leave him alone and not ask for autographs or photographs.

But Archie was well aware that NFL starting quarterbacks and their families were scrutinized. When his boys were young, he told Cooper and Peyton that people would be watching them. They needed to act with integrity at all times, he said, no matter the circumstances. Peyton the young perfectionist especially took the advice to heart. When he went to movies with his buddies, he didn't run up and down the theater aisles with them, because he didn't want anyone to say, *Just look at Archie's out-of-control boy*.

Peyton understood that because of his last name, the public camera lens was focused on him—and he hadn't even thrown his first touchdown pass in an organized football game yet. Years later, when he would drink beer at a high school party, he always put it in a cup.

Beginning with their earliest memories, the boys knew that their dad was a losing quarterback.

When Cooper was three the Saints hosted the Tampa Bay Buccaneers on December 11, 1977. The Bucs were in their second year of existence and had yet to win a game, fumbling and bumbling their way to an overall record of 0-26. The Saints were 3-9, and the New Orleans players were adamant about not becoming the first team to lose to the lowly Bucs. "I don't want to be the laughing-stock of the league, and that's what we'll be if we lost to Tampa Bay," Archie said on the eve of the game. He also said it would be "disgraceful" if the Saints were the first team to fall to Tampa.

But in front of the home crowd, Archie threw three interceptions before he was benched for backup Bobby Scott, who also
tossed three picks. Three of the Saints' interceptions were returned for touchdowns. By the fourth quarter Tampa Bay had a
26–0 lead. As the clock wound down, and with the New Orleans
fans loudly booing their team, a few Buccaneers defenders taunted
Archie, yelling, "It's disgraceful! It's disgraceful!" The final was
33–14.

"What a nightmare," Saints coach Hank Stram said in the
locker room. "It was the worst experience of my coaching career." Stram was fired the next week. When approached by reporters, Archie waved them away. "I've got nothing to say," he said. It
was becoming harder and harder to be the nice guy.

In the winners' locker room, coach John McKay thanked Archie for firing up his defense with his pregame comments and—
this zinger really touched a nerve with Archie—for his giving
nature on the field. Archie wanted nothing more than to go home
and disappear, but first he needed to drive some friends to a hotel.
They had watched the game with Olivia and Cooper.

At some point during the car ride a friend asked Archie, "Well,
who do you play next week?"

"The Atlanta Falcons," Archie replied.

Then Cooper, who was sitting on Olivia's lap, suddenly piped
up. "Yeah," he said, "and we'll beat the hell out of 'em too!"

Cooper, only a toddler, had already become the family comedian.

Shortly after he started speaking, Cooper had a name for his dad:
Archibald Watermelon. The parents had no idea why Cooper had
come up with this sobriquet for Archie, but every time he said it

Archie and Olivia couldn't help but smile. It was just Cooper being crazy Cooper.

Peyton followed his older brother everywhere, and if Cooper liked something, so did Peyton. Cooper was a standout at nearly everything he attempted. He had a comedic timing in telling jokes, could effortlessly perform a dance if a nickel was on the line, and had Archie's natural ability to spin a spiral. But little Peyton didn't possess his grace, at least not early on.

One afternoon Peyton was in the Saints' weight room with Archie when he fell, headfirst, onto a barbell. Peyton cut his head, and immediately blood gushed as if a 300-pound defensive lineman had just smacked him. But as Archie drove him to the emergency room for stitches, little Peyton's eyes never welled up with tears. He didn't even admit he was in the slightest bit of pain. He just bit his lip and said, "It doesn't hurt, it doesn't hurt, it doesn't hurt"—even though clearly he had to be suffering. It was the first time he tried to hide an injury.

As they grew older Cooper and Peyton spent more and more time in the Saints facility. A smooth talker even as a child, Cooper convinced one of the trainers to tape him up as if he were a member of the team. The trainer then wrapped his ankles and wrists in tape. When Peyton saw his brother getting worked on, he asked to be taped up as well. A tradition was born. Before many practices, the two boys would run through the locker room looking like miniature versions of their dad with their ankles and wrists mummified in tape. After practice they would jump into the whirlpool or walk into the sauna—just as the players did. The boys couldn't wait to grow up and become NFL quarterbacks just like their daddy.

Every night before bed, Archie had "man-to-man" talks with his boys. Archie told them how much he loved them and that the single most important thing in the world was to be kind to others. If they did that, Archie said, then, no matter what, he would be proud of them. *Be a nice guy,* Archie stressed. *Be a nice guy.*

During the football seasons Sunday nights were the hardest for Archie. He'd walk into the house after another loss and collapse onto the couch. Cooper and Peyton would run to their dad, anxious to hear all about the game. Archie would calmly explain that a quarterback can't win every game, and then he would challenge his boys to participate in a competition: who could best massage the bumps and knots out of daddy's aching arms and shoulders? Cooper and Peyton would then go to work, digging their fingers into their dad's beat-up body.

Archie spent most of his twelve seasons with New Orleans scrambling from defenders. He was sacked 340 times in his Saints career—in 1975 he was sacked an NFL record 53 times—and became a living, breathing, aching medical chart. In the mid-1970s many in the league believed his career was over when he underwent two operations on his throwing arm. In 1974 he was flattened by Chicago's Wally Chambers and tore cartilage in his left knee. In '77 Atlanta's Jeff Merrow crushed Archie with a hit so violent that it broke his jaw. The Bears' Alan Page smashed him so ferociously in '80 that Archie's nose was rearranged, breaking it clean.

On January 18, 1976, Archie and Olivia had finished watching Pittsburgh beat Dallas 21–17 in Super Bowl X in the den of their home when a league official called. Though Archie had been lustily booed throughout the '75 season by his home crowd, the NFL now wanted to know if he could play in the Pro Bowl, a week away in Honolulu. Two NFC quarterbacks—the Cowboys' Roger Staubach and the Vikings' Fran Tarkenton—had backed out. Archie hadn't been able to practice for stretches during the season because of his sore right elbow, but he told the league office to sit tight for a few minutes; he would call back.

He grabbed a ball from his trophy case and walked outside with Olivia into the cool New Orleans night. With his wife acting as his receiver, Archie reared back and tried to throw a spiral—but it traveled only a few feet, landing well short of Olivia. All he could do was lob the ball. His arm was shot. He called the league office back and thanked them for the offer, but said he wasn't physically able to play.

Archie would miss the Pro Bowl and the entire 1976 season with disabling tendonitis in his right shoulder.

The boys knew how much their dad was hurting. On many Monday mornings Archie couldn't even walk down the stairs; he'd slide down the banister. But Cooper and Peyton never heard their father complain about his football fate. His frustrations stayed at the Superdome.

After home games Archie One and Archie Two—if they weren't out running around in the dark of the dome field—would wait for their dad outside the locker room. They'd see Archie emerge, walking gingerly, often so sore it was difficult for him to move. But he would always give a big hug to Olivia, then wrap his arms around the boys before going to see the fans and signing every piece of paper or cap or jersey that was thrust at him. Peyton sometimes would grow impatient and say, "Dad, let's go home," but Archie would just smile at his son and tell Peyton to put a grin on his face. Archie was showing his boys that he was still playing the role of the quarterback, remaining upbeat and optimistic in public.

Archie never once enjoyed a winning season with the Saints,

but he never demanded a trade. Players around the league wondered why he was so faithful to the franchise and how he main-
tained such a positive attitude. Archie would always point to his
wife and kids, telling anyone who questioned his sanity for staying in New Orleans that his family was happy in the Crescent
City, that their roots were growing deep, and that was what mattered most. The smiles on the faces of his boys when they came
home from school—and the stories they told Archie about how
much fun they had with their friends—made the losing tolerable.

Archie's positive attitude made him one of the most well-liked
players in the NFL. Onetime Rams defensive end Jack Youngblood confided to New Orleans wide receiver Danny Abramowicz
that he couldn't bring himself to level Archie. "I can't do it to that
boy," Youngblood said. "So many times I've had a straight shot at
him when his back was turned, but I just can't do it."

After Abramowicz was traded to the 49ers two games into the
1973 season, he had some parting advice for Archie before flying
to San Francisco. "You better get out of this place," he told his
quarterback. "They're going to kill you here."

But Archie wouldn't leave. His kids loved New Orleans, and
that made it home.

CHAPTER 16

——

The Commuter QB

Houston–New Orleans. Fall 1981.

In 1978 Archie guided the Saints to a 7-9 record in his seventh year in the NFL. He completed 61.8 percent of his passes and threw for 3,416 yards—both career highs to that point. He tossed 17 touchdown passes and 16 interceptions. He rushed for 202 yards and 1 touchdown. He was sacked 37 times, the fifth most in the NFL. In the ultimate sympathy vote, the UPI named Archie the NFL's Most Valuable Player.

That year he also won the Justice Byron (Whizzer) White humanitarian award, given to the NFL player who had contributed the most to his team, his community, and his country. Archie flew to Chicago to accept the award at a black-tie banquet.

On his way to the stage, his thoughts traveled back in time to his father, to the conversation they had on the day Buddy drove Archie to Oxford for his first practice at Ole Miss. In this instant in Chicago, it was as if his dad were still speaking to him, his familiar voice echoing in his head once again. Archie was seized with emotion. The newly minted NFL Man of the Year realized that everything he had accomplished could be traced back to the wisdom of his father.

"He told me he knew I was going to Oxford to play football, but I should always remember that it was more important to be a nice guy, whether I turned out to be a great football player or not," Archie told the crowd. "I thought about what he said a lot after he died."

Archie didn't know why the image and memory of his father came back to him so vividly at the moment he mounted the stage in Chicago. "That had to be God-sent," Archie said. "I wasn't trying to be emotional, but it was an overwhelming moment. I finally was satisfied that I'd made an effort to do what my dad wanted."

Despite winning the UPI MVP Award and the Whizzer White Award, reporters in Chicago drilled Archie about the losing, about how it felt to play for the Saints. They pressed him to describe his private agony of being on the worst team in the NFL. "I'd like to win," he said. "I've thought about how nice it would be to play on a championship team, but I still think we can do that in New Orleans. If I didn't think we could win someday, I couldn't play here. I couldn't just pick up and go to another team, even if I were traded. I've made a commitment to New Orleans, and the community has been good to me. I would have to think long and hard before I could ever leave."

The lowest of all the professional valleys of Archie's football career arrived in 1980.

After the Saints began the season with seven straight losses, Robert Le Compte, a bartender in Di Liberto's bar in New Orleans, designed a brown paper bag with eyeholes and the word

"Aints" written across the front. As a stunt, Le Compte donned the bag and performed a eulogy marking the Saints' seventh consecutive loss, this one a 41–14 drubbing at home to Atlanta. Le Compte told his patrons that he would wear a bag every Sunday until the Saints won their first game.

Five weeks later, more than five thousand fans at the Superdome wore paper bags over their heads for the game against the Los Angeles Rams—the first time in history that paper bags made a widespread appearance at a sporting event. Team officials tried to dissuade fans from bringing the bags into the stadium because they constituted a fire hazard, but that only encouraged more fans to wear the bags.

The Rams' defensive front four dominated the game. All-Pros Fred Dryer and Jack Youngblood harassed Archie nearly every time he dropped back to throw—but they rarely hit him hard. With the Rams cruising to a 27–7 victory, the two stalwart defenders took it easy on Archie, whom they both respected as much as any player in the NFL. After the loss Saints head coach Dick Nolan was fired. Archie, for one of the first times in his professional life, cried at the news.

Life wasn't supposed to be this way for Archie. Before the season, Archie and Olivia had believed that the fall of 1980 was going to be magical. Olivia was pregnant with their third child, whom Archie optimistically called "our playoff baby." Archie had given up most of his off-the-field obligations to help Olivia with Cooper and Peyton. But by December, Archie was no longer using the playoffs to reference the baby; the child, who was due around the holidays, was now "our Christmas present."

On the first weekend of December, the 0-14 Saints flew across the country to play the San Francisco 49ers. Facing reporters before the game, Archie held his chin up and refused to admit he felt defeated. "It's hard to describe this thing," Manning said, "but the most fun is the two or three hours a week when you're playing the football games. Here we are 0 and 14 and the fans are on you and reporters, even the *Wall Street Journal,* are calling you, but at one o'clock every Sunday you have another chance to win a football game. That's the fun. It's just fun to play football."

During the first half against the 49ers, Archie played with sandlot abandon, scrambling around the field like he did at Ole Miss and rifling pinpoint-perfect passes into the arms of his receivers. He threw three touchdowns in the opening 30 minutes as the Saints charged to a 35–7 halftime lead.

In the locker room San Francisco head coach Bill Walsh paced and paced trying to figure out what to tell his players. Before he opened his mouth, the Saints emerged from their own locker room, yelling challenging words like, "Let's beat 'em 70–7." Walsh simply let his players listen; he didn't say a word.

That turned out to be a masterful motivational moment. The 49ers were transformed. Quarterback Joe Montana passed for two touchdowns and ran for another. Late in the fourth quarter San Francisco running back Lenvil Elliott plowed into the end zone to tie the score at 35. Then, in overtime, 49er kicker Ray Wersching drilled a 36-yard field goal to give San Francisco a 38–35 victory. The 28-point comeback remains the largest in NFL regular-season history.

In the locker room Archie didn't know if he should laugh or cry or maybe even put a bag over his head. In a lost year—the Saints had just tied the NFL record for the most defeats in one season—this had been the most absurd way to lose imaginable. On the cross-country plane ride home Archie lit a cigar and played poker with his teammates until they landed. "Otherwise," he said the next day, "I knew I'd never sleep when I got home. This season has given me insomnia."

The following Sunday afternoon the Saints played the New York Jets in a snowstorm at Shea Stadium in Queens. Before the game Archie spoke to Jets quarterback Richard Todd on the field. A former star at Alabama, Todd reminisced with Archie about playing in the SEC. Then Todd told Archie how sorry he was that the Saints' season had turned into such a disaster and that Archie should just keep fighting. At first Archie appreciated the kind words, but then he sensed Todd was belittling him.

"Richard, old buddy," Archie said, "we're going to whip your ass today."

Early in the first quarter Archie threw a 14-yard touchdown pass to Jack Holmes, giving the Saints a 7–0 lead. The game went back and forth, but New Orleans seized the lead in the fourth quarter on a 1-yard touchdown plunge by running back Tony Galbreath.

The seconds ticked away. With less than a minute to play and the Saints leading 21–20, Archie gazed at the scoreboard and saw what he later described as "a huge black cloud" descend from the heavens. He thought the apocalypse was at hand and "we're going to win a game but nobody's going to know it." But then the cloud disappeared, the final seconds evaporated from the clock, and the Saints captured their first victory of 1980.

Archie never won a Super Bowl and never experienced the excitement of a playoff game. But after the win over the Jets the party on the plane ride home—the cigars, the drinks, the toasts, the laughs—would stand out as the greatest moment of his NFL career.

No one—not even opposing players—could understand why Archie stayed in New Orleans. After hearing the home fans boo Archie in 1981, Eagles defensive end Claude Humphrey said, "Jesus Christ could be back there and if He didn't throw a touchdown pass, they'd boo Him."

Archie tried to explain his devotion to New Orleans earlier that year. "The number one question people ask me is: 'Why don't you leave? Why don't you get out of here?,'" Archie said in April 1981. "It's kind of hard to explain. I've put in ten years here, this team, this city. My kids are happy in school here; my wife is happy in New Orleans. Sure I want to win, but I want to be here, in this city."

Archie continued. "Coaches, players, they come and go so fast around here. I have this way of memorizing phone numbers. I'll remember the first three digits and then use the players' jersey numbers to help me recall the last four. Like 522-4210, that's 522, Charlie Conerly, Fran Tarkenton. Or 3203, that's O. J. Simpson, Daryle Lamonica. I used to do it with Saints players, but I was dialing wrong numbers, getting things screwed up because my teammates kept changing so often."

At the end of the preseason in 1982 New Orleans coach Bum Phillips named Kenny Stabler his starting quarterback. Stabler and Phillips shared a history: two years earlier Stabler led the Houston Oilers, who were then coached by Phillips, into the playoffs. Now Phillips was hoping that Stabler could spark a run to the postseason in the Big Easy.

Archie had just signed a five-year contract that annually paid him $600,000. He was the highest-paid player on the team—and now he was a backup. He figured his days as a Saint were numbered.

In the season opener New Orleans lost to the St. Louis Cardinals, 21–7. Late in the fourth quarter Archie entered the game. As he ran onto the field, a thunderclap of boos filled the Superdome. He had been the leader of the franchise for more than a decade, but now it was clear his time in a New Orleans uniform was coming to an end.

Five days later, on September 17, he was traded to the Houston Oilers for an over-the-hill defensive tackle named Leon Gray. Archie met with reporters shortly after the trade was announced. "It's kind of tough," he said on the verge of tears. "I've been here so long. I'm just going to look at it as something good and go over there and make a fresh start. They're not giving me a starting job. I'll just go over and find out my role."

Archie had never been cut loose from a team in his life, and it was a crushing blow. But his kids never lost their sense of humor. Archie asked Peyton, age six, what he thought about being traded to Houston, a team that finished the previous season with a 7-9 record. "Dad," Peyton said, "could you hold out for Dallas?"

What made the trade even more devastating was that Archie and Olivia had just purchased their dream home on First Street that sat in the heart of the historic Garden District. It had high ceilings, pretty flowers in the front yard, a swimming pool, and a view from the backyard of another immaculate house that would one day be home to musician Trent Reznor. Olivia was redoing the interior when the trade was announced.

With Cooper and Peyton already in school, Archie decided to lease an apartment in Houston. Southwest Airlines had a $29 one-way direct flight from Houston to New Orleans. So, many days after practice Archie would rush to his car, speed to the Houston airport, then catch the Southwest flight and be home on First Street by dinner. Then, late at night, he would return to the New Orleans airport and take the final flight of the day back to Houston at 10:30.

Archie, the commuter quarterback, sometimes took Peyton

and Cooper with him to Houston, easing Olivia's burden at home as she cared for infant Eli, who had been born on January 3, 1981. When Archie landed at the Houston airport, Oliver Luck, the Oilers' third-string quarterback, often would greet him. Luck had been conscripted into a most unusual duty: babysitter.

Archie would hand off his two oldest boys to his backup and then drive to the football facility; Oliver would chaperone Cooper and Peyton around town, stuffing them into his Mazda RX-7. The car was only a two-seater, so it was usually the younger Manning— six-year-old Peyton—who crouched in the hatchback as Oliver took the Manning boys to get ice cream, grab a hamburger, or play miniature golf.

Oliver couldn't ever have imagined that he was ferrying around a kid who would one day become the Colts' starting quarterback—or that his own then unborn son, Andrew, would replace that kid as the Colts' starting quarterback in 2012.

In the strike-shortened 1982 season, Archie started five games for the Oilers—and lost every one. The team finished 1-8 and at the bottom of the AFC Central. It may have been a new team for Archie, but it was the same lousy result.

Olivia spent most of the season in New Orleans. But she and Archie would talk for hours on the phone, reviewing virtually every move their children had made that day and all that was said. It was as if husband and wife were teenagers again, the way they gabbed over their rotary phones. Archie couldn't get enough of his family.

Archie was named the Oilers' starter before the 1983 season, and he believed he still had a few good years left. But after beginning the year with three straight losses, Archie received a phone call from head coach Ed Biles: Archie was being traded to the

Minnesota Vikings along with tight end Dave Casper for two future draft picks. When Archie broke the news to Earl Campbell,
the Oilers' star running back nearly fell to the ground in disappointment. Archie was so upset that he didn't even pack up his
apartment. He boarded a plane the next morning to Minnesota
and had a friend retrieve his belongings later.

Archie moved in to the Radisson Hotel in Minneapolis and
pored over his Vikings playbook. But after being in the Twin Cit-
ies for only a few weeks, Archie began to feel overwhelmed with
fatigue. He didn't know what was wrong. He was thirty-four now
and breaking down physically. Doctors at the Mayo Clinic eventually diagnosed Archie with a thyroid condition. He missed the
rest of the 1983 season.

The clock was running out on Archie's NFL career. He knew
1984 could be his final season, so he wanted to enjoy it with his
family. They rented a house on beautiful Lake Minnetonka; Cooper and Peyton enrolled in schools in September. Archie realized
that he hadn't developed a strong bond with little Eli, now three,
and so he spent as much time as possible with his youngest boy.
Shy and withdrawn, Eli could seemingly go for days without uttering a word. Archie wanted to change that by being more present in his life. In his free time Archie played with Eli and the two
went for walks around the lake.

On the field Archie didn't begin the year as the starter, but he
got a shot to play against the Chicago Bears on October 28 at
Soldier Field.

The Vikings had been dreadful in '84—their record at the time
was 2-6—but Archie took solace knowing that his boys were playing on winning teams in their youth leagues. Archie even got to
throw the football around with Cooper and Peyton in their yard.
And now Archie hoped that he could turn back time for one afternoon and play like he had at Ole Miss, dazzling the fans with

both his arm and his legs, and give his boys a poignant memory of their father playing at a high level in the twilight of his career.

But the Bears brutalized Archie. Linebacker Otis Wilson hit him so hard with his helmet that it busted Archie's chin open. As Wilson lifted himself off the turf, he looked down and saw the spreading pool of Archie's blood. Wilson looked at Archie with sincere sympathy and said, "Arch, these guys ain't blocking for you. You ought to just lie here and play like you're hurt."

Archie responded, "I'm thinking about it."

The Bears sacked Archie 11 times in Chicago's 16–7 victory. On the final sack lineman Dan Hampton eased up, just hugging Archie and not throwing him to the ground. It was clear that Hampton believed that Archie had been abused enough. The following day an image of a bloodied Archie sitting on the field with his eyes crossed appeared in newspapers from New York to California. He became the ultimate symbol of the beat-up quarterback.

Archie was benched the next week. "This has been especially hard on my boys," he said. "When I got home after the Bears game, they couldn't do enough for me—propping up pillows, make me comfortable. Cooper's fifth-grade football team was 5-0 this year; Peyton, who's eight, was the MVP of the New Orleans Little League team. We have man-to-man talks at bedtime. They ask why I'm not playing, and I tell them that everybody ought to sit on the bench for a while, that we become better people through struggles."

On the morning of Thanksgiving Eve in 1984, as Archie was still languishing on the bench, the family awoke to 14 inches of snow covering their backyard on Lake Minnetonka. It was the biggest snowstorm that the boys had ever seen.

Olivia looked out the window, staring at the pond in their backyard. Just twenty-four hours earlier it had been home to several ducks. "Where are all the ducks?" she said.

"It's cold, so I guess they flew south," Archie replied.

Olivia kept staring at the snow and the bleak portrait outside. She wasn't a fan of living in the North—people frequently told her that she talked funny—and now she was ready to go home. "They went south?" she said. "Well, so am I."

The end for Archie finally came on August 26, 1985. The family had moved back to New Orleans following the '84 season and Archie was in training camp in Mankato, Minnesota, when he realized that his right elbow had finally given out after years of throwing a football.

On a Monday afternoon Archie had been called into the office of Vikings coach Bud Grant. The two spoke for a few minutes about the toll that Archie's injuries had exacted on his body. Then Grant said, "You ever think of retiring?"

Archie smiled ever so slightly. "Not until now."

Relieved and excited to return to his family, Archie called Olivia and told her the news. She then informed Cooper, eleven, Peyton, nine, and Eli, four, that Daddy was coming home. The final whistle had blown on his football career.

The kids were devastated. "I think they thought their daddy could play forever," Olivia said.

Archie met with reporters in Mankato to announce that his playing career was over. "It's been a good trip," Archie said. "I don't think the good Lord meant a quarterback to do with his elbow what I did for twenty-six years. Maybe it just wore out. I wasn't able to tell Bud [Grant] he could depend on me."

After the press conference ended, Archie drove to the airport and returned to First Street, to the place that would soon become known around New Orleans as "the Manning House." He sat down with Olivia, Cooper, Peyton, and Eli for a family meeting. Archie had planned to move to Mississippi and finish raising his boys in the state where he had grown up. Now he asked his sons where in Mississippi they wanted to live.

"I don't want to live anywhere in Mississippi," Cooper said, speaking for all the brothers. "We like it here." The decision was made: the Mannings would stay on First Street. All those years of losing would not drive them out of New Orleans.

Soon Archie would begin playing a game called "Mazing Catches" with his three sons. Archie would stand on the porch and rifle passes to Cooper, Peyton, and Eli that were just in front of them as they sprinted across the lawn. The kids especially loved it when they had to dive to make the spectacular grab.

This was Archie's life now: his boys.

CHAPTER 17

―――
―――

Teaching Life―and
Football―Lessons

New Orleans. Autumn 1987.

From the time they started playing catch in their front yard, they were naturals.

Cooper enjoyed showing off little brother Peyton's football skills. When Peyton was three, he could take snaps from center and perform five-step drops, which he proudly demonstrated to Cooper's friends. Peyton also could execute seven-step drops. Mimicking his dad, he'd hold a Nerf football up close to his ear, run seven steps back, then throw the Nerf across the living room.

As he grew older, little Peyton would climb onto his dad's lap when Archie was studying game film. Peyton's eyes would grow as wide as twin moons as he watched the action, mesmerized by the violent ballet that danced on the screen. Peyton soon began asking questions about the game, about what his dad was looking at, why different players lined up in different spots on the field, who told them what to do and where to run. It wasn't long before Peyton was constantly firing the same query at Archie, no matter what his father was doing: *Daddy, Daddy, can we watch film?*

By the time Peyton was in second grade he could throw a tight spiral. One afternoon Archie went to a school event in Peyton's grade school cafeteria; Peyton went outside with his buddies to play. Out of the corner of his eye through a window, Archie saw a football travel the arc of a rainbow. He looked closer; surely an adult had thrown the pass. But no. He saw another spiraling ball soar through a bluebird Southern sky and Peyton's arm drop as the ball spun through the sunshine. "Did you see that?" another dad asked Archie.

Peyton was an intense boy, his internal furnace firing at full blast most hours of the day. One evening Archie invited Saints linebacker Rickey Jackson to come over for dinner. An All-Pro with a mean streak—he didn't even use knee pads or thigh pads and played most of the 1989 season with his jaw wired shut— Jackson was one of the NFL's most physical players. After dinner, Peyton asked Rickey to come upstairs to see his mini–basketball hoop that he and Cooper shot at every night. Minutes later Archie, in the living room, heard shouts and clanks and stomps and yells coming from Peyton's room. Rickey eventually walked downstairs, sweat pouring off him as if he'd just played five-on-five with a group of adults. Shaking his head, Rickey admitted to Archie that his boy had just trounced him.

When Peyton was in third grade, Archie saw more hints that his middle son was deeply serious about sports. Late in one of Peyton's basketball games the coach told Peyton to foul an opposing player to stop the clock. Peyton didn't just slap the player he was defending on the wrist; he kicked him in the stomach.

Archie had tried to coach Peyton's youth basketball team one winter, but Archie clashed with his star player. Before the season tipped off, the league coaches viewed all the players at a tryout, then drafted the kids onto their teams. But Archie couldn't attend the tryout, so he selected the players for his team based on whether he knew their parents, not on the kids' basketball abilities. He figured the boys just wanted to have fun, and if all the parents knew one another, it would foster a relaxed, convivial environment.

At the first practice the kids were told to dribble the ball. Some players had the ball bounce off their feet, others couldn't make it bounce more than two or three times, and still others chased their ball around as if it were rolling down a hill. Peyton was the only player who could control the ball. Seeing his struggling teammates, Peyton turned to his dad. "Why did you draft these guys?" Peyton asked. "What's wrong with you?" That was the last time Archie would coach his son.

Archie vowed not to be overbearing with his kids. His own father hadn't pushed him into sports, and Archie didn't want to influence whether his boys played or not. That was their call. Archie just wanted his kids to know one thing, and it was what he told them every day, whether over the phone or in person, whether he was in a good mood or bad.

He told them he loved them.

The gusts of little Peyton's temper didn't only blow at his dad. When he was eleven his youth basketball team lost for the first time. Archie had been in the stands, his eyes closely following the movements of his boy. Parents of other children in the stands often remarked about how intensely Archie watched his sons; it was as if he was scared to look away for even a moment, fearful he might miss something. It was an unspoken rule that Archie was never to be approached during a game, because he appeared as emotionally invested in the action as the players themselves. He certainly looked more nervous than he ever did when he was at Ole Miss or with the Saints.

After Peyton's basketball team was beaten, the volunteer coach, George Fowler, asked his players to gather around him. He then spoke to the eleven-year-olds. "The reason you lost," he said, "was that you didn't have your minds ready to play."

Peyton, furious about losing, piped up. "The reason we lost," Peyton declared, "is that you don't know what you are doing!"

Archie, standing out of earshot, saw Peyton and his coach jaw at each other, exchanging heated words. In the car, returning home, Archie asked his son what he had said to his coach. Peyton could not lie to his dad, so he told him the truth. Archie quickly made a U-turn. Minutes later Peyton was standing alone on the front porch of his coach's house. He rang the doorbell and, in tears, apologized for his outburst.

In the Manning way, sports were always a metaphor for life. Archie used games—and how his boys prepared for them and played in them—to teach valuable lessons, precisely what Buddy had done with Archie. One lesson Archie emphasized was the importance of respecting authority. He wanted his boys to be independent thinkers—especially when they were on the fields of play and were forced to improvise, which was Archie's hallmark athletic skill—but they also had to understand that the coach was ultimately in charge. Buddy had harped on this to Archie when he began playing football, and Archie repeated almost verbatim his father's words to his own sons.

But Peyton, more so than his brothers, sometimes resisted that mandate. As a kid he had been a quality pitcher in his organized baseball games. But when he finally decided that the sport he would focus on would be football, he opted to quit pitching. He had seen his dad's right arm break down after years of throwing, and he wanted to protect his own arm as best he could.

One day during a summer-league game, Billy Fitzgerald, the manager of Peyton's team, walked over to Peyton. Fitzgerald's pitching staff had been depleted. He knew that Peyton no longer wanted to pitch, but Fitzgerald was desperate. He asked Peyton if he would take the mound; Peyton said no. The manager then overruled his player; he ordered Peyton to pitch.

Angry, Peyton reared back and threw his first pitch—it soared over the batter's head by about ten feet and clanked against the backstop fence. Still seething and determined to make his point clear to his manager, Peyton fired another pitch. He hit his mark perfectly: the ball thumped the batter square in his back.

Fitzgerald was furious. He called time-out and stormed to the mound. He snatched the ball from Peyton's glove and told him to go to the bench. "That is the most bullshit thing I have ever seen in my life," Fitzgerald said.

Fitzgerald never asked Peyton to pitch again.

Fitzgerald also coached the Newman High School basketball team. At the start of Peyton's junior basketball season, Fitzgerald called Peyton into his office and told Peyton he wouldn't be a starter. Peyton was incensed; he had been the first man off the bench as a sophomore and now he believed he deserved to start. An argument ensued. Both agreed it would be in everyone's best interest if Peyton left the team, which he did, ending his basketball career.

But Peyton and Fitzgerald would remain close throughout the years. Peyton would always have a soft spot for the coach who never backed down to the stubborn high school pitcher and basketball player.

When Peyton was a teenager, he'd come home from school and review tapes of his own plays and the plays of other quarterbacks he admired. If he could find tapes of upcoming opponents, he'd study them over and over too. Archie saw his middle child holed up hour after hour, day after day. He wanted Peyton to have a social life, so he implored his son to enjoy his teenage years. "Get a girlfriend," he said. "Go to a movie. You need to get out more."

Peyton's reply was always the same: "Daddy, I've got to watch more film." They were the only movies that interested Peyton.

Though Peyton was serious as a judge about football, he still could be playful, especially when the opportunity arose to play a prank on his old man. One night Archie was on a local radio show in New Orleans when a young caller who referred to himself as Johnny from Chalmette phoned the station. This caller started discussing Archie's career, and Archie was shocked at how someone so young was so familiar with the arcane details of his life. The caller knew that Archie wore number 25 in basketball at Drew High and number 42 in baseball. *Man,* Archie thought, *this guy is a real fan of mine.* For several minutes, the caller stroked Archie's ego.

Late that evening Archie was lying in bed when Peyton strolled in to say good night. Just as Peyton turned to walk out the door, he said one more thing. "Hey, Dad, how was Johnny from Chalmette?" Peyton cracked a sheepish smile. Instantly, Archie started laughing. It had been Peyton on the line, and he had bamboozled not only Archie but also the entire listening audience.

Located in Uptown New Orleans, the Isidore Newman School was founded in 1903 and sat on a manicured campus of eleven and a half acres. The private secular school had a waiting list to gain admission and a reputation for being the domain of spoiled rich kids who were on the fast track to Ivy League schools. Newman boasted a rich history in academics—it had three Rhodes scholars among its graduates—but not in athletics. Newman had never won a football state championship.

Cooper was the first Manning to attend Newman. Before his sophomore year he told his dad he wanted to play on the Greenies football team. Archie was terrified. He knew the Manning name carried a burden of expectation, and he genuinely didn't know if Cooper had the skill to succeed. At 6'3" and 170 pounds, he was as skinny as a fence post. Archie thought, *He's not going to be good enough*.

He sat down with Cooper and spoke at length about working harder than anyone else, taking extra reps in practice, and studying the playbook like it was required homework. He told Cooper he'd do everything in his power to make him into a special player, throwing with him whenever he could and giving him pointers. Archie thought perhaps Cooper could catch on with a Division III college one day, but he didn't even know what constituted a good college player, because he hadn't closely watched a college game in years.

Cooper began his high school career aspiring to be a quarterback like his dad. He was the third-string signal caller as a sophomore, but when both the Newman starter and backup were injured against Redeemer High, Cooper took over. He attempted 14 passes. He completed only one throw, but it was good for a 99-yard touchdown. The Manning magic looked to be alive in Archie's oldest son.

Cooper again was thrust into action later in the season against Belle Chasse High—and was dreadful. He threw five interceptions. Archie had tossed five picks in a single game three times in his career, and against Tennessee as a sophomore at Ole Miss he had thrown six. Archie knew Cooper's agony. He planned to tell his oldest boy that he needed to learn from his mistakes and he would rebound just like his old man did.

When Cooper walked into the house, Archie lightheartedly spoke to his son. "You didn't beat me," Archie said. "I threw six against Tennessee in Knoxville one afternoon."

Cooper had a quick reply. "Well, they weren't my fault, Dad," he said. "I'm a receiver anyway."

The next year Cooper switched to wide receiver. He was one of several players to successfully lobby the Newman coaches to change the Greenies' offensive attack from a run-based Wing-T to a wide-open, pass-happy scheme. Cooper also spent hours with Archie and his brothers on the Newman field playing a game they called "Ten Balls." Archie would stand ten yards away and rifle all sorts of throws at Cooper—fastballs, over-the-shoulder balls, balls that forced him to dive, and balls that he had to snag with only one hand. If Cooper didn't catch ten in a row, they would start counting again at one and wouldn't quit until Cooper caught ten consecutive passes.

The results of their collective hard work were immediate: by his junior season Cooper had developed into a first-team all-state receiver. He ran routes—taught to him by his dad—that turned defensive backs in circles. By the end of the season coach Tony Reginelli, who had been the head football coach at Newman since 1968, told reporters that Cooper was the best route runner who had ever played on his team.

Cooper's hands were strong and reliable: he didn't drop a single pass during his junior year. Now at 6'4" and 180 pounds, he had a long gait, which was why he appeared slow, but he ran the 40 in 4.7 seconds, the same time Archie had clocked in high school. Cooper had trouble getting off the line of scrimmage quickly—it took time to get his legs to that 4.7 speed—but it gave him something to work on in preparation for his senior year.

Several Division I schools wrote letters to Cooper, expressing interest. He had a soft spot in his heart for Ole Miss—his parents had taken him to games in Oxford since he was a small boy, and he especially enjoyed watching the Rebel players walk through the Grove before they entered the stadium—but Cooper decided to wait until his senior year to commit to a school.

He believed his final season in high school was going to be his best. During the summer he would have a quarterback throwing to him daily, hundreds of times. He knew that QB especially well:

Peyton.

$$\equiv$$

The Most Magical Fall

New Orleans. Autumn 1991.

When Peyton became addicted to studying game film as an early teenager, Archie expressed another golden rule: *If you're going to watch film, do it the right way.*

By the right way, Archie meant don't keep your eyes on the ball like most fans do, but instead pay close attention to the defense. He instructed Peyton to focus on whether the defense played zone or man coverage, and in what down-and-distance situations. As the quarterback, Peyton needed to know how often the defense blitzed, in what situations they were most likely to blitz, what defensive formation was used the most, who the standout players were on the defense, and who were the weakest players on each level of the defense—the line, the linebackers, and the defensive backs.

Every play on film told a story to young Peyton; each snap was full of nuance, mini-plotlines, and layers of complexity. After practice, after games, on the weekends, Peyton would watch tape of his own games, opponents' games, and NFL games. His appetite for football information was enormous; he always wanted more, more, more.

Peyton also began examining his father's legacy. An Ole Miss fan had mailed audiotapes of the radio broadcasts of old Rebel games to the Mannings. Locking himself in his bedroom, Peyton would put a tape in his stereo, push "Play," plop down on his bed, and listen for hours. Closing his eyes, he would imagine he was in the crowd watching young Archie Manning, the gunslinger from Drew, emerge from the huddle and approach the line of scrimmage. The crowd roaring, Peyton would listen as his old man threw yet another touchdown pass against LSU or ran for a touchdown against Georgia. Over and over, for hours on end, Peyton would lie on his bed and replay his dad's long-ago games. Peyton eventually memorized the calls on the scratchy tapes and added his own commentary: *Manning, the 6'3" Drew redhead, brings 'em to the line. . . .*

He also pressed his parents about college game days and their experiences at Ole Miss. Archie and Olivia told their curious son what it was like back then, how every football fall Saturday was a waking dream, how they socialized with Archie's teammates, doubling on dates and going on ice cream runs. Archie played at the smallest school in the SEC on a team filled with nothing but native Mississippians, and this forged a closeness in the locker room that Peyton longed for. Peyton wished he could have played in the '60s at a place where the players spent their Saturday nights together after a game. Maybe he could recapture a slice of that era, he thought, if he went to Ole Miss and played with his brother.

———

When Peyton was a teenager, he also found a few dust-covered videos of Archie's old games at Ole Miss. Putting one in the VCR, Peyton was entranced by the grainy images flickering on the screen. There was his dad running around the field like he was a sprinter on the track team. He'd beat linebackers to the edge of the field on runs and he'd scramble in the backfield for what seemed like minutes at a time before throwing a pass. At one point, after watching all this fleet footwork, Peyton turned to his father and asked, "Why aren't I fast like that?"

"I don't know, but it might be a blessing," Archie said.

The father knew his sons would have to play the game differently than he did. Quarterbacks didn't rely as much on their legs as they once did. They played with multiple wide receivers and stayed in the pocket more now. Archie also insisted that throwing the ball down the field was the best way for an inferior team to beat a superior one, because if a throwing quarterback was special, he could carry the other ten players on his offense much easier than a running quarterback could.

Peyton cherished the times he talked football with his dad—but not as much as Archie did. He learned long ago that these moments, these otherwise innocuous interactions between father and son, were worth savoring. He believed a key to parenting was to never let a question from his children go unanswered, and he especially relished discussing quarterbacking with his boys—but only if they broached the subject.

In the summer of 1991 Peyton moved from Newman's freshman squad—where Peyton was known to look off receivers as a thirteen-year-old—to its varsity. After just a few weeks of practice the Greenies' coaching staff elevated him to first-string quarterback.

Cooper had been uncharacteristically nice to his younger

brother that entire summer and preseason camp. But he had an ulterior motive: he believed it was the only way he could entice Peyton to throw him the ball.

The two had been tangling for so long. It was Cooper who would hold Peyton down as a child and force him to recite every school in the SEC before he would let him go. Cooper, two years older, used his weight and height advantage to dominate Peyton in virtually every game they played, which imbued in Peyton an almost pathological hatred of losing.

When they were kids Cooper enjoyed tormenting poor little Peyton. One day Cooper spotted Peyton riding Cooper's tricycle in the driveway. Irate, Cooper hurled a brick at his little brother. And then another. Eventually Peyton ended up on the ground—Cooper claimed to his parents that Peyton had driven over a brick on the tricycle. Archie didn't buy it; later that night he spanked his oldest boy.

Archie didn't punish his kids often, but the fear of a punish- ment was ever present. When Archie was playing for the Saints, the family took a ski trip to Colorado during the off-season. Archie didn't hit the slopes, but one day he walked into a shop that sold belts and engraved initials on the buckle. Archie had a belt made with the number 8 on the buckle—his number with the Saints. He was too modest to ever wear it, but he hung it in the closet for his kids to see—and fear.

Buddy had used a belt to discipline Archie, and now Archie kept ol' number 8 visible as a reminder to his kids to stay in line. He would warn his boys, for instance, that if they crossed the street without an adult holding their hand, "Y'all going to get number 8." If Cooper and Peyton were bickering, Archie only had to say one thing to make them stop: "Y'all don't cut it out number 8 is coming out."

But the specter of the belt didn't always stop Cooper and Peyton from fighting. They were brothers, after all. One time Archie instructed Cooper, then ten, to let Peyton win a game of one-on-one on their driveway basketball hoop. After Peyton won, he ran up to Cooper and said, "I'm eight and you're ten and I beat you." This lit the wick of Cooper's rage. He charged at Peyton but was held back by his dad.

"You know how lucky you boys are to have each other?" Archie said. "I would love to have had a brother. Come on. You two need to appreciate each other more."

The two brothers would let their father's words blow past them as if they had been carried away with the wind. A few hours later, Cooper and Peyton would be back at it, playing and competing and trying to beat the snot out of each other.

Now, in the summer of 1991, the fighting stopped. For the first time in an organized game, they needed each other on the football field. They were teammates, which for them was a bond that ran deeper than blood.

Peyton spent the summer preparing for his first game as a high school starting quarterback by working out with Saints receivers. Jim Mora, then the New Orleans coach, often watched sixteen-year-old Peyton in these throwing sessions, and he was stunned to see that Peyton was calling plays and exhibiting the command and comportment of a quarterback twice his age. And Mora's breath was taken away at the sight of the bullets that the boyish-faced quarterback was firing with his right arm. Mora confided to friends that Peyton already looked like a starting SEC quarterback.

Archie didn't share much advice with Peyton before he began his high school career—it was the coach's job to coach, Archie said, and his job to be a dad—but he offered one lesson he learned the hard way. "You've got to know what you're doing out there because then you can get rid of the ball," Archie said. "And when you get rid of the ball you don't get hit."

This nugget of wisdom further fueled Peyton's obsession with preparation.

A few thousand local sports fans filed into the tiny stadium at Newman High for the Greenies' opening game of the 1991 season. Archie was still a legend in the Big Easy—he was working as an analyst for the Saints radio network and was a high-profile spokesman for several companies—and now curious fans of Archie's wanted to see the next generation of Mannings perform on the field.

Archie and Olivia usually sat in the top row of bleachers at Lupin Field. This afforded Archie the best perspective to film the games. Archie had been recording his boys in the front yard with his camcorder for years—the father wanted to preserve time because he knew well the transient nature of life—and now he lugged the video camera to Peyton and Cooper's first varsity football game together. Sitting in the top row allowed Archie to keep Cooper in his field of view; in the coach's game film Cooper often drifted out of the screen when he ran deep routes or patterns to the sideline. Archie wanted to make sure he had Cooper's every move on his personal film, enabling him to offer a critique of his down-the-field blocking and route running—if he was asked.

But taping the games meant it was often difficult for Archie to follow all the action on the field. On the various tapes Archie's voice runs alongside the action: *Nice block, Cooper. What happened there, Olivia? Great throw, Peyton. Excellent grab, Cooper.*

But as painstaking as it was to record the games, Archie would never stop. Sometimes parents of other Newman players would see Archie in the back row, the camera on his shoulder, the tape rolling, his face squinting in concentration. The parents would say aloud, *Boy, that Archie sure does love his kids.*

In the amber glow being thrown onto the field by the bank of lights atop the grandstands, Peyton and Cooper ran onto the field for their first series together as varsity football players. A murmur of expectation arose from the crowd. Then Peyton dropped back to pass. This was the moment that Archie had been waiting for— what everyone in the crowd had been waiting for—as Cooper sprinted down the field. He ran to the post, then cut sharply to the corner. It was a textbook post-corner route, and the defensive back was so faked out he nearly fell down. Cooper was wide open.

Peyton's first pass in high school was going to be thrown to his brother—and it was going to be a touchdown. They had run this play thousands of times in their minds and on their lawn. Every time Peyton threw a perfect ball and every time Cooper caught it for the touchdown. And many times Archie had been there to re-cord the event for posterity—just like he was doing now.

The boys knew each other like they had identical DNA. Peyton and Cooper had developed several hand and head signals and fa-cial expressions—their secret and unspoken football language— that they used during backyard games. Now, as he ran his pass pattern, Cooper, wearing number 18, his dad's college number, glanced back at Peyton, wearing number 14, his dad's high school number.

Peyton unleashed a perfect spiral, soft and catchable, the ball spinning through the steamy Southern air. Cooper raised his hands to grab the ball. The crowd rose to its feet, sensing that the dawn of a new era was about to arrive, that the Manning brothers were about to fulfill their destiny, claim their birthright.

And then it happened: the ball traveled straight through Cooper's fingertips and fell to the ground. The perfect moment became nothing more than an incomplete pass.

"What was that?" Olivia asked Archie up in the stands.

By her count and that of everyone else who had paid attention the previous year, Cooper didn't drop a single pass, even in warm-ups. Olivia immediately suspected he'd done it on purpose as a way of reminding Peyton who really was in charge.

That night Cooper caught every other ball his little brother threw in his direction—including a few gravity-defying grabs that prompted a chorus of *ohhhs* from the crowd—and number 18 went on to record nine receptions in the first half alone as Newman rolled to an easy victory. But it was *the* ball that slithered through Cooper's hands that would remain under discussion at the family breakfast table for the duration of the fall. When asked about the play, Cooper would say that he simply misplayed the ball, but his beaming grin suggested he was holding on to a secret—one that he had no plans on spilling.

Before every game, Archie told his boys the same thing. "Have some fun out there," he would say. "Remember to always have fun." It was a ritual that he would continue for the next two decades.

That was easy to do for the balance of that 1991 season, as the Manning boys were virtually unstoppable, putting on aerial shows at different high school stadiums in front of crowds that grew increasingly large. Communicating with hand signals at the line of scrimmage that they had perfected on their yard—if Peyton touched his nose, it was a comeback pass; if he tapped his helmet, it was a curl—Peyton and Cooper would change plays after reading how the defense had lined up. Other times just a knowing glance from Peyton would tell Cooper to run a fly pattern, an out, or a post-corner.

In the huddle Cooper was constantly jabbering in Peyton's ear, proclaiming that he would be open on the next play. If Peyton had just thrown an incompletion, it was Cooper who would badger him more than any other player. "Throw it again," he would say. "Hey, come on, throw it to me again, Peyton."

One time a defensive back covering Cooper began talking trash, telling Cooper in R-rated language that he wouldn't be catching any passes against him. Cooper relayed his words to Peyton, who quickly resolved to throw the ball to Cooper on nearly every play to shut that player up. Even if Cooper was covered, Peyton would just loft the ball up to his brother, who was 6'4" and towered over the smaller defensive back. Peyton always knew that Cooper would either catch the ball or bat it down to make sure it wasn't intercepted. By the end of the first half Cooper had over 100 yards receiving, and the defensive back had nothing to say about it.

The Newman coach, Tony Reginelli, was in awe of Peyton's knowledge of the game. Only a sophomore, Peyton played like he'd been studying defenses for over a decade, which in some ways he had been. In the middle of a game it wasn't uncommon for Peyton to come to the sideline with something urgent on his mind. "Coach, every time we're in third and long, they're playing three-deep. I think our square-ins will work," Peyton would say. Coach Reginelli, who believed his sophomore quarterback could read defenses as well as he could, almost always agreed with Peyton.

Immediately after games, Peyton would still be consumed with needing to improve. Peyton was slow of foot in high school, but he was determined to become faster. Late one night, hours after a game had ended, Reginelli returned to school and spied a tall, lanky teenager running up and down the dark football field. The stadium lights weren't even on, but he could see the silhouette of Peyton, illuminated by the moonlight, performing sprints on the field—just like his old man used to on that dusty high school field in Drew.

On many Saturday mornings, only hours after their games had ended, Newman coaches would be in their offices when they would hear a knock on the door. It would be Peyton asking for the game plan for the next opponent. At the sight of Peyton on these Saturday mornings it was clear to Reginelli that the value of hard work Archie had preached had taken root inside Peyton and was growing like a springtime garden.

Peyton also learned from his dad that it was important to acknowledge the work of his offensive linemen. When Archie was in the NFL he once took his O-line to a steak house for dinner, laying out over $1,000. Mimicking his father, Peyton wanted to treat his offensive linemen to lunch at a restaurant of their choosing, but sophomores weren't allowed to leave campus at noon. So instead he purchased each of them a pair of Isotoner gloves, which had been made popular by quarterback-pitchman Dan Marino, one of Peyton's favorite players. If the gloves were good enough for Marino, Peyton figured they were good enough for the guys charged with protecting him.

That fall, as the temperatures dropped and the Newman offensive linemen donned their Isotoners, Archie and Olivia couldn't have been happier when they trekked to the stadium. They would arrive early for games and tailgate in the parking lot with friends, as if they were back in Oxford in the Grove. Then they would take their seats high in the stands, where Archie would film his boys and Olivia would fret and pray they wouldn't get hurt.

Archie told his wife that he was having more fun watching his boys than he ever did when he was playing ball. It felt like only minutes ago to Archie that Cooper and Peyton were two feet high and chasing each other around the yard, but now here they were, star attractions on Friday nights under the high school lights. His boys were growing up before his eyes. As he watched them dominate on the field, his camera rolling, Archie overflowed with more pride than he thought possible.

There were a few times when parents of other players on the team would shoot Archie and Olivia exasperated looks, because their kids weren't getting the ball. Peyton wasn't shy about making it obvious that Cooper was his favorite target on the field; sometimes he even threw it to his brother when he was covered and another receiver was open. But Peyton knew his time on the field with his brother was limited, and there was no feeling in the world that was more powerful to Peyton than completing a pass to his best friend.

It was a magical fall for the Mannings. Even little Eli was on a roll: the ten-year-old threw 20 touchdown passes in five flag football games.

At one of Newman's games a friend of Archie's pulled him aside and shared his feelings on Peyton. "He's going to be a college star," the friend said with certainty.

The one thing that could raise Archie's blood pressure like almost nothing else was putting expectations on his kids. Archie quickly replied, "You don't know that; you're not a college scout. You're not a coach. How do you know that? Be quiet." Archie didn't anger often—this was why his words were freighted with so much vehemence when he was upset—but he would unleash his wrath on anyone who suggested his boys were going to follow his path to stardom.

In the semifinals of the state playoffs Newman faced heavily favored Haynesville, a state power. Late in the game, trailing 27–

21, Peyton was driving his team down the field. With less than two minutes to go, Peyton fired a pass to his tight end. But a linebacker from Haynesville leaped high to intercept the ball. Upset with his little brother, Cooper said, "Blame it on the sophomore!" But after he cooled down, Cooper approached Peyton and put his arm around him. "Don't worry about it, Peyt," he said. "It was a great year."

Newman's season was over. Peyton and Cooper had become one of the most prolific pass-and-catch tandems in Louisiana history. Cooper, who had 76 catches for 1,250 yards and 13 touchdowns, was named the team's MVP. Scholarship offers for Cooper started to arrive in the Manning mailbox: Texas, Virginia, and eventually Ole Miss were interested in him.

In December, after their high school season was over, a reporter asked Cooper where he was going to college. He was still undecided, he said, but he was confident of one thing: his brother would follow him to whichever college campus he attended. "I definitely want Peyton to come with me, no matter where I go," he said.

Together, the brothers believed, they would achieve things on the football field that not even their famous father had accomplished during his college career. Together, they would make Archie proud. They were sure of that.

CHAPTER 19

A Note for Peyton

New Orleans. Winter 1992.

The discussion raged at the breakfast table, the place where the Manning family did a lot of their talking: Why had Cooper dropped that first pass from Peyton in their only season of football together at Newman High?

Cooper had other uncharacteristic drops that fall, especially when the weather cooled late in the season. He told Archie that his right hand occasionally felt frozen and he had trouble gripping something even as small as an orange. It was strange, but nothing that triggered alarm bells.

The dullness in his right hand didn't stop Cooper from continuing his athletic career. After his final football game, Cooper became a starting guard on Newman's basketball team. Shooting right-handed, he averaged 12 points a game. His right hand was still numb at times, but he didn't tell anyone for fear that defenders would catch on to a secret that only he and Archie knew: Cooper struggled dribbling and driving to his right. A solid shooter, Cooper was a complementary player on the team—the star was forward Randy Livingston, a *Parade* all-American who would be named the 1993 Naismith Prep Player of the Year—but as the season progressed Cooper appeared to lose his soft-touch shooting skill.

In February of his senior year Cooper signed a letter of intent to play at Ole Miss. He welcomed the expectations his last name carried, even coveted them. He knew he wouldn't impact the games the way his dad had—a wide receiver couldn't influence the action like a quarterback—but he grew up hearing stories about how idyllic and perfect Oxford was on fall football Saturdays. He dreamed of striding through the Grove as a player and slapping the hands of the fans who lined the entrance to the stadium. Then, once out on the field, he hoped to become a receiver who caught everything thrown into his zip code. Up in the stands, his mom, dad, and baby brother Eli would see it all.

The best part: he already had convinced Peyton to join him in two years. Even Peyton told friends that it was only a matter of time before he and Cooper would be moving their game of pitch-and-catch to Oxford. The tricks they developed and honed in their yard—their secret language, their knowing glances—would soon be on display at the campus where their parents first met. It would be the story of all football stories: A Tale of Two Mannings.

But something still was wrong with Cooper's right arm and hand. Late in the basketball season—Newman would win its second straight Class 2-A state title—Peyton and Archie could see from the stands that Cooper couldn't shoot his usual jump shot. Instead of the ball spinning out of his hands like it used to, the ball fluttered and floated with no spin. From behind his video camera, Archie knew that something was amiss with his boy.

Concerned, Archie took Cooper to see the Saints' team orthopedic surgeon. An MRI revealed that Cooper had an injured ulnar nerve in his right elbow, a relatively common ailment among football players. A minor surgery was performed, and only weeks after his cast was removed, Cooper was cleared in July to play football in the Louisiana High School Coaches Association All-Star Game.

A quarter century earlier, Archie had entered the Mississippi High School All-Star Game as a virtual unknown. He then threw five touchdown passes, won the MVP award, and caught the attention of his coaches at Ole Miss, who quickly elevated Archie on their preseason depth chart. Now Cooper hoped that his performance in the all-star game would launch his college career.

Cooper impressed his teammates in practices. "He runs great routes," said East quarterback Eric Randall. "He's got a lot of good technique. I can tell he's been to some camps, and he's been coached by great coaches. He's a great target. I like his speed. He gets open on time, and that's good."

Cooper told reporters he ran a 4.7 40 in high school. "But out here," he said, "I'm probably running a 4.5 because I'm so fired up."

He was asked about his surgery on the ulnar nerve in his right arm. "My whole hand seriously has atrophy and has lost a lot of strength," Cooper said, showing reporters the five-inch scar from the surgery. "I can barely even hold a ball with my right hand. So it's hard to work like that. But I just use my left hand and kind of guide the ball in with my right."

Cooper continued. "You've really got to concentrate on your routes and make every move count. Because any little step you can get counts in this league, and Ole Miss is going to be even bigger. So, I've got a lot of work ahead of me and a lot to look forward to. . . . I've got to perform. All that stuff about following in my dad's shadow, I've said before that we're totally different people.

Being a receiver helps a lot. But you never know. I'm wearing 81, the opposite of 18, so it's still there a little bit."

In the all-star game Cooper made two spectacular catches, rising above defensive backs to snag the ball both times. He didn't appear the least bit injured. To the Ole Miss coaches who watched Cooper on the game tape, he looked like a player destined to have a wonderful college career.

Peyton adjusted to football life without Cooper. Over the summer he organized Sunday workout sessions. He'd call his teammates on Friday, tell them what the plan was, and then early Sunday morning Peyton would lead them onto the practice field at Newman.

If a teammate failed to show, Peyton would light into him on Monday, telling him he didn't have the dedication of a champion. To Peyton, high school football was serious business, worthy of being at the top of the priority list—ahead of girls, ahead of spending time with buddies shooting pool, ahead of . . . well, just about everything. When Archie overheard Peyton excoriate a player over the phone, he finally sat his son down, explaining he needed to throttle back the intensity.

"Look, for sixteen-year-olds, a lot can come up between Friday afternoon and Saturday night," Archie said. "A chance to go fishing. Surprise tickets to an event of some kind. A girl. Or just the chance to hang out."

Archie then shared a piece of advice that his own father had dispensed to him: "It's better to be a good person than a good player."

Lesson learned, Peyton calmed down—a little.

———

Cooper arrived at Ole Miss shortly after the Louisiana All-Star game. Like all the incoming freshmen, Cooper shaved his head—and loved every second of the tradition, just like Archie had two decades earlier when he arrived on the tree-lined, manicured campus. Cooper relished his new home, the place his mom and dad had romanticized for years. The next Manning was finally in Oxford.

On August 5, 1992, the Ole Miss squad held "Meet the Rebels Day" on the field. Hundreds of fans surrounded Cooper, wearing his number 81 jersey. Olivia stood nearby, watching Cooper deliver gut-busting one-liners to fans, pose for pictures, and sign autographs. He was a natural interacting with the public; Cooper had been telling jokes to anyone who would listen for as long as Archie and Olivia could remember.

Five-year-old Cooper once surprised a group of strangers at the Neshoba County Fair in Mississippi with this joke: *A man dressed like a cowboy walks into an ice cream store and orders an ice cream cone. The lady behind the counter says, "Do you want your nuts crushed?" The man pulls out his gun and says, "No, do you want your boobs shot off?"*

That was Cooper—always dancing around the line between funny and vulgar. But now as Olivia watched him being surrounded by fans, she smiled like only a proud mother can. Her son was formally welcomed into the homeland of his father.

"The most popular player [at Rebels Day] was a lanky 18-year-old who hasn't played a down yet," wrote columnist Mike Talbert in the *Daily Journal*. "Cooper Manning, his freshman scalp hidden under a white cap, was swamped by fans wanting an autograph or to get their pictures taken with 'Archie's Boy.'"

Cooper desperately hoped that the pain in his arm would subside, but it persisted through preseason camp and into the first week of the season. Something, he sensed, was seriously wrong.

Cooper finally confided to the team doctor, who phoned Archie and told him that Cooper should see a specialist. The Ole Miss doctor also informed Archie that the medical staff was now so concerned about the numbness and atrophy in Cooper's right arm that he was being held out of practice.

Now a danger signal flashed in Archie's head. If Cooper wasn't practicing, then his injury must be significant. Archie made one phone call after the next, trying to connect with the brightest medical minds in the country. He and Cooper flew to Dallas and met with a neurosurgeon and orthopedist at the Baylor Medical Center. Then father and son traveled to the Mayo Clinic in Rochester, Minnesota, where a team of doctors put Cooper through a battery of tests. The staff at Mayo told Archie they would call him when they had the test results.

Cooper returned to Oxford, still unable to practice or play. Ole Miss had an open date a week after Cooper was back on campus. Instead of hanging out with his college buddies, he drove home to New Orleans, where on Friday night, September 21, Peyton had a football game. The older brother wanted to check in on his old quarterback.

That Friday afternoon a doctor from the Baylor Medical Center called Archie with the knee-buckling news: Cooper had a congenital condition called spinal stenosis, a narrowing of the spinal canal. Cooper could never play football again, and he would need surgery. Cooper was lucky, the doctor emphasized, that he was still walking; one collision on the football field at any point in his life, dating back to pee-wee ball, could have left him paralyzed. The doctor recommended a surgery that would require drilling a hole in Cooper's head. After hanging up the phone, Archie, trembling, nearly fell to the floor.

Unaware of the life-altering conversation his father had just had with the doctor in Dallas, Cooper arrived home in time for

Peyton's game. He sat in the stands on a rainy Friday night at Fisher High School in Lafitte, Louisiana, and watched Peyton play one of the worst games of his young life. Newman's junior quarterback—the one already being touted by several recruiting analysts as the nation's top overall player in his high school class—finished 8 for 32 for 35 yards. Newman lost 8–3. Peyton's mind wasn't singularly focused on the game; he was worried about what the doctors were going to say about Cooper.

Peyton returned home after the game. Archie pulled his middle son aside and, his eyes welling with tears, told Peyton about Cooper, that he needed a significant surgery and that he would never put on a football helmet again. Archie wanted to know if Peyton would like to be at his brother's side when he laid out the situation to Cooper.

"I can't," Peyton said, holding back tears. "I'm sorry, but I just can't do it." It was just too hard for Peyton. Too many dreams were about to be shattered. Peyton then had to leave the house. He told his dad that he was going to get some food and he'd be back later.

Archie and Olivia sat down with Cooper. The sadness leaked out of Archie's eyes as he somberly explained to his son that his football career was over. He told Cooper that he was actually lucky he was still walking. Yes, he would need surgery, but Archie and Olivia assured their boy that he would also be able to live a happy, full life.

Archie was so delicate, so tender, so compassionate with his oldest boy. His heart ached, but Archie fought through his own sorrow to be strong for Cooper, hugging his son and keeping his chin up as he delved into more details about the surgery, the recuperation, and moving on from football. Olivia later called Archie's words to Cooper his "finest gathering of thoughts."

Cooper sobbed at the news. Football was his everything. His

fondest life memories, stretching back to being in the Saints' locker room with his dad to throwing the ball around with Peyton on the front yard, were wrapped around football, the sport he loved almost as much as family. He was devastated. It wasn't the winning and losing he was going to miss the most, he told friends; it was just being around the guys in the locker room, the camaraderie, the sense of being a part of something bigger than himself. There was no feeling more powerful in the world, nothing more intoxicating, than walking shoulder-to-shoulder with teammates onto a football field. It was those moments—the ones that take place before the game, which were always the most intense to Cooper—that he would really wish he could relive just one more time.

But Cooper also understood the gravity of his condition. He had been hit hard so many times, and any one of those collisions could have put him into a wheelchair. Eventually, he would feel like he was the lucky one in the family—but that feeling didn't fall over him on this night.

When Peyton returned from his late dinner, Cooper already was asleep. The brothers talked the next morning, and Peyton was more upset than Cooper. This wasn't supposed to happen, Peyton said; it just wasn't, not to his older brother. Archie was worried sick about both his boys—about the physical health of Cooper and the mental health of Peyton.

The next day Archie drove Cooper back to Oxford to begin his college life as an ex–football player. Cooper left behind a note for Peyton. It would change Peyton's life.

It said, in part:

I would like to live my dream of playing football through you. Although I cannot play anymore, I know I can still get the same feeling out of watching my little brother do what he does best. I know now that we are good for each other, because I need you to be serious and look at things from a different perspective. I am good for you, as well, to take things light. I love you, Peyt, and only great things lay ahead for you. Thanks for everything on and off the field.

As Peyton sat in his bedroom and read the words, tears streamed down his cheeks. He never knew he could love and admire his brother so much.

He now had his life's mission.

CHAPTER 20

—
—

"The Bad Thing Happened
to the Right Guy"

New Orleans. Autumn 1992.

Just after midnight on a Saturday in September, a little more than twenty-four hours after he learned his brother would never play football again, Peyton sat down and began writing his own letter to Cooper in longhand. Seated at a desk in his upstairs bedroom, darkness falling outside the window, Peyton poured his heart onto the page.

Peyton was exhausted. The night before, his sleep had been stalked by nightmares of a strange world—and of a changed relationship with his older brother. The afternoon had been emotionally draining as well. Peyton asked Newman's offensive coordinator, Frank Gendusa, if he could change his jersey from number 14 to Cooper's number 18. When Peyton brought his new football jersey home at lunchtime and showed it to Olivia, the two hugged and cried.

Now, his head buried in a circle of lamplight on his desk, Peyton began to express his own thoughts to Cooper, spreading them across the page in his meticulous handwriting. The words flowed easily as Peyton told his brother just what he meant to him.

"What I'd do to have you back again as a receiver I don't know," Peyton wrote. "But this is all part of growing up—learning to cope with change. I'll be seeing you plenty, I know, but things will be different. I know other people have gone through losing their older brother or sister before, but I think me and you are different. We're not average. We're Coop and Peyt. We always have been and we always will be, thank God."

At the end of the missive Peyton told Cooper he loved him—something he'd never done before in print. He signed the note, "Your bro and pal, Peyt."

On Monday, September 28, 1992, Ole Miss officials announced that the football career of Cooper Manning had come to an end. "Cooper had a bright future as a wide receiver at Ole Miss," Rebel head coach Billy Brewer said. "For his age, Cooper is a mature young man, and I know he will deal with this setback. He was fulfilling a dream, and I am sure this is a difficult thing for him to handle."

"It's been a tough week for us," Archie said. "Our concern is for Cooper. What hurts the most is knowing how happy he's been the last two months just being in the Ole Miss family and being a player there. . . . It's been tough on him, and it's been tough on us, but the paramount thing is to get the problem corrected for him to carry on a normal life."

"He took it hard but he took it good," Archie told a reporter. "Cooper's always been so upbeat and free-spirited, but it hurts him. He was really happy at Ole Miss. . . . [But] thank goodness we found this thing. As much pleasure as we had watching him play, it's scary to think back to him running those slant patterns."

Peyton was deeply upset that his brother's football career was over. "This is just not fair," he told his dad. "Life's not fair for football to be taken away from Cooper." Peyton took the news harder than anyone in the family, Cooper included, stewing for weeks over the realization that his best friend had lost his dream. Even as a boy Peyton sought to control situations, but now for the first time in his adolescent life, he experienced an emotion he detested: helplessness.

Once Cooper returned to Ole Miss as an ex–football player, he attended football practice every afternoon as if it were his personal mass. His surgery was a few months away, and Cooper wanted to feel like he was still part of the team. This was what he loved most about the sport, being one of the guys, and he wasn't prepared to give that up just yet. He always was ready with a quick answer when someone asked him if he was a football player—he'd joke that his eligibility had run out or that he was now a bowler or a pianist—but the truth was he missed the game dearly, like a part of him had died.

He'd stand on the sideline and intently watch the action during practices. He'd hang out in the locker room and shoot the bull with the players, cracking jokes and talking about upcoming opponents. Cooper had been spending time in locker rooms since before he started preschool—Archie even let him stand on the sidelines of home Saints games—and he began playing pee-wee football in fifth grade. Now, even though he knew he'd never play again, he couldn't let go of the rhythms and sounds of the game. The pull was still too strong.

Then before practice one afternoon senior defensive end Jack Muirhead walked up to Cooper in the locker room. Cooper was chatting with other players when Muirhead interrupted. "What the hell are you doing here?" the burly defensive player asked, not intending to be hurtful.

"What do you mean?" Cooper asked.

"You should be out fishing, you should go play golf or something, go chase some girls," Muirhead said, laughing. "Instead you're in the locker room shooting the breeze with guys before practice."

For one of the few times in his life, the quick-witted Cooper didn't have a comeback. He mumbled "oh" and walked out of the locker room, never to return. That was the end of football for Archie's oldest boy, the final break.

In June 1993 Cooper underwent a three-hour surgery on his spine at the Tulane Medical Center in New Orleans. Peyton always was busy in the summer—throwing to high school teammates, throwing to Saints receivers, playing other sports—and on the day of the surgery he had a baseball game. His parents told him to go ahead and play; he could come to the hospital later to check on his brother.

But during the game the Newman coach, Billy Fitzgerald, approached Peyton with a look of concern on his face. "Peyton, you need to go with my wife, Peggy," Fitzgerald said. "Your mom called. She wants you at the hospital."

Still wearing his cleats, Peyton rushed into the hospital, his heart pounding with fear. He was guided to a small room where Archie, Olivia, and little Eli were praying with a chaplain. Peyton was told that, after the surgery, doctors had found a blood clot in Cooper that required an emergency operation. There was a possibility that Cooper could be paralyzed.

The Mannings dropped to their knees in prayer. The second

surgery took two hours—the most harrowing two hours Archie and Olivia and Peyton and even little Eli had ever endured. It was two hours during which everything hung in the balance for their beloved Cooper, and the entire family. Archie desperately wished it were him on that operating table, not his boy. He'd already lived a good portion of his life, but Cooper had only taken his first few steps into adulthood. There was still so much for Cooper to accomplish and enjoy in life—getting married, having kids, raising his own family. Archie's past experiences taught him that life could be cruel, but the specter of Cooper never walking again was more unthinkable, more terrifying to Archie than losing his father.

They all felt utterly helpless. Archie fought to be positive. That was how he had pushed through those dark, devastating days after Buddy died, and now he told his family they had to believe that Cooper would be fine, that he would still be able to walk. But still Archie prayed for his oldest boy and pulled his other two sons, both racked with fear, tight to his chest.

Peyton thought of Archie, of how difficult it must have been to lose his dad at such a young age. Peyton then swore that football would never again be as important as his family. Like most seventeen-year-olds, he had taken his family for granted. But never again, he vowed, never again.

The doctor returned, and the relieved look on his face said it all: The surgery was a success; Cooper would be fine. The blood clot had dissolved and the possibility of paralysis vanished. Cooper would never play contact sports again, but he would walk and run and live a normal life.

Standing in the soft light of the hospital, hearing these words, Archie felt a once-in-a-lifetime relief course through his body. Then his thoughts turned to one question: *What do I need to do to help Cooper get better?*

———

Cooper could barely move when he opened his eyes. He needed a wheelchair for a brief time—he couldn't move his right leg, and his left leg was numb—and he had to learn how to walk again. He fell repeatedly during his rehabilitation and he couldn't shake hands firmly, like his dad had taught him to do. But not once did Cooper complain about his new lot in life.

He steadily improved, moving from a walker to a cane to needing only the support of his two legs to walk. In early 1994, after months of rehab, he returned to school. He kept a picture in his wallet that was his official dining pass at Ole Miss, taken only weeks before he was forced to give up football. The snapshot captured Cooper with a shaved head as a freshman, his neck bulging with muscles, his shoulders broad, his football future so full of promise. The picture was a reminder of the fragility of life, that everyone's path can be altered in a heartbeat, and that it was critical to savor those pinch-me moments that can pass by at warp speed. It was a lesson his father had learned at virtually the same age as Cooper.

With football gone, Cooper was a changed young man. But of the three Manning brothers, it was the fun-loving, joking, carefree Cooper who was best equipped to deal with a life that didn't include putting on shoulder pads.

"Maybe the bad thing happened to the right guy," Cooper said. "I'm just a big believer that things happen for a reason. I don't sit and dwell, whether it's good or bad. You can walk around and be a sad guy, but that never appealed to me."

Cooper moved on with his life, rarely looking back—just like his old man.

CHAPTER 21

═══
═══

The Decision

New Orleans. Winter 1993–94.

Each senior in the Isidore Newman class of 1994 selected three quotes to appear in the school's annual yearbook. The quotes could be about anything—life, love, motivations, inspirations. Peyton didn't have to thumb through Bartlett's to find his favorite trio of sayings, because he had three that he could recite by memory.

One quote centered on the nature of losing.

> *"I hate to lose more than I like to win. I hate to see the happiness on their faces when they beat me."*
>
> **—JIMMY CONNORS, TENNIS PLAYER**

Another probed the nature of pressure—and the importance of preparation.

> *"Pressure is something you feel only when you*
> *don't know what the hell you're doing."*

—CHUCK NOLL, STEELERS HEAD COACH

The third quote contained the words most important to Peyton—precious, resounding words that would rest in his heart and echo in his head for the next two decades.

> *"I would like to live my dream of*
> *playing football through you."*

—COOPER MANNING

Even when Cooper was away at college, he was Peyton's biggest influence. If Peyton was tired at a football practice during his senior year and didn't want to push through another rep, he'd think of Cooper—and suddenly he'd find the energy. If Peyton felt the urge to quit studying the film of an upcoming opponent, he'd think of Cooper—and then comfortably settle in for a few more hours of tape-watching. Cooper was 350 miles away at Ole Miss during his sophomore year, but he was still the fuel that powered Peyton's internal engine. It was a dynamic that would never change.

Peyton already was one of the most highly recruited players in the nation. In his junior year he completed 168 of 265 passes for 2,703 yards and 39 touchdowns, leading the Newman Greenies to an 11–2 record. He was named the state player of the year by several publications and the national high school player of the year by the Columbus, Ohio, touchdown club. A few months after the season, Archie received the first of several calls from college coaches from California to the Carolinas who wanted to "talk about Peyton."

Peyton was bigger and stronger than Archie at seventeen, but not as fast. Peyton's throwing motion, honed for years by his dad on the yard on First Street, was by-the-book perfect—precise, pure, faultless. It was the epitome of the instructions and illustrations in the how-to football manual Archie received more than two decades earlier from his old coach John Vaught. And Peyton already could hit a receiver 60 yards away. The summer before his senior year Peyton worked out with the Saints. Gazing at Peyton, New Orleans coach Jim Mora was in awe of the kid's throwing mechanics and arm strength. Mora turned to Archie and said, "The way he looks, the way he throws, I would have thought Peyton was a junior in college, not in high school."

Peyton was a gem, polished by Archie, who believed there were four common fundamental mistakes that young quarterbacks frequently committed: They weren't perfectly balanced when they received snaps from center; they stutter-stepped after receiving snaps; they looked into the backfield when dropping back; and they patted the ball before throwing it, disrupting the timing with receivers. These flaws were football sins according to Archie's pigskin bible, so he taught his boys how to avoid each of them, emphasizing the importance of proper footwork and maintaining balance. By the time Peyton was seventeen, coaches like Mora graded Peyton's drops and throwing mechanics equal to those of elite college quarterbacks.

The summer before his senior year Peyton flew across the country to attend a football camp at Stanford University in Palo Alto, California. This was Peyton's chance to sample the West Coast lifestyle and see if he'd one day like to play college ball in the Pac-10 Conference. On the camp's first day a coach told all the quarterbacks that practices would start at 9:00 a.m. but they should arrive at 8:45 to loosen up their arms.

Four days later, on the night before the final practice, the same coach gathered all the older players and asked them what they thought of the experience. Peyton had been bothered about something the entire time during his stay, and now he wasn't shy about expressing himself—one of Peyton's defining personality characteristics.

He raised his hand and was called on. "Remember the first day when you said practice starts at 9 and you want the quarterbacks there at 8:45 to get their arms warmed up?" Peyton asked.

"Yeah," the coach replied.

"Well," Peyton said, "it's pretty hard to get our arms warmed up when we don't get any footballs until 9:15."

That was Peyton being Peyton, the same player who often started practices fifteen minutes early at Newman before the coaches walked onto the field. Now, in Palo Alto, he was right, of course, and the next morning balls were available at 8:45 to all the quarterbacks. But Peyton had seen enough of the West Coast to know he'd never attend college in that region of the country. "Dad," he said, "those kids out there are *different*."

"Yeah," Archie replied, "and they think you are *different*."

By the time Peyton was a senior, he already had a pre-snap routine. After calling a play in the huddle, he would walk to the line of scrimmage. Before putting his hands under center, he would survey the defense to see how it was deployed, his eyes darting from one side of the field to the other, two, three, sometimes four times. Then, from memory, Peyton would quickly replay the tapes he had watched of the opposition's defense, trying to recall when he had seen that specific alignment. Once he pulled up the align-

The First Family of football. From left to right:
Cooper, Peyton, Eli, Olivia, and Archie.

Archie and Olivia first lost themselves in each other's eyes
at a fraternity dance at Ole Miss in 1968.

Archie's favorite pastime as a parent was playing games with his boys. Cooper, a blossoming wide receiver, catches a pass from his dad and sprints past Peyton (far right) and a friend for a touchdown.

Peyton first displayed his cerebral approach to the game—which would become his hallmark in the NFL—and his powerful right arm at Newman High in New Orleans.

The number one recruit in the nation as a senior in high school, Peyton received hundreds of letters from colleges across the country. He picked Tennessee because of his instant connection with David Cutcliffe, the team's offensive coordinator.

Archie had a rule when it came to sports with his kids: he would teach them but only if he was asked. Here he shows Eli the proper two-handed grip for holding the ball in the pocket.

Many Manning family discussions took place in the kitchen. And when one of the boys needed to make an important decision, Olivia was there for support and guidance.

As a boy, Peyton once fell on a barbell in the Saints' weight room and
cut his head—but he never cried, even when he was stitched up
at the hospital. As a young man at Tennessee, he always
worked out like he had something to prove.

Peyton's obsessive study habits—coaches at Tennessee nicknamed
him "the Computer" and "R2-D2"—would fuel
his ascendance in college and the NFL.

Archie, who had only a sister, often reminded his boys how lucky they were to have one another. Though they sometimes fought growing up, in the end, Peyton, Cooper, and Eli always had each other's back.

ment from his mental catalog, Peyton would try to remember what the defenders had done once the ball was snapped. Based on that, Peyton would try to picture where the defenders were about to move once the ball was hiked.

In mid-September, Isidore Newman played Country Day High. As usual, Archie was one of the first fans to arrive. An hour before kickoff he walked to his normal seat in the top row of the bleachers, turned on his video camera, and started to film Peyton warming up. Archie was secretly hoping that Country Day would jump to an early lead, which would put pressure on Peyton and force him to throw. But soon after the opening kickoff it was clear that Peyton was in full control, accurately reading the Cajun defense before the snap and knowing exactly where the defenders would move once the play began. At halftime Newman led 34–7.

Early in the third quarter, as Peyton continued to guide Newman ruthlessly up and down the field, the Country Day head coach started screaming at the referee. "Hey, stripes! Why don't you stop watching Manning and start watching the game? You'll get to watch him the next four years on TV!"

Up in the stands, Archie was still filming with a documentarian's zeal. Archie didn't really know why he was recording his son's games—he'd been behind the camera for years now—but it felt comfortable to him, natural, as if it was part of his fatherly duty. Peyton had noticed that his father had been hugging him tighter recently and telling him that he loved him more frequently. It eventually dawned on Peyton that he was approaching the age that Archie had been when he lost his own father, and that Archie wanted to make sure all his boys knew precisely the boundless love he had for each of them.

Late in the third quarter, still filming, Archie spotted something on the field that made him rise to his feet.

Peyton faked a handoff to his running back, hid the ball on his hip, then sprinted around the end and up the sideline for a first down. Peyton had ignored the play call—he was supposed to hand the ball to his running back—and bolted against the grain. "The blind bootleg," Archie said aloud, pointing at Peyton. "Did you see that, Olivia? It was the blind bootleg!"

Peyton had been watching his dad's old game tapes and seen him run the blind bootleg when he was at Ole Miss. Peyton had never thought to replicate the play, but then at the line of scrimmage, as he was assessing the defensive alignment, the thought popped into his head: *The blind bootleg will work here.* So without telling anyone, Peyton kept the ball and ran like he was a young Archie tearing up the field in Oxford. The play wasn't even in the Newman playbook.

After Newman's 46–7 win, the sweat-drenched quarterback couldn't contain his enthusiasm when he spotted his dad on the field. "Did you see my blind bootleg?" Peyton asked excitedly.

"I sure did, Peyton," Archie said. "I saw it, all right."

Peyton then retreated into the locker room to shower. As Archie waited, three boys who looked to be Eli's age—ten— approached him, one carrying a football. They asked Archie to throw them some passes; the old quarterback was happy to oblige.

Standing near midfield, Archie threw a few short passes. Then he told a kid to start running down the heart of the field. He was at the 30. The 20. "Keep going," Archie yelled.

When he was at the 10, Archie reared back and unleashed a bomb. The ball traveled high into the black sky, spiraling beautifully, arching like a bottle rocket shot into the night, climbing as high as the stadium lights. Archie had the same throwing motion as his middle son, and the same motion of his youngest boy, Eli. The ball continued to spin through the air, as if it had been thrown by Archie in his prime, in front of 70,000 fans, all of them putting some of their hopes into the ball along with Archie.

The kid was at the goal line as the football fell from the heavens and landed softly in his arms—the final perfect strike of the night by the Manning family.

Late in Peyton's final season at Newman the team's offensive coordinator, Frank Gendusa, turned over the two-minute offense to his quarterback and allowed him to call the plays—a first for Gendusa. Before Peyton stepped into his life, Gendusa, who described Peyton as being "as serious as a heart attack" in his approach to football, never could have imagined letting a high school quarterback run the show; the burden was simply too immense for a seventeen- or eighteen-year-old. But Peyton knew the playbook as well as any of his coaches. Handing Peyton the keys to the two-minute offense was Gendusa's way of acknowledging that Peyton was a once-in-a-generation quarterback.

Newman's longest play of the season was a result of Peyton's quick thinking. In the state playoffs against Northeast High of Baton Rouge, the Greenies had the ball on their own 1-yard line. Peyton looked to the sideline for the play call, but Gendusa was slow to relay what he wanted. With the play clock running down, Peyton ducked into the huddle and told his offense that they would run one of his dad's favorite plays: the blind bootleg.

The ball was snapped. Peyton faked a handoff, hid the ball on his right hip, then sprinted out to his right. But the outside linebacker didn't bite on the fake; he charged at Peyton. Then the cornerback on that side of the field saw that Peyton had the ball, and he left the receiver he was covering to try to make the tackle. Just before Peyton was hit, he dumped the ball to his suddenly uncovered receiver, who ran for a 99-yard touchdown. The blind boot had worked again.

Peyton passed for 395 yards and three touchdowns in the game, but Newman lost to Northeast High 39–28. As Peyton walked off the field, teammates, rival players, rival coaches, and hordes of fans circled around him. They all wanted to know the answer to the same question: *Hey, Peyton, where are you going to go to college?*

The first handwritten letter arrived from Bobby Bowden, the Florida State head coach, when Peyton was a sophomore. Then more came to the house on First Street. A steady trickle became a downpour that turned into a deluge, like Christmas shopping catalogs in December. During his junior year, Peyton—the consensus number one player in his class, according to most recruiting analysts—received about twenty-five letters a day from coaches across the nation. He stored the missives in four large boxes, which he placed on Eli's Ping-Pong table up on the second floor in the sunroom.

Every night, Peyton took his recently received letters up to his parents' bedroom. Lying across the foot of the bed, Peyton would talk about the new offers. Archie and Olivia would ask their middle child if anything had resonated with him, and Peyton would usually shrug his shoulders and shake his head. There was just so much information to consume.

The plan, since he had been a small boy, had been clearly laid out: Peyton would follow Cooper to college, and the two of them would form a brother-to-brother pass-catch combination like no other in college football history. When Cooper chose Ole Miss, Peyton intuitively knew that he too would become a Rebel—the third Manning man in Oxford.

But that plan was derailed the moment Cooper's football career ended. Now unsure of where to go, Peyton applied the same intensity to his recruitment as he did to game preparation. When a coach called the house, Peyton didn't merely listen; he quizzed the coach at length—sometimes for more than an hour—about how he would develop him into an NFL quarterback, what type of academic support he would get, where the library was in relation to the football facility, what the weight room was like, how early he could play, who the receivers were on the roster, and who the playmakers were that were being recruited. Bobby Bowden was so taken with Peyton after speaking to him by phone that he felt like an FBI investigator had him under an intense light.

Archie pursued the same hands-off approach with Peyton that he'd taken when Cooper started playing football; Archie was there to answer questions and offer guidance, but he wasn't going to be heavy-handed and direct his son to a particular school, even though Ole Miss alums were pressuring Archie to push Peyton toward Oxford. Old friends whom Archie hadn't talked to for years were now phoning the Manning home and telling Archie to keep Peyton "true to the Red and Blue." Archie secretly hoped that Peyton would stay in the South because the Mannings were a Southern family and Archie wanted his boy to be close to home. But Archie never even shared that with Peyton; in the choppy waters of recruiting, Peyton was the captain of his own ship.

On one spring weekend of his junior year Archie and Peyton hopped into a car and, with Peyton behind the wheel, drove to Gainesville, Florida. For a few hours father and son sat with Gator coach Steve Spurrier and watched film of Spurrier's Fun 'n' Gun offense. The folksy Spurrier put on the hard sell, explaining how Peyton could be the perfect quarterback for this offense: Peyton would put up historic numbers and, Spurrier stressed, he would make Peyton NFL-ready. After the film session, Peyton and Archie stood on the sideline and took in Florida's final spring practice.

The next morning father and son cruised 150 miles to Tallahassee, making it onto campus in time for the Florida State spring game. A staffer guided Peyton into the locker room, where a Florida State number 18 Manning jersey was hanging in the locker of the reigning Heisman Trophy winner, Charlie Ward. After the spring game Peyton sat down with Bobby Bowden and viewed more film. Bowden was as persuasive as Spurrier, telling Peyton that he could win multiple national titles for the Seminoles. Just as he had done on the phone, Peyton grilled Bowden about everything from the practice schedule to the quality of the dining hall. Bowden left the meeting believing he'd never met a high school player as meticulous and thorough in decision-making as Peyton.

During the summer Peyton and Archie took another long car trip, driving to Austin, Texas, to meet with Longhorns coach John Mackovic. Then they moved on to College Station, Texas, to sit down with Texas A&M's R. C. Slocum. Peyton and Archie had more visits mapped out, but Peyton grew tired of driving, and the grind of gathering information wore him down.

But Peyton still was capable of having youthful fun—especially when Cooper was around. Cooper was by his younger brother's side when they rolled into South Bend, Indiana, for Peyton's recruiting visit to Notre Dame. When they spotted the historic stadium rising out of the Indiana farmlands, the brothers grew giddy. As soon as they strolled into the House That Rockne Built and were by themselves, they imagined they both were playing for the Fighting Irish. Three times they sprinted down the tunnel from the dressing room, slapped their hands on the iconic "Play Like a Champion Today" sign, and ran onto the field, pretending the sold-out stadium was thundering with pregame excitement. It had been a decade since the brothers had played one-on-one football in the empty Superdome, and now they were together again on another empty field in another stadium. At this moment, here in the Indiana quiet, Peyton and Cooper may have been the two happiest young men in America.

When Peyton finally met with Notre Dame coach Lou Holtz, Peyton flooded him with questions, asking about the offense, the weight room, the quarterback coach, the wide receivers, the running backs, the offensive line, even other recruits. Holtz, like Bowden at Florida State and Spurrier at Florida, was blown away. He'd never been around a more inquisitive high school player than Peyton. The kid's thirsty mind made him even more appealing to Holtz, who promised Peyton immediate playing time.

On the morning of January 2, 1994—just hours after Florida defeated West Virginia 41–7 in the Sugar Bowl on New Year's Day—Gator coach Steve Spurrier dropped by the Manning house on First Street. The third-ranked Mountaineers had entered the game undefeated with an outside shot of winning the school's first national title, but Spurrier's Florida offense moved the ball with ease, scoring the last 41 points of the game. The coach reiterated to Peyton that he would make him a star who shined even brighter than his daddy had at Ole Miss.

On January 14, 1994—several weeks after Peyton had completed his senior season—Peyton and Archie flew to Oxford for an unofficial visit to Ole Miss. The two met with offensive coordinator Larry Kueck and then walked around the leafy campus. Peyton was introduced to several longtime football staffers and Ole Miss employees who had worked at the school when Archie was a student. Peyton dazzled each of them; in their eyes, he seemed to be the Second Coming of the old man. The voice was the same, the squinting eyes, the round face, the perfect teeth, the square jaw, the prominent nose—all 100 percent Manning. He said "yes sir" and "no sir" just like his daddy. And based on the game film—Manning, the sequel—there was no mistake he had Archie's magical right arm. Suddenly long-ago echoes were once again reverberating in Oxford.

Archie's former coach, John Vaught, who still lived outside of

Oxford on his farm, stopped by to shake Peyton's hand. Ole Miss hung a number 18 Archie Manning jersey in the locker room, and told Peyton they would bring the jersey out of retirement for Peyton to wear. The Rebel staff even made an audiotape for Peyton that featured him leading a game-winning drive over Auburn—the Rebel's first opponent next season. The tape ended with Peyton tossing a touchdown pass.

Ole Miss coaches spoke as if it was a foregone conclusion that Peyton would honor his father by committing to Ole Miss. "Peyton's a player who will have the most impact of any player in the history of Ole Miss," Billy Brewer said after Peyton's visit. "If Peyton and his daddy were the same age, his daddy would have to watch him play because Peyton would beat him out. He's the best high school quarterback I've ever seen."

Almost as soon as Peyton had thrown his first high school pass, Archie had been hearing from Ole Miss folks. Archie never led the Rebels to the SEC title or the national championship, and now prominent Ole Miss alums believed that Peyton would finish his father's business in Oxford. Even Olivia thought that Peyton would become a Rebel.

Archie refused to intervene—exactly how his father had acted during his own recruitment. "I love Ole Miss, but I love my son more," Archie said. "I want him to go where he'll be happy."

The day after visiting Oxford, Peyton and Archie traveled to Knoxville, Tennessee, to meet with the Volunteer coaches. There was an ice storm pelting the Neyland Stadium natural grass when Peyton and Archie walked into the building, a place Peyton had never visited before. Then, for several hours, Peyton talked with David Cutcliffe, the Tennessee offensive coordinator. Sitting in the darkness of a meeting room, the two watched game film and spit-balled philosophical ideas. Something happened during this chat—neither Peyton nor Cutcliffe would ever be able to articulate exactly what, but it was palpable to both of them—and the two just clicked, a Plato finding his Socrates. Cutcliffe later commented that he'd never spent so much time in his life with a quarterback breaking down tape on a recruiting visit than he had with Peyton.

They were so much alike. Cutcliffe told Peyton about sitting in the Legion Field stands in 1969 and watching Archie run and pass for 540 yards against Alabama. That night Cutcliffe couldn't take his eyes off the quarterback from Drew, and now Peyton was riveted to Cutcliffe's recollections of that long-ago game, as if history came alive for Peyton. "I couldn't believe Archie Manning," Cutcliffe said. "He was the best-looking quarterback I'd ever seen." Peyton's father, Cutcliffe believed, was the ultimate prototypical quarterback.

Cutcliffe was a perfectionist like Peyton. When Cutcliffe was a kid growing up in Birmingham, his father, Raymond, the manager of a grocery store, would ask him to wash his car. The father demanded it be spotless, and one time it took David nine attempts before his father was satisfied—the boy's introduction to chasing perfection. When he was put in charge of taking care of the yard, he wanted it to look as pristine as a golf course, no matter how long it took him to finish cutting the lawn and trimming the hedges. And when he played imaginary football games by himself by throwing a ball at tree limbs in a pasture, he continually focused on honing a quick-twitch release and visualizing he was in a game.

Peyton couldn't get enough of Cutcliffe. When Cutcliffe later visited Peyton in the Manning home on First Street, Tennessee head coach Phillip Fulmer was by Cutcliffe's side. Yet Fulmer said only a few words to Peyton; he turned the show over to his offensive coordinator, who had an obvious rapport with the middle Manning.

Fulmer called Archie the next day. "Ya know, I didn't really talk to Peyton," Fulmer said. "I didn't want to interfere."

Olivia saw the instant connection between Peyton and Cutcliffe. She had wanted to cook a meal for the two Tennessee coaches, but she had to take Eli to an event at First Baptist Church. She left a hot dish for them to eat, and when Olivia returned home she spotted Peyton on the edge of his stool in the kitchen locked in an eye-to-eye, passionate conversation with Cutcliffe. They were so engrossed in talking that they still had food on their plates.

Olivia was struck with one thought: *Peyton is really interested in Tennessee.*

The Ole Miss coaches dropped by the Manning house. Billy Brewer, the head coach, already was smitten with Eli. He had arrived early in the afternoon to watch Eli's grade school basketball game—he was the first college coach to express interest in Eli—and later Brewer and Peyton talked offensive philosophy in the family dining room, sketching out X's and O's on Olivia's linen napkins.

Peyton narrowed his list of potential schools to six: defending national champion Florida State, Notre Dame, Florida, Tennessee, Michigan, and Ole Miss.

On January 16, nine days before Peyton was set to announce his decision, a reporter asked thirteen-year-old Eli where Peyton should go to school. "Tennessee or Notre Dame," Eli replied, "because they always have great receivers." After Eli weighed in to the news media, Peyton cut his list to three—Florida, Ole Miss, and Tennessee.

——

Archie didn't share it with his son, but he wished Peyton would choose Ole Miss. Many of the defining events of Archie's life had occurred in Oxford—meeting Olivia, navigating the hurricane of grief from his father's suicide, developing into an elite quarterback, maturing into a man—and Archie silently dreamed about sharing more memories with his boy at the place that meant so much to him. The Ole Miss program was struggling—the Rebels hadn't won a conference championship in thirty years and there were whispers that the program was about to be placed on probation, which Peyton was aware of—but perhaps more than anyone in America, Archie didn't view success in terms of wins and losses. Football was a means for personal growth, for bonding with friends, for discovering values, and Archie was sure there was no finer patch of land in the world to experience all of this than in Oxford, Mississippi.

Never one to shut off his mind, Peyton kept asking himself questions, day and night: *Where will I be the best fit? What coach do I click the best with? What school will I enjoy the most? Where will I develop the best?*

After his final official visit, which was to Florida, Peyton said he would announce his decision one week before the official signing date. Peyton had a motive for making his plans known early: he hoped his commitment would entice a few of the nation's top receivers to follow him to the school he selected. As always, Peyton was thinking a step ahead.

Peyton needed to clear his head. So he and Archie spent the Sunday and Monday before D-Day—decision day—at the downtown Hilton Hotel. Father and son checked in under assumed names.

Early on Monday evening, about twenty-four hours before Peyton was to stand before a small army of reporters, he called his mom from his hotel room and told her his plans. Then he spoke to Archie. "Dad, I've decided I want to go to Tennessee," Peyton said. "I think that's the place for me. But I told Mom and I'll tell you. If you'd rather I go to Ole Miss, that's what I'll do."

Archie was so happy that his boy had made a decision that he hugged Peyton tight. "Don't even think about it, son," Archie said. "You go where you want to go. It's your life, not ours. We're with you all the way."

Peyton then called Cooper, who was a sophomore at Ole Miss. The older brother was thrilled. "Yessss," Cooper said. "I like it. I like Tennessee. Great receivers. Big stadium. This is terrific."

The next day Peyton held a press conference at the Hilton. Dozens of reporters from Mississippi were in the room when Peyton said he was heading to Tennessee. The Mississippi reporters were stunned.

Peyton had no interest in being a campus celebrity, which was what he feared he would be as an untested freshman if he signed with the Rebels. (Ole Miss was placed on probation and wasn't allowed to play in bowl games in '95 and '96 and couldn't appear on television in '95.) Later that day Archie began receiving phone calls from irate Ole Miss fans. Angry letters soon filled the Mannings' mailbox. "I hope you get hurt," one Ole Miss supporter wrote to Peyton. Another letter, addressed to Peyton, read: "We always loved your dad. But not after this." Another stated: "I hope you break your leg." The owner of a gas station in Oxford, where Archie always stopped when he visited the school, told the family never to come back.

Once Cooper was told about the backlash, he handled it the only way he could: he put on a bright orange Tennessee baseball cap and proudly walked around the Ole Miss campus, practically daring someone to say something to him. His brother was a Vol, which meant he was too.

Weeks after Peyton committed, Cutcliffe traveled to New Orleans to talk to Peyton. Sitting in the living room with his new quarterback and Archie, Cutcliffe launched into a review of plays, formations, and the unique language of the Tennessee offense. Minutes into his soliloquy, Cutcliffe glanced over at Archie. He was slumped on the couch and fast asleep.

It was unintentional, but Archie had just communicated a long-held principle to the Tennessee offensive coordinator: he had no plans to be a micromanager—or even a manager, for that matter—of his son's football career.

CHAPTER 22

===

The Mamma's Boy

New Orleans. Winter 1994.

From the very moment he came into this world, Eli was different.

For weeks leading up to his birth, Olivia daydreamed of having a little girl. They would spend their days together as Archie would be off playing with the two boys. There were so many things to do in the Big Easy with a girl—shops to visit, art galleries to explore, antiques stores to rummage through—that had no appeal to Cooper or Peyton. The thought of having a miniature version of herself excited Olivia, who often felt she had two younger, slimmer incarnations of Archie terrorizing their house.

On January 3, 1981, three weeks after the Saints won their only game of the 1980 season, Olivia went into labor. Her hope for a girl suddenly changed when she looked down and saw a "big fat bulldog face." She said aloud, "Oh, Lord, let this be a boy."

Elisha Nelson Manning weighed 9 pounds, 14 ounces at birth,

considerably less than Cooper and Peyton, who both tipped the scales at over 12 pounds when they were born. No, Eli wasn't a girl, but unlike Cooper and Peyton, from the instant he first laid in Olivia's arms, he was very much a mamma's boy.

Growing up, Eli spent most of his time with his mom; he inherited her mild-mannered temperament. Five years younger than Peyton and seven years younger than Cooper, Eli was often left behind when his older brothers went out with their friends to play sports and carouse around New Orleans. So Eli frequently went antiques shopping on Magazine Street with Olivia, always on the lookout for bargains. Years later, when he was a college freshman, he decorated his room with items he bought with his mom in antiques stores.

Little Eli didn't talk much. In fact, he didn't say any intelligible words until he was about three years old. Eli's first word wasn't "mamma" or "daddy"; it was "ball." In his crib he slept with a football and a basketball, which soothed him more than any stuffed animal.

Archie described Eli to friends as "distant." During the first decade of Eli's life, he essentially spoke in monosyllables and was so quiet as a child that his parents often didn't know if he was in the house or outside. Archie and Olivia couldn't figure out why their youngest was so shy and reticent. Eli didn't even like to attend his brothers' basketball and baseball games; he often begged his parents for a babysitter so he could stay home. Archie began to think that perhaps sports wouldn't interest Eli.

On other occasions Archie confessed to his friends that he was afraid he'd never understand Eli and have a sense of what made him happy or sad, angry or fulfilled. There were times Archie feared he'd never be able to pull back the curtain that hid Eli's thoughts. In the very low moments, Archie felt concerned that he'd lost Eli, that he'd never connect with him the way he had with Cooper and Peyton. He worried that their relationship would be as distant as his was with his father, Buddy.

First-grade math came easily to Eli, as if numbers spoke volumes to him. But reading was difficult; the words and sentences on the page often were difficult to comprehend. The prospect of being called on in class to read aloud horrified Eli because it was so hard for him to get through even a few sentences. His classmates teased him, which caused Eli to withdraw even more. When Olivia visited Eli's first-grade class one afternoon, the teacher asked Eli to introduce his mom to the class. Eli became so paralyzed with fear that he could barely force the words from his mouth.

Eli struggled to keep up with the other students in his grade school classes at Newman, the same elite private school where Peyton and Cooper were students. Eli's teacher eventually suggested to Olivia and Archie that Eli be held back a year to allow his mind to develop. But Olivia wouldn't hear of it; she instead enrolled him at St. George's Episcopal School, a smaller school that had a specialized reading program.

Eli's friends at Newman ribbed him about leaving, but the change in schools was just what he needed. Eli learned that, if he had a test on Friday, he needed to start studying for it on Monday, so he wouldn't be surprised by any of the questions—the beginning of Eli's education in the art of how to prepare, which his middle brother had already perfected. Eli was open to this new approach to studying because he was so terrified of being embarrassed in his classes again. Plus, he wanted to earn good grades so he could return to Newman and be back with his classmate buddies—and prove to them that he was their intellectual equal.

In seventh grade Eli tested back into Newman—Olivia had never been prouder of any of her boys' accomplishments—but the reserve had now become ingrained in Eli's personality. He was still so shy that, on occasion, he didn't even finish his sentences.

But the one thing that now emerged and excited him—a first— was his desire to play football with old friends. Though Eli never verbalized it to his parents, he wanted to be like his older brothers and play high school football for Newman. So he consistently pestered Peyton to play catch with him. One late afternoon the older brother finally obliged. Out on the lawn Peyton fired one hard pass after the next to Eli. Little brother couldn't hold on to the ball, so Peyton came up with an idea: he removed the pillows from a living room couch and taped them to Eli's arms and chest, making him look like a tiny Michelin Man. Eli then gobbled up passes from his older brother for the rest of the afternoon.

Eli largely lived in the long shadows cast by Cooper and Peyton as he grew up. He was the classic tagalong baby brother, always wanting to be included but never sure of his welcome. His older brothers usually dominated the backyard games and the dinner table conversations. But there were some weekend nights that Cooper and Peyton stayed home with Eli and his friends, causing Eli to think he was finally being accepted; only later did he learn that his brothers had been grounded and ordered to babysit.

From an early age, Eli preferred to blend in to the background rather than hover near the epicenter of conversations. During Cooper's senior season at Newman, as he was catching balls from Peyton, a local reporter dropped by the house to interview the family. Olivia flashed her Southern hospitality by cooking a big spaghetti dinner and inviting the reporter to join the family in the dining room. But eleven-year-old Eli refused to play along. He insisted on eating his peanut butter and jelly sandwich in the kitchen. The specter of the reporter asking him a question was as frightening to Eli as a bogeyman in his bedroom closet.

Even when Eli succeeded in sports, his emotional equilibrium never changed. One time, when Cooper was in high school, Eli walked through the front door after playing in a baseball game. "How'd it go?" Cooper asked.

"Good," Eli replied as he walked upstairs to his room, maintaining his usual hangdog expression. It wasn't until later that Cooper learned Eli had hit the game-winning home run in the final inning—a feat that if Peyton or Cooper had achieved would have resulted in them yelling "Guess what I did!" the moment they stepped inside their house. Eli's happiness was more of an internal joy.

One night Archie had a heart-to-heart with his youngest. He told Eli that he didn't have to play sports if he didn't want to, and that he shouldn't feel any pressure because his brothers played or because of his last name. Eli listened, stone-faced. Unlike Cooper and Peyton, who grilled Archie about what it was like to be the starting quarterback at Ole Miss and then the Saints, Eli never once asked Archie about his past. It wasn't that Eli didn't look up to Archie—his dad was his hero—but Eli wanted to live life in the present, not the past. He also just wasn't overly interested in the NFL. Cooper and Peyton could name virtually every starting player in the NFL; the older brothers wondered if Eli could name even one.

Archie continued to talk to Eli. He told his boy that he wanted him to pursue whatever made him happy—that was all. "I want you to know this: you don't even have to play football," Archie said. "If there's ever a day where you say I really don't like this, if you want to play basketball or other sports, or if you don't want to play quarterback, don't."

Eli had virtually no reaction. He politely thanked his father and quietly went back to what he was doing before the one-sided conversation.

The Mannings were a hugging family—except for Eli.

Archie constantly told his boys he loved them, and in return Cooper and Peyton hugged Archie and Olivia in the morning, during the afternoons when they would greet one another, and always at night before bed. The two oldest boys were never shy about showing their emotions and telling their mom and dad precisely how much they cared for each of them.

Not Eli. As a kid he wore a poker face, rarely revealing if he was content, happy, glad, sad, or mad. He avoided affection like it was a blitzing linebacker. Eventually little Eli instituted a rule that he insisted both Archie and Olivia abide by: he could be kissed only on Sunday nights. That was it. And the kiss could be given only before bed.

The rule was law in the Manning household—one of the first signs of Eli's resolve.

CHAPTER 23

Easy Rider

New Orleans. Autumn 1990.

Kids who rarely speak are usually stuck on the offensive line in pee-wee football. The linemen simply have to try to get in the way of the defense, and they don't have to open their mouths in the huddle or at the line of scrimmage.

The talkers play quarterback. Even on grade school teams, the quarterback needs to show snippets of possessing a personality. The fifth-grade quarterback must be seen as a leader by his teammates because he's the one all eyes turn to when things don't go as planned on the field. At the very least, the pee-wee QB typically needs to say more than a few words at practice.

The reticent Eli would have been the last kid a pee-wee coach would want as his quarterback except for one thing: his last name. He was the son of the most famous quarterback to ever play in New Orleans. The flag football coach at St. George's Middle

School would have been considered a fool by every parent in the league if he didn't tap Eli to be his quarterback.

So when Eli was in the fifth, sixth, and seventh grades he was the quarterback of the school's football team. His skill at passing the ball was unmistakable—he could spin a spiral better than any other boy on the roster—and there was zero doubt he was a Manning. Though Eli only occasionally flexed his vocal cords, it was clear he had eagle-eyed his brother Peyton. Eli's throwing motion, his body language, and his sixth sense for understanding where his receivers were supposed to be when it was time for him to throw were virtually mirror images of Peyton's when he was a pee-wee player.

But Peyton rarely let Eli play quarterback during their back-yard games. Little brother typically lined up at center. When older brother allowed Eli to play receiver, Peyton didn't throw the ball to his brother very often because little Eli dropped more passes than Peyton's older friends—shared last name or not, catching the ball was the most important thing to Peyton the quarterback. Sometimes Peyton conjured up a trick play for his baby brother: he'd tell Eli to run about ten yards, fall to the ground, act like he twisted an ankle, then hop up and run a deep post pattern. When Eli caught a touchdown on a play like that from Peyton, he jumped up and down as though he had just conquered the sporting world. But when he dropped the pass—and he dropped balls often—he'd want to run into his house and hide under his bed in embarrassment.

Eli looked up to his brothers—he silently watched their high school games with as much intensity as Archie did—and he grew especially close to Peyton. When Peyton left for Tennessee in the summer of 1994, Peyton would have Archie film Eli's games. Peyton would watch the tape at night in Knoxville and then call home to offer pointers to his little brother. Other times Peyton would analyze Eli's drops in the pocket and critique them. "This is what we're learning at Tennessee," Peyton would say. "On your three-step, make that second step real short and quick to get the ball out." Everything Peyton learned, he wanted to pass on to Eli.

Peyton was like a second father to Eli. Away at Tennessee, Peyton would call Eli at random times and pound him with questions: *What did you do for your last workout? How is your five-step drop progressing? Are you studying the playbook? Are you keeping your grades up?*

Cooper, conversely, was more of an avuncular figure. He'd ask Eli, even when he was underage, "You got enough beer for tonight?"

A college football history buff, Peyton tried to teach little Eli a few lessons. When Eli was ten, Peyton would wrestle his little brother to the ground. After Eli was pinned, Peyton—just as Cooper had done to him years earlier—would thump his little brother on his chest and not stop until Eli had named every SEC school and where each was located. This was the only reason why, by the time Eli was a senior at Newman, he had memorized the schools of the SEC.

When Peyton was in high school at Newman he sometimes drove Eli in the mornings to grade school at St. George's Episcopal. Nearly a dozen times during Eli's fifth-grade year Peyton became so lost in thought—worrying about an upcoming game or a test or mentally reviewing the homework he'd done the night before—that he'd drive past Eli's school without stopping. The ever-quiet Eli didn't tell his older brother that they had cruised by St. George's Episcopal. Reaching Newman and realizing that Eli was still in his car, Peyton would snap out of his own world and quickly call his mom, asking her to come get Eli; Peyton didn't want to be marked tardy for his own first-period class. The one time Olivia wasn't home, Peyton shoved Eli into a cab, telling the driver to take care of his little brother and to please make sure he arrived safely at his fifth-grade class.

A year later—when Peyton was seventeen and Eli was twelve—Peyton came home from school a few times and felt the need to throw. Cooper was away at Ole Miss, so Peyton asked Eli to act as his receiver. The two had played catch before in the yard, but now Peyton really wanted to air it out, to let it rip, so they needed more space. They moved their game of pitch-and-catch to the street. As in the past, Peyton put a large T-shirt on his little brother and stuffed it with padding and pillows and wrapped tape around his brother's body.

Peyton told Eli to move far away from him; Eli waddled down the street like a plump penguin. Peyton then let a ball fly. As it whistled through the air, Eli moved to catch it with his extra padding. But the laser throw knocked him to the ground. This would be repeated several times in front of tour buses that rolled by the Manning home on their way to see writer Anne Rice's mansion down the street. The tourists would be wide-eyed as they watched little Eli get rocketed to the pavement, with some wondering, *What is wrong with this kid who keeps getting hit by balls on purpose?*

Peyton also was a role model to Eli. One afternoon when Eli was seven, Peyton stood under the basketball hoop on the family's court rebounding balls for Eli and passing back to him so Eli could work on his shot. Over and over, little Eli launched bricks that banged off the rim. But Eli kept shooting, determined, and he kept missing. Peyton finally took the ball himself and unleashed a long shot from the doorstep to the house. *Swish.* Not saying a word, Eli quickly grabbed the ball, went to the precise spot where

Peyton had hit his jumper, and heaved a shot. He made it. The pattern of trying to match his brother had already begun.

Eli, the baby of the family, got away with things that Cooper and Peyton didn't. As a teenager, he'd sneak out of the house, drink beer with his buddies, host parties at his house when his parents were out of town, and go off to Bourbon Street to make merry. When he wanted to stay out past curfew, he'd call home. If Archie answered, Eli changed his voice to pretend he was someone else and ask to speak with "Miss Manning." Once Olivia—Eli's usual partner in crime—was on the phone, Eli asked to spend more time with his friends, an appeal that Olivia most often granted.

There were times when Olivia covered for Eli, but there was one rule that all the boys had to observe at all times: Mom and Dad had to know where you were, no exceptions, no arguments. Eli obeyed this directive, though usually he spoke to his mom if he was going to be late arriving home.

The expectations for Eli always were high—he had to follow in the footsteps of two pairs of shoes—and Peyton poured fuel on the flames of hype when Eli was only thirteen years old. Writing in his Newman High School yearbook as a senior, Peyton had a message about Eli printed next to his senior picture: "Thanks to the best lil' brother Eli. (Watch out, World, he's the best one.)"

At Newman High, coach Frank Gendusa nicknamed Eli "Easy Rider" for his laid-back, unaffected approach to life. It soon was shortened to "Easy," and it was perhaps the most appropriate nickname ever given a player at Newman. How even-keeled was Easy? In high school he once scored 29 points in a basketball game and then, the following evening, he failed to sink a single shot. The only thing consistent about Eli on both occasions was his reaction: after each game, he didn't utter a word to Archie about his performance.

But with the passing of time, Eli slowly emerged from his shell. After Cooper graduated from Ole Miss, the oldest Manning son moved back home and began spending more time with seventeen-year-old Eli. They became so close that Cooper went to a few parties with his baby brother. Sometimes Cooper would pull back from the crowd and watch Eli interact with his friends. He saw that Eli was growing up: he could charm a room with his dry sense of humor and his boyish smile. Eli had hordes of friends, though whether or not he actually knew their names was a subject of debate in the Manning household.

Eli was becoming tougher too. When Eli was a junior in high school Peyton flew home one weekend from Knoxville. Shortly after his older brother stepped inside the house, Eli asked Peyton if he'd like to play a game of one-on-one basketball on the court in their driveway. Sure, Peyton replied.

The brotherly battle quickly devolved into a game of tackle basketball: every layup was contested, every foul more jarring than the last. Eli had been the "littlest" of the three brothers for as long as he could remember, and now it was as if he was trying to prove to Peyton that he was just as strong and ferocious as his famous older brother.

Eli claimed he won when he blew past Peyton for a game-clinching slam dunk—Peyton would dispute that for years—but afterward Olivia ordered Archie to take down the hoop. She feared that a rematch between Peyton and Eli would be even more combative, and that her boys would seriously hurt each other.

Slowly, and not as quietly, Eli was coming of age.

———

Archie and Olivia never missed one of Eli's games. On Friday nights they'd sit in a tiny high school stadium and watch their youngest fling the ball all over the field. On Saturday mornings they'd fly to Knoxville—or to the city Tennessee played in—to watch Peyton lead the Volunteers out of the locker room and onto the field.

Archie, working on the Saints' radio broadcast team, would then fly wherever the Saints were to play the next day. By Sunday night, Archie would be exhausted—but always looking ahead. He'd board the Saints' charter flight back to New Orleans and, just after liftoff, begin scribbling his upcoming schedule on a yellow legal pad. Preparation and attention to detail were two of Archie's hallmarks as a player, and now he used those skills as a dad to make sure he never missed a down of his boys' football games.

As Eli developed into one of the most highly recruited quarterbacks in the country, he wasn't as hyper-obsessed with the game as Peyton was. One of Newman's games took place on a Thursday night. Eli was in the team training room when a wave of panic suddenly hit him: it dawned on him that he would miss his favorite television show, *Seinfeld*.

It was only four p.m. and the show didn't begin until eight. He called home, hoping his mom would answer. Eli didn't want to explain the situation to his dad, who he knew would be mildly appalled that his son was thinking about a sit-com when he should be concentrating on playing—and winning—a football game.

Alas, Archie picked up the phone at home. As soon as he heard Eli's voice, he immediately became concerned, figuring something must be very wrong for his son to deviate from his pregame routine by making a phone call. Eli assured his father that everything was fine, but didn't explain the reason for the call. "Can I speak to mom real quick?" Eli asked.

Archie eventually handed the phone to Olivia, who promised her youngest that she would take care of his request. But later, when Archie questioned his son about the call, Eli confessed two things: he wanted to tape *Seinfeld* and, at the time he made the call, he didn't even know who Newman was playing that night.

That was Eli being Eli.

≡

CHAPTER 24

"I Only Had Dogs and Cats Named After Me"

Knoxville, Tennessee. Autumn 1994.

It was a shocking sight.

On November 19, 1994, as one a.m. approached in Knoxville, the party was just revving up throughout the college town. The Volunteers were hosting the Kentucky Wildcats later this very day, and orange-clad fans from across the state now filled the town's bars. The night was ripe with possibility.

The Tennessee faithful had a lot to celebrate this fall. A freshman quarterback had revived the program. His name: Peyton.

After starting the season as the Vols' third-string quarterback, Peyton was thrust into the lineup in the fourth game against Mississippi State after knee injuries knocked out quarterbacks Jerry Colquitt and Todd Helton. Manning struggled at times as a starter—he was booed against Memphis on November 12, causing Peyton to ask Archie afterward, "It wasn't pretty, was it?"—and many callers to local radio sports shows clamored for coach

Phillip Fulmer to start freshman Branndon Stewart. But Peyton won five of his first six starts, even if his play was inconsistent.

Just hours before he would make the sixth start of his college career against the Wildcats, Peyton was supposed to be in his bed just like every other Tennessee player. On Friday nights before games Fulmer instituted a 10:30 p.m. curfew. Peyton had been present at his bed check in the team hotel.

As the clock neared 1:00 a.m., inside a crowded, dimly lit bar in downtown Knoxville, a few fans spotted a tall, lanky, lean college student wearing a baseball cap. Through the smoky haze, the fans could see his hands clutched around a drink and puffs of white smoke rising from a cigar in his mouth. The fans approached and—*oh my gosh!*—he looked like their starting quarterback.

"Hey, Peyton!" one yelled. "What are you doing? It's one in the morning!"

Manning casually straightened up, looked the fans squarely in the eyes, and smiled like he didn't have a care in the world. He took a big drag on his stogie, the red-orange ember glowing in the dark, and then exhaled long and slow, letting the string of smoke drift near their faces as he continued to lock his eyes on theirs.

Manning finally said, "Hey, we're just playing Kentucky tomorrow. What's the big deal?"

The fans were flabbergasted.

Cooper had hoodwinked all of them.

Peyton arrived in Knoxville early in the summer of 1994, weeks before most of the incoming Tennessee freshman football players. The day he walked onto campus he was fourth on the team's depth chart.

In the film room Peyton filled up notebook after notebook, studying the nuances of David Cutcliffe's offense. The strategy of football always sparked a fire in Peyton's imagination—that was why he so enjoyed watching his dad's game films of his Ole Miss days, to see how Archie had flourished in that early version of the spread offense. Now he couldn't load information on Cutcliffe's pro-style offense into his mind fast enough.

The coaches started calling Peyton "the Computer" and "R2-D2" because of his compulsive study habits. During one cram session in the quarterback meeting room junior Todd Helton appeared to be daydreaming. When Helton failed to answer a question from Cutcliffe in a timely fashion, Peyton chimed in, offering his own answer. Peyton then responded to another query directed at Helton, who quickly grew irritated with this know-it-all freshman.

"Damn it, Peyton," Helton finally said. "I can answer my own questions, thank you."

Peyton wasn't bashful about calling out his coach when he believed Cutcliffe had made a mistake. If Cutcliffe told his quarterbacks to do one thing on a certain play, Peyton would check his notes to make sure that Cutcliffe had given the same instructions for that particular play weeks earlier. When Cutcliffe contradicted himself, his freshman signal caller would raise his hand and tell his coach that he was either making a mistake now or had committed a blunder weeks earlier. As the other quarterbacks in the room rolled their eyes, Peyton said he wanted to know what his coach really intended.

Peyton was a note-taking machine even when the topics weren't about X's and O's. When the other freshman football players arrived on campus before the start of the fall semester, Peyton and the members of his class took a three-hour orientation seminar. Taught by Carmen Tegano, an associate athletic director, the seminar introduced the freshman players to life on the Tennessee campus and laid out the expectations of the Volunteer student athletes. At the start of the session, Tegano asked all the players to please take notes. At the end he picked up every spiral notebook. Later, as he reviewed what the players had scribbled down, Tegano was stunned by Peyton's effort: the young quarterback, writing feverishly, had filled thirty pages.

That evening, Tegano related Peyton's attentiveness and mastery of detail to his wife. "If God is willing and I live long enough," Tegano said, "I'll either work for that kid or vote for him."

Before the fall semester began at Tennessee, Peyton went to a fraternity party, one of the few he would attend in college. Wearing a pastel shirt, he was introduced to Ashley Thompson, who had grown up in Memphis and was visiting friends in Knoxville. When Ashley first laid eyes on Peyton, one thought rushed into her head: *This guy is a nerd.*

But Peyton was enchanted at first sight. After explaining that he had a curfew because he was on the football team and they were in preseason workouts, Peyton told Ashley that he would sneak out of his dorm room once the coaches finished bed check. Then they could talk deep into the night and really get to know each other.

But Peyton chickened out; once he was in his dorm room he didn't dare break a team rule. Peyton wouldn't see Ashley, who was a student at the University of Virginia, for several weeks. Yet Peyton was persistent; he couldn't get the beautiful, blond-haired, brown-eyed Ashley out of his mind. Ashley agreed to go out with him on a return visit to Knoxville. On their date Peyton was the perfect gentleman, asking her questions of her life, her hopes for the future, and even pulling out chairs for his date, holding open doors for her, and rising from his seat when Ashley excused herself from the table. His refined Southern manners—taught to him by Archie and Olivia—won her over.

When Ashley returned to Charlottesville, the two began a relationship largely through the written word. Peyton and Ashley penned letter after letter to each other, spilling their thoughts, feelings, and dreams onto the pages. Ashley, thought Peyton, was very much like his mom: caring, empathetic, and thoughtful.

Peyton reminded Ashley of . . . well, no one. At age eighteen, he was already a celebrity throughout the South, but he also could come off as endearingly youthful at times. He once arrived for a date with Ashley decked out head to toe in denim—and thought he looked ready for the red carpet. Another evening, as Peyton spoke to Ashley over the phone, he said that he was in the mood for Chinese food and he was going to have it delivered. After he hung up Peyton then fumbled around trying to figure out how to place an order. He finally gave up, called Ashley back, and convinced her to phone a Chinese restaurant in Knoxville and order dinner for him from her apartment in Charlottesville. Ashley was happy to oblige her clueless boyfriend, her way of taking care of Peyton and nurturing their budding relationship.

Ashley also invaded Peyton's heart by speaking his language: football. Her grandfather, Van Thompson, had played for General Bob Neyland at Tennessee in 1939 and '40. And her brother, Will, played football at Virginia. Ashley had been around the game her entire life, and had a keen understanding of the sport. Just as Archie had been attracted to Olivia's football knowledge all those years ago in Oxford, so too was Peyton captivated by Ashley's pigskin smarts. Almost from the very beginning, their friends said they were a perfect match for each other. One day, they believed, Ashley would walk down the aisle toward her man who—bless his heart—struggled to operate a can opener.

——

During his final two years at Ole Miss, Cooper often boarded a plane on Fridays after his classes in Oxford and flew to Knoxville, where he enjoyed hitting the bars with Peyton's friends. Cooper and Peyton were spitting images of each other, and Cooper relished pretending he was his little brother during those Friday night sojourns before Volunteer games.

On more than one occasion when Cooper was in a bar past the bewitching hour, a well-served Vol fan stumbled toward him and asked, *What the hell are you doing here, Peyt?*

Cooper typically looked the inquisitor in the eyes and said with a straight face, *Oh, just hitting the scotch.*

One night, on the eve of a Tennessee–Alabama game, Cooper was walking down a Knoxville street when a Ford Expedition pulled up next to him. A Tennessee fan stuck his head out the window and shouted, "Hey, Peyton, what are you doing out here on a Friday night?"

"Oh, I'm just getting drunk and chasing women," Cooper replied casually. "Go Vols!"

On Friday nights in Knoxville, Cooper, masquerading as Peyton, signed autographs as Peyton, had conversations as Peyton, shook hands as Peyton, and even talked to women as Peyton. For the first time in his life, Cooper was now known as "Peyton's brother," and he handled the new role well. He proudly wore a Tennessee hat when he was on the Ole Miss campus, and he frequently talked to Peyton by phone, checking in on him and encouraging him. Cooper's football dreams had ended when he was given the news that his next hit on the field could be his last, but that unlucky break didn't turn him bitter or fracture his relationship with Peyton. Instead, it transformed him into Peyton's number one fan.

But Cooper still enjoyed needling Peyton. During Peyton's

sophomore year in Knoxville, Cooper secured a sideline pass for the Kentucky game at Commonwealth Stadium in Lexington. After Peyton threw an interception, he marched to the sideline, his face scrunched in a scowl. Cooper stepped forward. Peyton didn't know his older brother was at the game. Cooper shouted, "Hey, Peyton! Get your ass in gear!" Peyton looked up and argued with Cooper in front of 65,000 fans. The two bickered like they were kids out on the front lawn at their home on First Street. Peyton yelled that he would wave the state troopers over and have Cooper forcibly removed from the sideline if he didn't shut his damn mouth.

After the game—Peyton led the Vols to the game's final 18 points and Tennessee won 34–31—the brothers hugged. The best of friends realized again what Archie meant when he told his boys how lucky they were to have each other.

Tennessee's opening game of the 1994 season was in the Rose Bowl against UCLA. A third-stringer and a true freshman, Peyton was bug-eyed during pregame warm-ups. He waved to ABC announcers Keith Jackson and Bob Griese—he had known both since he was a boy—and he gazed in wonder at the grandstands, which seemed to stretch up, up, and up to heaven. He was so nervous that he asked starting quarterback Jerry Colquitt if he had put his pants on the correct way. Laughing at the baby-faced kid, Colquitt assured him he had.

Peyton expected only to hold a clipboard and stand on the sideline during the game. But on the seventh play of the first quarter, Colquitt suffered a knee injury and limped to the sideline. Now Peyton was second string. Minutes later head coach Phillip Fulmer walked over to Peyton and said, "Be ready."

The Vols fell behind 17–0. Cutcliffe, up in the press box,

phoned down to the sideline and asked to speak to Peyton. "All right, Peyton, you're up," Cutcliffe said. "Get us going."

Peyton strapped his helmet on and loosened his arm up on the sideline. Sitting in the stands, Olivia noticed her boy throwing passes behind the bench. She turned to Archie. "Peyton's going in!" she screamed.

"It's not going to happen," replied Archie.

Minutes later, the quarterback from First Street jogged onto the field, his heart jackhammering, his eyes wide. As he neared the huddle, Peyton could hear his father's voice echoing in his ears, telling him that when you're the quarterback, you have to act like you're the general and in complete charge, no matter if the game is in the front yard, in an empty high school stadium, or in the sold-out Rose Bowl in front of a nationally televised audience.

Peyton reached the huddle. He clapped his hands and confidently said, "All right, guys, I know I'm just a freshman, but we're going to take it down the field on this series and score!"

Senior lineman Jason Layman looked at Peyton like he was a kid who had just run onto the field from his mother's lap. "Shut the fuck up and call the play!" Layman said.

On that note Peyton's career as a college football player got under way. Sideline reporter Lynn Swann climbed into the grandstands and asked Olivia how she thought Peyton looked. She had a one-word response: "young."

Peyton was in for only three plays—all handoffs that netted 9 yards—and Tennessee lost the game 25–23. But Peyton would start the final eight games of his true freshman season, leading the Vols to a 7–1 record over that stretch. He threw 11 touchdown passes and 6 interceptions and was named the SEC Freshman of the Year.

—

During his first year of college Peyton was as stressed as he'd ever been. He unloaded his worries and fears every night during phone calls to Archie, who listened patiently as Peyton went on about adjusting to life in Knoxville, about being away from his mom and dad for the first time, and dealing with the finger-pointing and arched eyebrows every time he stepped out of his dorm room—experiences Archie understood well. Peyton also talked to his dad about the quarterback competition he was having with fellow freshman Branndon Stewart.

Peyton viewed Stewart—a big-armed kid from Stephenville, Texas—only as one thing: a rival. When Stewart would ask Peyton if he wanted to study and watch film together, Peyton would say no. Then later, after Stewart had retreated to his dorm room, Peyton would walk to the football offices and view film for at least an hour. Peyton never wanted to give Stewart any insight into his preparation or how he viewed opponents or what he looked for when he broke down their tendencies. To Peyton, Stewart represented a roadblock that stood between himself and the starting position. One evening Peyton only half-jokingly locked Stewart out of a meeting the quarterbacks had with Cutcliffe.

Peyton had immediate chemistry with his offensive coordinator. Archie had repeatedly told his son about the importance of developing a trusting relationship with the coach who calls the plays, and Peyton took that advice to heart: he spent more time with Cutcliffe than any other person on the Tennessee campus, friends included.

Cutcliffe became a virtual second father to Peyton. He invited him to his house for dinners, introducing Peyton to his wife and kids, who enjoyed horsing around with the young quarterback. Cutcliffe's office door was always open to Peyton, who would stroll in at all hours to talk about an upcoming opponent or a play design that Peyton really liked. The coach and quarterback had so much in common—dissecting the X's and O's of the game and bantering on about football history were their shared favorite subjects—that by the start of his sophomore year Peyton could practically finish Cutcliffe's sentences. On the field, he could often anticipate what Cutcliffe was going to call from the press box based on down and distance and field position—the same intuitive talent that Archie displayed at Ole Miss, where he consistently predicted what play Vaught would call before he sent it into the huddle.

At age nineteen, Peyton was becoming even more like his father. Like Archie, Peyton was a neat freak. One of his first roommates at Tennessee was sloppy and routinely left his belongings scattered throughout their dorm room, as if a cyclone had blown through. In response, Peyton cleaned and organized the room like a housekeeper; in a few instances he made his roommate's bed. In every aspect of his life, Peyton—like Archie—liked order and structure and routine. It was one of the reasons why Peyton compulsively updated his to-do list, a habit he inherited from his father, and why growing up he checked to make sure all the doors were locked before he went to bed. The list was Peyton's compass; without it, he had no magnetic north. He felt lost if it wasn't updated in the morning.

When speaking to reporters Peyton often repeated phrases and maxims that he first heard Archie articulate, such as always giving credit to his teammates and rarely using the word "I" in his responses. Peyton had watched his dad talk in front of television cameras and tape recorders for years—Peyton's media training started in the Saints' locker room when he was no taller than Archie's thigh pads—and so Peyton knew at a young age the importance of not saying anything controversial to reporters. But he would gush about his dad to the local media, so much so that the summer before Peyton's sophomore year Archie asked Peyton to stop mentioning him. Archie didn't want anyone to think that he was coaching his son from afar.

"Now, son, when you go back to school this year, and you talk to the media, please stop saying, 'As my dad would say, . . .'" Archie told Peyton. "I'm not your coach. I just want to be your father."

As far back as he could remember, Peyton had wanted to be like Archie. When he was a kid playing in pickup games on the front lawn, Peyton would walk up to the center slightly bowlegged even though Peyton's legs were perfectly straight. This was the way Archie had approached the line of scrimmage—Peyton saw that on the old videotapes—and while friends would laugh and mock Peyton for his bowlegged imitation, he would never stop mimicking his old man when he ambled to the line.

In his sophomore year Peyton's preoccupation with preparation was growing into the stuff of local legend. On the night before Tennessee played Arkansas in Fayetteville, a reporter called Cutcliffe's hotel room. Peyton answered the phone; he was reviewing some last-minute changes to the game plan. The extra time with his coach paid off the next day when Peyton threw for 384 yards and 4 touchdowns in the Volunteers' 49–31 win.

As Peyton guided Tennessee to an 11-1 record and final AP ranking of number 3 in 1995, he still routinely called Archie, who always seemed to have pitch-perfect advice at the ready. Peyton was his own worst critic—his roommate, Will Newman, often could hear Archie's voice on the other end of the line, telling his son, "Quit being so hard on yourself, Peyton"—but Archie would remind his boy of the beautiful throws he had completed, the proper audibles he had called, the correct reads he had made, the wise decisions to throw the ball away rather than forcing it into tight coverage. Archie was the reassuring, confidence-building voice that his son needed to hear.

But still Peyton brooded over his mistakes, a perfectionist always searching for improvement. That was the key to Archie's rapid development in college, and now his middle son was replicating his old man's behavior in Knoxville.

Near the end of Peyton's sophomore season, he emerged as a Heisman contender. Reporters from across the country flew to Knoxville to interview this second-generation Manning quarterback, who would complete his second season at Tennessee by throwing for a school-record 2,954 yards and would finish sixth in the Heisman Trophy voting. Peyton rarely dug deep with reporters; he was purposefully bland during interviews. To try to understand what made Peyton tick, reporters often called Archie, who, with Peyton's growing success, suddenly was reborn as a public figure.

Archie relished his "second life" as a regular Joe, blissfully recapturing the ability to walk through an airport without being asked for an autograph or even being recognized. But now, in a matter of months, a new narrative of Archie was emerging. He was Super Dad, a parent who molded an all-American kid without ever pushing him into anything he didn't want to pursue.

That fall Archie sent his second-born an email. "Peyton," he wrote, "you have screwed up my fleeting fame."

On October 14, 1995, the Vols traveled to Birmingham, Alabama, to face the Crimson Tide at Legion Field. In this rivalry game between the two winningest teams in SEC history, Tennessee hadn't beaten Alabama in a decade.

On the first play of the game, Peyton spotted wide receiver Joey Kent streaking across the middle of the field. The throw hit

Kent in the hands, and the wide receiver ran untouched into the end zone for an 80-yard score. Up in the radio booth, Tennessee announcer John Ward joyously screamed, "Touchdown on play one!"

Later in the first quarter, with the ball on the Alabama 1-yard line, Peyton called a play from Archie's past: the blind bootleg. Taking the snap, Peyton faked a handoff to the right, put the ball on his hip, and then sprinted to the left. By the time the Tide defenders realized Peyton had the ball he was pumping his fist in the end zone. On the field where his father first commanded the attention of the country against the same opponent twenty-six years earlier, Peyton finished the game 20 of 29 for 301 yards and 3 touchdowns. The Vols won 41–14. Fans across the Volunteer State celebrated deep into the night.

Ten months later, in the fall of 1996, doctors and nurses at hospitals throughout the South started to notice a new trend: in startling numbers, parents were naming their newborns Peyton. From 1985 through '95, only ten children had been named Peyton at the University of Tennessee Medical Center. But from the time Archie's son guided the Vols to the win against Alabama in 1996 through the year 1998 there were sixty-eight Peytons born at the UT Med Center.

By Peyton's junior year, fathers clutching their newborns began coming to Vol practices and asking Peyton to hold their "baby Peyton," who was usually dressed in a bright orange onesie. The two Peytons would then pose for a picture. Day after day, more parents arrived with their babies named after Archie's boy. "What am I supposed to say?" Peyton asked his dad.

"I don't know," Archie replied. "I only had dogs and cats named after me."

As time passed families became more creative about paying homage to Peyton the football player and role model. A mom and dad in Knoxville named their twins Peyton and Manning. Another family named their son Peyton Cooper as a reminder that nothing should ever be taken for granted in life.

Peyton was far from a sure bet to make it as an NFL player when many of these families named their child after him—he'd yet to even win an SEC championship—but mothers and fathers throughout the South already felt like they knew Peyton and the values for which he stood. To his most devout fans, Peyton represented something far more significant than mere athletic talent: he was the personification of hard work, preparedness, and dedication. Nearly three decades after an entire region had revered Archie, his boy had replaced him on the pedestal of fame.

With each completion and each victory, Peyton's story began to blend more and more with Archie's. Peyton had yet to eclipse his father's level of regional fame, but in his sophomore year Peyton had won more games in a single season than Archie ever had—in high school, college, or the pros. There was a powerful feeling throughout the South that Archie was owed this bright time with his son. If anyone deserved a moment in the football sun, it was that lovable loser Archie Manning.

By the spring game before Peyton's junior year, he was so popular in the hearts of fans that he had to part the sea of admirers who gathered outside the locker room after the game to reach Archie, Olivia, and Eli, as well as Ashley, who had driven from Charlottesville to see her boyfriend. As he signed autographs and smiled for photos, Peyton remembered what it was like years earlier waiting for his dad outside the Saints' locker room, watching him scribble his name on every last piece of paper. Archie told Peyton back then that a quarterback doesn't stop being a leader once he steps off the field, but now Peyton began to feel like he was missing out on the authentic college experience.

He couldn't go to the mall or walk around campus without

being recognized and hounded by fans. His dad had romanticized college life at Ole Miss—hanging with buddies and teammates at frat parties, going on dates with the homecoming queen, hearing about his friends going on panty raids—but Peyton's experience was far different. "Peyton has this ideal of college life where he can hang out with everyone, make friends, go to parties, have great moments," Ashley said. "He feels like he's missing out on that."

One of Peyton's favorite times as a college student would come late on Saturday nights after home games. Once he had showered, dressed, and signed dozens of autographs outside the locker room, Peyton would go out with friends. Then, around two a.m., they'd return to their off-campus house. The just-completed game would be replaying over and over on one of the channels, and Peyton and his buddies would pull up chairs and be hypnotized by the action, as if they were experiencing the emotions of the game for the first time. Here, surrounded by his college buddies, his face pressed close to the glow of the screen, Peyton was just one of the boys.

These were the times that Peyton especially cherished. Finally he was living the vision of college that his dad had described to him all those years ago when he was just a boy on First Street.

However, Peyton was far from perfect.

On February 29, 1996, Peyton had an ankle injury. Jamie Ann Whited, the university's director of health and wellness, examined Peyton in a training room in the Neyland-Thompson Sports Center. As Whited was bent over looking at his ankle, a cross-country runner named Malcolm Saxon was on the other side of the training room. Peyton later said he attempted to play a practical joke on Saxon by pulling down his shorts and mooning the runner.

Whited had a different interpretation of what happened: She eventually alleged that Peyton placed his naked testicles on her face. Within hours, Whited said she reported the incident to the Sexual Assault Crisis Center in Knoxville. The police were never called.

Whited then took a medical leave of absence, citing what had happened with Peyton. In May 1996—three months after the incident—Peyton left an apology on Whited's answering machine. He also sent her a written apology by registered letter. "I was clowning around in the training room with a good friend of mine and she happened to see it," Peyton said at the time. "By no means was anything directed at her. It was nothing more than a joke toward somebody else. My practical jokes have come to an end."

Whited then sued the University of Tennessee, claiming thirty-three incidents of sexual harassment, including what had transpired with Peyton in the training room. In August 1997 the school reached a $300,000 settlement with Whited. "I know that around the country people kind of put their own headlines on stories," Archie said after the settlement was reached. "But that's just the way it is. I'd just like for it to die now. I believe it will."

But it didn't. The settlement included a nondisclosure agreement that forbade all parties involved from discussing the incident. But in September 2000, Archie, Peyton, and ghostwriter John Underwood collaborated on the book *Manning: A Father, His Sons, and a Football Legacy*. Before the book was published, an excerpt was mailed to Florida Southern, where Whited then worked and went by Naughright, her maiden name that she reclaimed after going through a divorce.

The excerpt included five paragraphs from the book that detailed the "mooning" incident. Peyton wrote that Naughright had a "vulgar mouth" and that she "had been accumulating a list of complaints against the university that she intended to take action on—alleged sexist acts that, when her lawyer finally put it together, resulted in a lawsuit."

Shortly after Naughright received the excerpt—it was addressed to "Dr. Vulgar Mouth Whited"—she sued Peyton for defamation. Naughright also claimed that the excerpt was circulated to her bosses at Florida Southern and within months she was demoted and then lost her job as director of the Athletic Training Educational Program.

In a court deposition in the defamation case, Naughright— who had never before publicly said Peyton had made physical contact with her—now stated under oath that Peyton had scooted down the training table toward her as she examined his ankle and put his naked testicles and buttocks directly into her face, an act known in the parlance of the locker room as "tea-bagging."

Naughright said she removed her head from under him. "It was the gluteus maximus, the rectum, the testicles and area in between the testicles," Naughright said in a court deposition. "And all that was on my face when I pushed him up. To get leverage, I took my head out to push him up and off."

Peyton admitted to mooning Saxon in the training room, but Peyton said in court documents that he didn't realize Whited had seen his exposed posterior. Peyton once again denied any wrongdoing, and the court case was settled.

But Saxon disputed Peyton's version of events. He wrote a letter to Peyton in 2002 stating, "Peyton, the way I see it, at this point, you are going to take a hit either way, if you settle out of court or if it goes to court. You might as well maintain some dignity and admit to what happened. . . . Your celebrity doesn't mean you can treat folks that way. . . . Do the right thing here."

Through the entire experience Peyton learned a valuable lesson: if he wanted to maintain his sterling reputation, he needed to act like a television camera was trained on him at all hours. For his role in the 1996 incident, the punishment for Peyton the football player was minimal: he was banned from the training table and he had to run at six a.m. for two weeks. But the hits to the reputation of Peyton the person would keep coming for decades.

In February 2016 a New York *Daily News* reporter resuscitated the 2003 Whited court documents, questioning Peyton's white-knight, boy-next-door image. For weeks, on talk radio throughout the nation, Peyton was cast as the villain for the first time in his career—all for a prank, a mistake he had made as a nineteen-year-old sophomore at Tennessee.

Peyton, in 1996, had forgotten the Mannings' guiding life principle, first articulated by his grandfather Buddy to Archie almost three decades earlier when he went off to college: *Be a nice guy.*

Peyton had other missteps in Knoxville, albeit none as serious as what transpired in the training room with Whited.

After an overweight Florida Gator fan heckled him mercilessly, Peyton did what his dad always told him not to do to an obnoxious fan: he responded. Peyton asked her, "What position did you play? Guard or tackle?"

In the middle of games it was prudent to stay out of Peyton's way. Country music singer Kenny Chesney once had a field pass to a Tennessee home game. Born in Knoxville, Chesney was a lifelong Volunteer fan. After Peyton threw a touchdown pass, Chesney cheered along with the chorus of the other 100,000 fans in Neyland Stadium. Moments later Peyton was on the sideline talking to a coach when Chesney, wearing his trademark cowboy hat, enthusiastically bounded over. He slapped Peyton on the shoulder pads and yelled, "Good job, buddy!"

Peyton shot a death glare at the country star. "Get the hell out of here!" Peyton yelled.

Football was serious business to Peyton, but he soon forgave Chesney for his sideline interference, and the two struck up a friendship. Years later Peyton went on tour with the country music star, donning a cowboy hat that he pulled down low and strumming an unplugged guitar at the back of the stage. Peyton blended in to the background with the rest of the musicians, and no one in the crowd knew he was there until Chesney introduced him late in the show.

Peyton loved every minute of it—just as his dad had relished singing songs and dancing around with his buddies at the Sigma Nu fraternity back in Oxford. For a brief amount of time, as the music flowed around Peyton, he was in a state of being that he coveted more than he ever let on. As it had been with his dad a quarter century earlier, Peyton often was happiest when he felt like a "regular" guy.

When Peyton contemplated entering the NFL draft after his junior season, he pulled a classic Peyton: he collected as much information as possible before making his decision.

He consulted Michael Jordan, Tim Duncan, Phil Simms, and Troy Aikman, among others. The majority of the people he interviewed on the subject told him to turn pro and collect that multimillion-dollar jackpot. Others implored him to think about Cooper, and how the story of his brother should remind him that he's only one hit away from never throwing another pass. But Peyton really only listened to one person: himself.

"I can't wait to get there, and I want that challenge," Peyton said of the NFL when he announced he was returning to Knox-ville for his senior year. "But I want it with every bit of ammuni-tion I've got. I have the opportunity [to stay]. I'm entitled to play four years, so I'm going to."

Peyton was offended at suggestions he was dismissing the pos-sibility of serious injury, especially after what happened to his older brother five years earlier. Peyton understood the vagaries of football more than most. "I've counted every day of football since my junior year in high school as lucky," he said.

Dating back to when he was six years old and listening to the old radio replays of his dad's games at Ole Miss, Peyton had dreamed of playing college football. Now he wanted a few more months of the college experience. He wanted to be able to walk around campus and hear his fellow students wish him good luck. He wanted to join his parents' tailgate after games and then grab dinner with them. He wanted to listen to the school band play "Rocky Top" after Tennessee victories. He wanted to drive his Oldsmobile Bravada around campus and see the students playing Frisbee on the sprawling green lawns. He wanted to see the orange-clad Vol fans cordoned off in the nosebleed seats at SEC road games, and he wanted to spend more time in the locker room, talking and horsing around with his teammates. He wanted to savor one more autumn in Knoxville, to push back adulthood for a few more months and be a college football player a little longer. No amount of money was worth forfeiting that.

On game days his senior year—before facing the likes of Alabama on the third Saturday in October in 1997 (a 38–21 Vols win) or Auburn in the SEC championship game (a 30–29 Tennessee victory)—Peyton sat in front of his locker and read the official program. He'd flip through the pages, cover to cover, gaze at the pictures of his teammates, and read the heights and weights of the opposing starting players. Once finished, he'd put on his pads and then, typically, for a few minutes talk SEC history with Cutcliffe.

Before kickoff, out on the field, Peyton sometimes would find Cooper, who would have a sideline pass. Standing together, the two would share a few moments, joking about old games or times when they pulled a fast one on Archie as kids. Planted next to his brother, the stadium filling up, Peyton would fantasize for a few minutes about what could have been. In his imagination he could see himself threading passes through the defense and into the arms of his older brother, his best friend, who then would outrun everyone into the end zone.

In their dreams they always saw each other. "I always see us playing Georgia, in the daylight, always in the daylight," Cooper said. "We're driving down the field, the place is packed. Peyton hits me on a little post-corner route. . . ."

"We're both in Ole Miss uniforms, gray and red," Peyton said. "I picture how it would have been. He comes into my dream, catching a pass. Then he throws the ball up into the stands."

Together, the brothers always scored a touchdown to win the game. Through it all, the dream—seeded in the front yard on First Street—never changed.

CHAPTER 25

——
——

A Coach Just Like Archie

New Orleans. Autumn 1998.

The fall of 1998 marked the end of an era for the Manning family. It was their final season of high school football.

There was virtually nothing about prep football that Archie and Olivia didn't enjoy. They loved the carpooling, the tailgating in the parking lot at Newman, seeing and talking to their friends in the bleachers, and sitting in their customary perch in the top row of the stadium, the ideal roost for Archie to flip on his video camera and record his boys' football history for posterity.

Why was Archie always filming? Because of time—and the sense of it slipping away.

He felt robbed of time with his own father. Their ongoing conversation had been halted in the midstream of Archie's life. Even years after his father had died, Archie continued to wish that he could see his old man once more, to tell him about everything he had missed, from his own success in football and life, to the birth and lives of his own boys, to the kind of father he had become. The plight of many children left marooned by suicide—to wish for more time—was a burden that Archie carried throughout his life, according to friends. It was a weight that never really lightened with the passing of years.

But there was one way Archie did control time—with the video camera. On those tapes he would always have the ability to freeze the most precious moments of his life with his boys: Christmas mornings, first days of school, birthday parties, games in the yard, homecoming dates, proms, and Friday night high school games. These moments in time could always be replayed because Archie—the proud father and wounded son—captured them.

Archie and Olivia savored every game of Eli's senior season in what was the most hectic autumn of their lives. After watching Eli sling passes around the field on Friday nights in rickety high school stadiums, mom and dad often jetted to Indianapolis on Saturday, where on Sundays they'd take their seats in a luxury box suite in the RCA Dome and cheer for Peyton, who had been selected by the Colts as the number one overall pick in the NFL draft earlier that spring.

Yet even as they saw their middle boy performing in front of 70,000 fans in the dome and millions more on television, Archie and Olivia often talked about how much they relished the entire high school football experience, especially Eli's games. That was where dreams first stirred, where lifelong relationships were formed, where the game was learned—so many firsts. The realization that it would all soon end pained both Archie and Olivia. That was why, for this one final season of high school ball, Mom and Dad were more emotionally invested in their Friday nights than they were in their Sunday afternoons.

Wearing number 18 to honor Cooper, Eli could read defenses with ease, and he had an arm that was accurate and developing more strength by the month. Eli started his first varsity game as a freshman after the senior starter was injured. Eli had known for days that he would make his varsity debut on the coming Friday night, but he kept that to himself until about forty-eight hours before kickoff. Sitting at the dinner table with Archie and Olivia, Eli in the middle of the meal nonchalantly said, "Looks like I'm going to be starting Friday night."

"What!" Archie replied. "Friday night? On the varsity!"

A three-time all-state selection, Eli finished his high school career with statistics almost identical to those of Peyton, who was also a three-year starter but was named all-state only twice. At Newman, Eli threw for 7,421 yards; Peyton threw for 7,528 yards. They both completed over 60 percent of their passes, and they both had more than 80 touchdown passes. At the end of the 1998 season, Eli was named all-state and *Rivals.com* ranked him the top pro-style quarterback recruit in the nation. One of the schools that pursued him most relentlessly was the University of Texas.

One Saturday afternoon during Eli's senior year, Archie was in the living room watching the Texas Longhorns on television when Eli plopped down on the couch next to him. Archie and Olivia abided by the same rules with Eli as they had with Peyton when it came to recruiting: they would offer advice only when asked, and they would stay out of the way and let their child make his own decision.

Peyton had occasionally spoken to his parents about the different schools he was considering, but Eli never opened his mouth on the subject of recruiting, as if he were guarding a state secret. But that was typical Eli. Archie later described Eli's indifference to recruiting as "monumental."

So when Eli slid onto the couch next to his father, Archie figured he wanted to watch the Longhorns game because he was interested in going to school in Austin. Texas had always been one of Eli's favorite teams. But after the first quarter Eli rose to his feet and—without uttering a word to Archie—walked upstairs to his bedroom, shut the door, and began playing videogames, not caring whether the Longhorns won or lost. The clock was ticking for Eli to make a decision, but neither Archie nor Olivia had any clue where he'd be attending college.

Instead of leaning on his parents for advice, Eli reached back into his recent past to find a confidant. When Peyton had been at Tennessee, Eli attended a few summer football camps in Knoxville. For years Peyton had raved to Eli about the teachings of Volunteer offensive coordinator David Cutcliffe, and when Peyton finally introduced his kid brother to Cutcliffe at these camps, the two immediately hit it off.

Cutcliffe was a master at teaching quarterbacking fundamentals—such as proper throwing mechanics and footwork—and he was as Southern as a tall glass of sweet tea. Born and raised in Birmingham, Cutcliffe was reserved and thoughtful, preferred substance over style, and could break down a quarterback's strengths and weaknesses after just a few minutes of watching tape. He was, in other words, just like Archie.

So now Eli called Cutcliffe at Tennessee. Peyton had flourished under Cutcliffe's guidance and play calling, and the older brother told Eli about Cutcliffe's coaching ability—Cutcliffe always said to Peyton, "On first and 10, there's a completion out there somewhere; let's find it"—and how Cutcliffe had turned Peyton's own potential into production. Peyton didn't lobby Eli to follow him to Tennessee, but Eli began to imagine what it would be like to become the second Manning to play quarterback in Knoxville.

One evening, as Tennessee was recruiting Eli, the oldest Manning brother was in Knoxville when a group of Volunteer fans spotted him. One of them approached Cooper. The fan mistook Cooper for Eli, and boldly asked if he was coming to play for Tennessee. Without missing a beat, Cooper replied, "How much money you got for me if I do?"

But the more Eli pondered playing in Knoxville, the more intimidating it became. Sure, Cutcliffe had worked wonders with Peyton, but Eli didn't want his every move to be measured against what his older brother had accomplished; he'd already had enough of that at Newman.

Eli phoned Cutcliffe in December 1989. "I don't think I can go to Tennessee," he said. "I'd be under too much pressure."

Eli, who unlike his brother never let recruiting infiltrate or disrupt his personal life, then narrowed his list of possible schools to three: Texas, Virginia, and Ole Miss—with the Rebels being a distant third. Ole Miss had the same thing going against it that Tennessee had: Eli was reluctant to walk into a situation where he'd be compared to a former quarterback named Manning.

But then three weeks after Eli told Cutcliffe he wouldn't attend Tennessee, the phone rang in the Manning home on First Street. It was Cutcliffe, who asked to speak with Eli.

"I'm recruiting you again," he said, "this time for Ole Miss."

Cutcliffe, who'd just signed a contract to become the Rebels' head coach, then flew on a private jet to New Orleans to have dinner with Eli. The two talked for hours—about Peyton, growing up a son of Archie, what Cutcliffe was planning to build at Ole Miss—and the coach's words resonated with Eli. It was as if he'd found the coaching version of his dad.

Cutcliffe explained at length what he believed made Peyton so good. He called it his "fast-twitch thinking ability," and he gushed about what Peyton could do when he approached the line of scrimmage. He first would assess where the safeties were lined up and, based on that, where they were likely to move once the ball was snapped. He would examine the defensive front seven, and, if he was anticipating a blitzing linebacker, he would set the proper pass protection with a running back. He would determine, based on the entire defensive alignment, if he needed to take a five- or seven-step drop. Then, in less than two seconds after the ball was snapped, as he was dropping back to pass, he would read the defense and figure out where the weakness was in the defense and where the ball needed to be thrown. Cutcliffe emphasized that he taught Peyton how to think and act in those ways, and now he wanted to pass such knowledge and skills onto Eli.

The youngest Manning was intrigued. Eli's earliest memories of Ole Miss were wrapped around being in the Grove with his family, tailgating and being tackled by his older brothers in games of pickup football. Oxford had always suited his personality; the slow-as-molasses pace of life was perfect for the kid dubbed Easy. And now that Cutcliffe had replaced coach Tommy Tuberville, who hadn't vigorously pursued Eli and had left for Auburn after the 1998 regular-season finale against Mississippi, Eli began to picture himself at Ole Miss. The more he considered that—and the more the mental pictures came into focus—the more Eli liked what he saw.

Maybe the Manning family would return to where it all began.

CHAPTER 26

===

The Past Is Never Dead

Oxford. Winter 1998.

The private plane touched down in New Orleans early on a Sunday morning. The passenger cabin door swung open and the pilot welcomed the eighteen-year-old aboard with a warm smile. He was precious cargo.

The jet then lifted and soared into the wintry Southern sky. The flight was quick—only about one hour—before it ended outside Oxford. It was December 13, 1998, just weeks before Archie's youngest, a high school senior, had to make a momentous decision.

Everywhere Eli went on the campus of Ole Miss during his recruiting trip he was reminded of his father's legacy. The posted speed limit on campus was 18 mph in honor of Archie and his football jersey number. There was an Archie Manning Room near the football stadium, where Eli was told he could conduct his post-practice interviews while sitting close to his father's old cleats, old jerseys, old press clippings, old trophies, and other memorabilia from his college career, including the purse Olivia had taken to homecoming her senior year. And pictures of Archie still were plastered all over campus. Three decades removed from his playing days, Archie remained the king of Oxford. Now the question was: Did Eli want to play in the shadow of his dad's legend?

Eli spent the day meeting with coaches, talking with players, and touring the grounds, including the Grove, those ten acres shaded by oak trees where he had tailgated before games—often with linen tablecloths—with his family for years. The school felt like a second home to the youngest Manning.

David Cutcliffe, the new head coach at Ole Miss, had been on campus for only nine days when Eli arrived in Oxford. Cutcliffe had a hard time reading Eli—his ho-hum body language suggested he could take Ole Miss or leave it—and Cutcliffe later privately wondered aloud to friends how serious Eli was about football and if he had the commitment it took to flourish in the Southeastern Conference. When Peyton visited Tennessee for his recruiting trip, he amazed Cutcliffe by how much he knew about the Volunteer program, from its record on the road against various teams to the depth chart at every position. But Eli acted like he may not have known the name of a single player on the entire Rebel roster, much less whether the team had a winning or losing record the past year. When Eli finished his visit, Cutcliffe wasn't certain he would ever see the young quarterback again.

What Eli didn't share with Cutcliffe was that he had genuine doubts about his own ability. According to friends, he didn't think he would ever be as good as Peyton, and questioned if he would be good enough to contend for a starting QB position in the SEC. Eli masked his fears behind his emotionless face, but they traveled with him during every step of his recruitment. Eli never was as engrossed in the entire process as Peyton had been—it was more important to Eli to play basketball with friends or hang out at a buddy's house than take a call from a college coach—but that didn't mean he didn't have more deep-seated anxiety about playing college football than his brother.

Eli returned to New Orleans that evening. He opened the front door to the house on First Street and, in silence, walked directly to his upstairs bedroom. Olivia was desperate for information. She wanted her youngest to attend her alma mater—she even dreamed of Eli committing to Ole Miss—and now she wanted to get a sense of how Eli felt after his visit to Oxford. Finally she turned to Archie and said, "Why don't you ask him? You're his father!"

Archie rarely said no to his wife, but he wouldn't budge on this. He wasn't going to influence Eli one way or the other about his college choice. He told Olivia that they needed to leave their youngest boy alone.

So they did.

Almost a week later Eli returned home from basketball practice. Looking around, he asked Olivia, "Where's Dad?"

She informed him that Archie was on a duck-hunting trip with Bert Jones, an old buddy from Ruston, Louisiana, who from 1973 to '81 had been a quarterback for the Baltimore Colts.

"Why?" Olivia asked.

"I need to ask him about putting together a press conference for this announcement," Eli said.

"Okay, we can reach him at [the hunting] camp," she said.

The room fell silent. Eli was lost in his own world, oblivious that he still hadn't shared any news with his mother.

"Do you mind telling me where you're going?" Olivia asked.

"Oh," he said. "Ole Miss, of course."

Olivia hugged Eli tight, relief washing over her. Eli explained that the school just felt right, and his choice had had nothing at all to do with their family history in Oxford or in Mississippi.

Olivia didn't care what the reasoning was behind his decision; she was overjoyed that she would be able to watch her son play on the same field where her husband had brought happiness to her and so many others. It was almost as if Olivia and Archie were being given a second chance to return to their school and experience college again through the life and times of their youngest boy.

Several hours later, a dozen television and print reporters began setting up in a room at Newman High. With the press conference slated to start in a few minutes, Archie hustled through the school's front doors. He had lead-footed it home from his hunting trip. Like his wife, he couldn't have been happier with Eli's decision.

"Am I supposed to make a statement or something?" Eli asked his dad over the phone.

"Just give 'em a couple of sentences on why you picked Ole Miss and then let 'em ask questions," Archie said.

Eli, who looked so young that he could have been chewing on a blade of grass, took a seat in front of the cameras. Several of his Newman teammates stood nearby, riveted to the scene. Then, without notes, Eli spoke continuously for nearly five minutes—it may have been the longest soliloquy of his life—about why he decided to attend Ole Miss.

"This really didn't have anything to do with my father playing at Ole Miss," Eli said. "That was over thirty years ago."

Everyone in the room laughed, but no one harder than Archie. He was so proud of his son—Eli had come so far from those days of being a painfully shy six-year-old—that his eyes moistened with emotion. It was one of the finest moments of Archie's life.

Shortly after Eli moved in to his dorm room in Oxford, he began reading about his father's college playing days. He pored over old stories that detailed Archie's thrilling playing style, how he scampered all over the field like a tailback and then how, just before being tackled for a loss, he'd flick the ball 40 yards down the field for an improbable completion. He learned about the night in 1969 when Archie threw and ran for 540 yards against mighty Alabama in the first prime-time broadcast of an SEC game. And he discovered that Archie was a Heisman Trophy favorite heading into his senior year, a quest that was derailed by injury.

Eli phoned home late one evening to share his new knowledge with his old man. Peyton and Cooper had virtually memorized everything about Archie's career by the time they were twelve, but Eli never quizzed his dad about anything from his past. Now Eli wanted to let his father know exactly what he thought about all that he had accomplished at Ole Miss.

"Dad," Eli said. "You know, your numbers weren't very good."

Archie, on the other end of the line, let out a belly laugh. Finally his college-aged son was turning into something of a historical scholar. But the remark also was comforting to Archie because it showed that Eli was embracing his dad's past, that he could use his dry sense of humor to deal with the inevitable comparisons, and that he was fully ready to follow the path that Archie had blazed three decades earlier.

By enrolling at Ole Miss, Eli chose to put himself in the most demanding and stressful environment possible. The boy who once struggled to read—and was deeply humiliated when he stumbled over written words in front of the class—was now in a place where the expectations on him were so high that a degree of failure seemed inevitable. The shy Eli of a few years ago would have run from this pressure.

Yet Eli still was plagued with doubts. Ole Miss officials had retired Archie's number 18 jersey, but the coaching staff offered to dust it off and allow Eli to wear his dad's Rebel number. Eli turned it down because of his greatest fear: disappointing his family. "What if I went out there my first game and threw six interceptions and never played again," Eli said. "It was almost like I was setting myself up to be bad."

Eli chose to wear number 10. In typical Eli fashion, he picked that number for no specific reason.

Gangly and needing to gain 20 pounds of muscle, Eli was redshirted his freshman year. Like many first-year college students living away from home for the first time, Eli sampled many of the forbidden fruits of college life. He sometimes partied late into the night and was overserved a time or two. In February of his freshman year he was arrested for public drunkenness at a fraternity party and briefly jailed.

But there was more going on than just Eli spreading his wings at college: he was now more frightened of failing than ever before. The prospect of not being as productive as Peyton, who made playing the game look so simple and easy, terrified Eli. And now that he was face-to-face with his father's legacy every day at Ole Miss, he felt increased pressure to live up to his last name— emotions he rarely experienced when living in New Orleans. Eli became so consumed with not failing that he didn't like going to class or even being seen on campus, for fear that someone would point at him and say, *There's Archie's kid* or *There's Peyton's little brother.*

But Eli kept his anxiety in check, never sharing it with Archie, Olivia, or any of his friends. He knew he was going through a "bad stage"—his words—and he was embarrassed that his picture was in the local paper after his arrest. He talked to Archie, but didn't tell his dad that he wondered if he had what it took to be a successful college quarterback.

Cutcliffe finally intervened. That spring he called Eli into his office. "I need to know, and I need to know the truth: Do you want to be a starter at Ole Miss?" the coach asked. "Do you want to be all-conference? Do you want to be an all-American? Or do you want to be the best who's ever played here? If you do, you're going to have to change your ways. Do not answer me right now. Go home and think about it. I want a conscious answer."

Eli retreated to his dorm room. Not one prone to introspection, he forced himself to search his soul, asking himself, *What do I want out of my life?* He knew he enjoyed practice, but he also admitted that his effort had been only half-hearted, like he was a player who was on the field only because his scholarship required that, not because he wanted to get better.

He also thought about what his life would be like without football, if he one day held a nine-to-five job like Cooper, who now worked in finance in New Orleans. And he spent hours pondering Peyton, how his life had turned out, the work he had put in, the joy the game continued to give him. Peyton was as much a father figure to Eli as Archie; Peyton called his little brother at least once a week during his freshman year to check in on him. In Peyton, Eli saw what he wanted the most—a quarterback who continually chased one goal: perfection.

Three days later Eli returned to Cutcliffe's office. Looking his coach in the eyes, Eli asked him for a second chance and told him that he would never lose focus again. "I want to be able to say that I went for it," Eli told Cutcliffe. "I want to be the best that ever played here."

The following autumn, when Eli's teammates saw him driving his SUV across campus, they wouldn't know what to make of him. Behind the wheel of his expensive car, Eli typically had a blank expression on his soft and gentle face. Peyton had recently signed a contract extension with the Colts for $100 million, but to veteran players like running back Deuce McAllister, it appeared that Eli was no Peyton. The older brother already was a legendary leader. There was even a framed picture of Peyton in Cutcliffe's office with a handwritten note that read: *To Coach Cut, all my best—Peyton Manning #18 (Eli's brother)*. But Eli? To the upperclassmen on the team, he looked like he'd have trouble deciding whether to buy premium or regular gasoline for his fancy car that they assumed was a gift from his daddy.

Because of Cutcliffe's connection to the family—the coach was now in his fifth year of tutoring a Manning boy—Cutcliffe had grown close to Archie. The two spoke frequently and candidly. Before Eli had played a down at Ole Miss, Archie had a strange request of Cutcliffe: he wanted Eli to sit on the bench.

Archie was concerned how the older players would react if Eli was handed the starting job, as if it was his birthright. The starting quarterback at Ole Miss at the time was senior Romaro Miller, who had led the Rebels to two straight bowl games. He had an NFL arm—he would play three seasons with the Minnesota Vikings, backing up quarterback Daunte Culpepper—and he also was black.

The first black football player at Ole Miss was Ben Williams, who played in 1972, the year after Archie graduated. The image of a privileged white quarterback with no college experience supplanting a successful black quarterback at a school that was last in the SEC to integrate its football team was something Archie wanted to avoid. Cutcliffe agreed that it would be in everyone's best interest for Eli to sit and watch his redshirt freshman year.

In the first eleven games of the 2000 season, Eli played sparingly, attempting only 33 passes. But then on December 28—on a cold and windy night in Nashville—the Rebels faced West Virginia in the Music City Bowl. Ole Miss trailed 49–16 in the fourth quarter when Cutcliffe motioned for Eli to put on his helmet and go into the game.

With Archie, Olivia, and Cooper watching from the stands—and Peyton transfixed by his television in Indianapolis—Eli jogged onto the grass field. Eli, the onetime tagalong brother who grew up playing with bigger boys, looked perfectly calm as he completed one pass after the next: lasers over the middle, deep outs to the sidelines, floaters down the seam, rainbows over the top, and darts into the flats. He escaped oncoming rushers like his dad and read the defense like his brother.

Eli's first drive against West Virginia ended with an Ole Miss touchdown. As Eli walked to the sideline, Cutcliffe waved him over. The coach asked his young quarterback what he saw on a particular play during the drive. Gesticulating his arms to illustrate his points, Eli articulated a detailed account that lasted for 30 seconds; the play itself took only 2.5 seconds. As Eli walked away, Cutcliffe grinned as if he'd just discovered the Holy Grail for a second time. The coach turned to an assistant and said, "We got us one. No one on earth could do that other than Peyton."

Eli engineered two more scoring drives. He finished 12 of 20 for 167 yards and 3 touchdowns. The Rebels lost 49–38, but in the span of 15 minutes Eli had infused the Ole Miss fan base with the same thing his father had many years ago: hope.

Peyton, watching from afar, was so happy that he was near tears. He later equated what he had seen to a father witnessing a son succeed at something for the first time, like taking a first step.

On December 30, 2000, two days after Eli's breakthrough performance in the Music City Bowl, Archie's mother, Sis, passed away at age ninety-four. The funeral in Drew was a celebration of Sis's life. She was hailed for her strength, her ability to hold her family together after Buddy pointed that gun at himself, and for never leaving Drew. Even when the farming industry withered and people fled the town, Sis remained in her old house. In the year that she died she penned a letter to a friend who lived a few blocks away. "Drew has been good to me and I say thank you each day for my life and being fortunate to spend the happiest part of my life here," she wrote.

In the midst of the funeral celebration, Archie looked over at Eli. What he saw stunned him: tears streaming from his eyes, dripping like candle wax. Archie hadn't seen his youngest cry since he was spanked as a child, but now Eli couldn't hold back the emotion. At this moment Archie realized just how much family meant to his youngest boy.

Eli moved in to Cooper's old apartment on the square in Oxford—the town's cultural and social hub that was lined with shops and boutiques—with the help of Olivia, who made the arrangements. Eli liked to hang out on the balcony veranda, with its view of the landmark Lafayette County Courthouse and of the statue of William Faulkner seated on a bench in front of City Hall. Farther beyond was St. Peter's Cemetery, where Faulkner is buried. Out on the veranda, Eli could imagine Cooper once looking out at the same vistas as he was, which comforted the youngest Manning.

The apartment was located close to the office where Faulkner, alone with his typewriter, wrote several of his books and short stories. Some of the Ole Miss faithful now quoted Faulkner in relation to Eli and Archie. "The past is never dead," Faulkner wrote. "It's not even past."

The past came alive for Archie and Olivia. They bought a condo on University Avenue between the square and the campus. Archie sometimes dropped by Eli's apartment to check on his son. If the place was messy—and it often was—Archie would tidy up by putting magazines in stacks, organizing the papers on Eli's desk, and picking up clothes that had been scattered about. Sometimes Eli quietly followed behind Archie, dropping the magazines back on the floor and messing up his desk. Archie would then pick up the same things two or three times before realizing that Eli was pranking him. He'd then turn to Eli, who looked at his dad with a blank face, feigning innocence.

On Friday nights before games in Oxford, Archie and Olivia often went to City Grocery restaurant on Courthouse Square. The patrons would let Archie eat his meal in peace—he'd have the shrimp and grits, the house specialty—but he would invariably end up working the room, shaking hands with old friends, signing autographs, and posing for pictures. For Archie, the past was not dead.

On the mornings of games Archie and Olivia could walk to the Grove from their condo. The Grove, to all the Mannings, was paradise found, one of the most magical places on earth. A forest of giant, arching oak trees in the middle of campus, the Grove was one of the premier tailgating spots in the nation. There, under a sea of red, white, and blue tents, finger sandwiches were served on sterling-silver platters, the drink of choice was bourbon, and the snack du jour was boiled peanuts. Everyone's manners were impeccable.

The Mannings had a tent in the Grove for years. Olivia would go all-out. She typically served a shrimp dish, sandwiches, chili, fried chicken, vegetable spreads, and, of course, boiled peanuts and all sorts of drinks. Eli's first memory of the Grove dated to his middle school days. Wearing his dad's old number 18 Ole Miss jersey that fell to his knees, he would go play pickup football with other kids his age. Hours later Archie and Olivia would search for Eli and typically would find him slathered in mud and begging to throw one more pass.

Now that Eli was an Ole Miss player, the Mannings' tent was more popular than ever. On home game days Archie and Olivia welcomed hundreds to their tailgate. Olivia made sure to cook a new meat every week to go with pimento cheese, marinated shrimp, a special punch, and a basket filled with buttons that featured the smiling face of her baby boy. About two hours before kickoff the entire group would make its way over to the Walk of Champions to catch a glimpse of Eli.

Before entering the stadium, the team always strolled along the brick path that cut through the east side of Grove. Lining the path, the fans were so close they could touch the players, who were dressed in coats and ties. When Eli was a first-year freshman and not playing, he got pulled into the crowd before a night game against LSU. Once off the path, the cherubic-faced Eli looked like every other student in the crowd. He struggled for a few minutes to squeeze back into line.

Now, before his first game of his sophomore year against Murray State—it would be the first start of his career—Eli walked confidently through the Grove. He strode past Archie, the aging

Huck Finn, who gazed lovingly at his youngest boy. Eli carried his playbook in his right hand to prevent people from shaking his throwing hand, and he had a thin, easy, and confident smile spreading across his face. Exuding a sense of tranquility in the limelight had always been a Manning family trademark, and now Eli looked ready.

After he disappeared into the stadium, his entire family soon followed him. Peyton's season with the Colts didn't begin for eight days, so he sat with Archie, Olivia, and Cooper in the stands. The family was more nervous than Eli, who started his first game since high school. Eli was nearly flawless, completing 20 of 23 passes for 271 yards and 5 touchdowns. At one point in the 49–14 victory he connected on 18 straight passes, a school record. Up in the stands, Archie was astonished by Eli's poise. Archie had completed 8 of 14 passes for 116 yards and 2 touchdowns in his college debut in 1968 against Memphis, which Ole Miss won 21–7, but he didn't look as comfortable and as seasoned as his youngest boy on this day.

Before the game Eli had met with Cutcliffe to discuss the great expectations fans had of Eli. The coach told his quarterback to concentrate only on what he could control. The simple advice had a calming effect on Eli. "I didn't expect to throw five touchdowns," Eli said after the game. "But I do know regardless of what happened tonight I was prepared for this position."

He'd spent virtually his entire life preparing for the moment.

The fans in Oxford who had seen Archie on the field now thought his ghost had returned, that they were seeing him again.

University chancellor Bob Khayat couldn't take his eyes off Eli on the sideline during Eli's first start against Murray State. Khayat, who played for the Rebels in the late 1950s and was a kicker for the Redskins from 1960 to '63, swore he had traveled back in time when he gazed at Eli. He had his father's square jaw. He stood just like his old man, with his legs slightly bowed, and he put his hands on his hips the way Archie always did. The resemblance was uncanny.

Cutcliffe saw a lot of Peyton in Eli. Throughout Eli's first year as a starter, Cutcliffe broke down game film with his quarterback, asking Eli to describe what he saw on certain plays and what worked, what didn't, and why. The average play occurred in 3.2 seconds, but it would typically take Eli 25 to 45 seconds to describe the thoughts that ran through his head in those 3.2 seconds. Cutcliffe never dreamed he would coach another quarterback as intellectually gifted as Peyton, but now he believed Eli had a chance to be just as successful as his older brother. Cutcliffe even described Eli's brain as possessing the same "fast-twitch mental fibers" as Peyton's.

"Eli has great football thinking ability," Cutcliffe said. "He has instant recall and is able to use it. In that three to five seconds of a play, he can have 45 seconds worth of thoughts go through his head." The only other quarterback that Cutcliffe personally knew who had this gift was Peyton.

In other ways, though, Eli was not at all like Peyton. When Peyton was at Tennessee, he and his offensive coordinator would walk together into the opposing team's stadium on Friday night. If the Vols were about to play Alabama, Peyton would talk a blue streak about past Tide players—from Joe Namath to Kenny Stabler to Jay Barker—and about the great moments that had occurred inside Tuscaloosa's Bryant-Denny Stadium. A lover of SEC history, Peyton would go on about how special the different castles were in the SEC kingdom and how, as a boy, he had lain awake at night dreaming of playing in these venues.

But when Cutcliffe strolled into these stadiums on Friday nights with Eli, his quarterback only wanted to know where the 25-second clocks were located. Cutcliffe would try to engage Eli by telling him about the legends who once roamed these fields, but Eli would look at his coach like he'd never heard about any of them, which he hadn't. The only reason Eli had learned the names of all the schools in the SEC was because, when he was young, Peyton used to hold him down and pummel him on the chest until he could name them all, but Peyton never forced him to recite any of the history.

But in terms of on-the-field comportment, Peyton now admitted that Eli was his clone. During an Ole Miss spring game Peyton stood on the sideline close to Cutcliffe. The older brother watched his sibling closely, studying his mannerisms and his countenance. The more he looked, the more Peyton realized that he shared not just physical traits with his brother, but also an important emotional trait: success was Eli's default mode. It was his expectation, his presumption. Archie was that way, Peyton was that way, and now it was clear to Peyton that Eli also was that way.

At one point during the spring game Peyton shared his observations with Cutcliffe. "It's like an out-of-body experience," Peyton said. "It's like I'm watching myself play."

Eli had always been a heavy sleeper. And so on the October 2001 afternoon before Ole Miss hosted Alabama—a team that the Rebels hadn't beaten since 1998—backup quarterback David Morris expected to find his roommate soundly napping after a walk-through practice. But when Morris entered the room, his eyes grew wide at the sight before him: Eli, in his boxer shorts, bouncing up and down on the bed, pulling his knees to his face over and over. Eli simply couldn't contain how happy he was to have a chance to slay mighty Alabama in twenty-four hours.

The two quarterbacks eventually began testing each other with their weekly play-calling signals, which were delivered in a complex sign language. They always made a game out of this, trying to trick the other. One would signal the play and then the other would have to articulate it: *Gun, flop right, duo, X-jet, roll 98, X-flood.* In their four years together, Eli beat Morris in every test.

The next day—with Archie, Olivia, and Cooper sitting in Vaught-Hemingway Stadium—Eli led the Rebels on a 59-yard drive in the last 1:34 of the fourth quarter, delivering a 27–24 win. The victory raised the Mannings' family record against the Tide to 6-2. "We hit Manning a lot of times," Alabama coach Dennis Franchione said. "That might have rattled a few quarterbacks. He just stayed in there and made one more play than we did."

After the game, trailed by a crush of adoring fans, Eli ran off the field with the game ball in his hands. Later that night he met with his parents at his apartment—Eli didn't have much to say about his performance—and then put on a cowboy hat and headed to a country-western concert. As Eli walked out the door, Archie and Olivia didn't know what Eli considered the highlight of his day: the game or the concert.

In his first year as a starter Eli threw for 31 touchdowns and nearly 3,000 yards. He directed three fourth-quarter comebacks against SEC teams. Off the field, he was a film junkie just like his dad and brother.

"I don't know of anyone since I've been here who studies as much film, who critiques himself as hard as Eli does," said senior center Ben Claxton before Eli's junior season.

By the time Eli was a junior, NFL scouts began showing up at his games. On November 2, 2002, New York Giants general manager Ernie Accorsi flew to Oxford to watch Eli and Ole Miss play

Auburn. Accorsi had seen Eli play on television, but he wanted to see him in person. Accorsi was contemplating picking him in the 2003 NFL draft, if Eli decided to turn pro after his junior season.

It was a frigid fall Saturday in 2002. Accorsi had hoped to sit in the press box, but wound up standing outside on the photographer's deck. By Accorsi's count, Auburn had a dozen NFL prospects; Ole Miss had two. Accorsi figured that the Tigers would win in a blowout.

Auburn rolled to a quick 14–0 lead, forcing the Rebels to essentially abandon the run on offense. In the second quarter Eli threw a gorgeous 55-yard strike to a receiver, prompting Accorsi to quickly scribble in his notebook that Eli had a stronger arm than Peyton.

Against the superior Auburn team, Eli single-handedly kept Ole Miss in the game. He threw precise passes to receivers tightly covered by exceptional athletes. Even with defensive linemen directly in his face, Eli kept his eyes downfield and delivered accurate throws. Several times, a second after Eli released a pass, a defender flattened him to the ground, but Eli never flinched or developed a case of jittery feet. Accorsi had never seen a college quarterback complete so many difficult throws in his life. The general manager noted Eli's ability to manage risk as well.

In his report, Accorsi wrote, "Rallied his team from a 14–3 halftime deficit basically all by himself. Led them on two successive third-quarter drives to go ahead 17–16, the first touchdown on a streak down the left sideline where he just dropped the ball (about 40 yards) over the receiver's right shoulder for a touchdown . . . called the touchdown pass (a quick 12-yard slant) that put them ahead at the line of scrimmage himself."

Accorsi was in deep lust with this quarterback. He was tall and strong and looked as natural playing the position as anyone Accorsi had seen since the great Johnny Unitas. Later that night, after Ole Miss had lost the game 31–24, Accorsi wrote in his diary, "He's the complete package. . . . He has a feel for the pocket. Feels the rush. Throws the ball, takes the hit, gets right back up. . . . Has courage and poise. In my opinion, most of all, he has that quality that you can't define. Call it magic. . . . Peyton had much better talent around him at Tennessee. But I honestly give this guy a chance to be better than his brother."

Eli would eventually score a 39 out of 50 on the Wonderlic intelligence test given to NFL draft prospects. Of the 2.5 million people worldwide who took the test that year, Eli had a score ranked in the 99th percentile, further deepening Accorsi's infatuation with the youngest Manning.

It was one of those perfect fall weekends in the South. The air was cool, the sky was blue, and the Alabama Crimson Tide were in Oxford for a football game—the final time a Manning would square off against the team from Tuscaloosa.

On October 18, 2003, Eli led the Rebels to a 43–28 win over Alabama. The 43 points scored by Ole Miss against the Tide were the second most in school history, five fewer than the number Archie's team had laid on Alabama when, as a senior, the elder Manning propelled the Rebels to a 48–23 win.

After the game Eli rushed from the locker room and joined his family in the Grove at their normal tailgating spot. They wanted to enjoy this time of triumph together, so they cordoned off their tent and, alone together, Eli, Archie, Olivia, and Cooper all reveled in the moment. It marked the end of something—the last time the Manning family would feel the excitement of beating Alabama—as well as the start of something: before their eyes, Eli had grown up and was now on the fast track to join his brother in the NFL.

A few weeks later, before Ole Miss hosted LSU, Archie walked through the Grove and around campus. On one street he saw about a dozen kids playing in a pickup football game. Eight of them were wearing an Ole Miss number 10 jersey.

Archie smiled and waved at the boys. The college years were almost over for his kids. Eli had matured so much that he was now a younger version of Peyton. He had also become a hero Southern quarterback like his dad.

Archie kept watching the boys adorned in Eli's number. For several minutes, filled with pride, he soaked in the scene.

Then he moved on. He knew there was still more—so much more—for his sons to accomplish.

CHAPTER 27

———

A Combination of Archie
and Peyton

New Jersey Meadowlands. Winter 2016.

He sat in the front row of the media room at MetLife Stadium in New Jersey's Meadowlands, his eyes misty with emotion. Eli Manning looked up at the dais at his head coach, Tom Coughlin—the only head coach he'd ever played for in the NFL—and he couldn't conceal his sadness as Coughlin announced he wouldn't return to coach the New York Giants for the 2016 season.

Coughlin spotted Eli, his bottom lip aquiver. The coach quickly deviated from his notes and looked directly at the player he had spent more time with than any other in the past decade. Coughlin knew that Eli personally blamed himself for the Giants' 6-10 record in 2015. Eli, the youngest Manning, had always aspired to please the important male figures in his life with his play on football fields, but now he felt he had failed Coughlin. For Eli that was tantamount to disappointing Archie and Peyton.

"Eli, it's not you, it's not you—it's us," said Coughlin, staring at Eli. "We win, we lose together. When we lose, I lose. When we win, you guys win. That's the way it is. That's the game, I know what it is. I got what I got."

Eli, the highest-paid quarterback in the NFL, was a full-grown man now, thirty-five years old, but there was still an innocence in his boyish face, like he should be out in the yard blowing bubble-gum bubbles and chucking around the football with Peyton. Family was always first for Eli—his mom and dad imbued him with that—and now he was devastated that he couldn't rescue his professional father from losing his job.

"He has not failed," Eli said of Coughlin. "We, as players, failed him."

Days later Eli penned a note to Coughlin, which appeared in *The Players' Tribune*. The Manning boys always preferred the written word in times of trial.

"Thank you, Coach, for being that role model to a young quarterback and not only allowing me to grow as a football player and as a man, but being that example and displaying those characteristics I wanted to emulate," Eli wrote. "At first, I just saw you as the 'head coach.' But since then, you've been that and so much more to me and the rest of the guys on this football team. We'll miss you."

Eli arrived in New York in 2004, the same year as Coughlin. As Eli sat in the press conference at the Giants' training facility in the Meadowlands on that cold January morning in 2016, he had come so far from his college days at Ole Miss. He was now the quiet leader of a team in America's largest city. Eli wasn't as glamorous as Tom Brady of the Patriots, he wasn't the smooth advertising pitchman that Peyton had become—Peyton was now the face of Nationwide Insurance and Papa John's Pizza—and he wasn't a larger-than-life character like "Broadway" Joe Namath had been for the Jets back in the 1960s and '70s. But Eli had evolved into a modern-day Bart Starr, a low-key quarterback who excelled at one thing: playing his best in the biggest moments of his career. He had become a combination of Archie and Peyton.

Eli was one of only five quarterbacks in NFL history to capture two Super Bowl MVP trophies—in 2008 and 2012. He bested Brett Favre in overtime in the 2008 playoffs, and he beat Tom Brady and the Patriots three consecutive times despite trailing with under two minutes to play in each game. And Eli piloted the Giants' offense in 2015 when New York scored more points (35) on the eventual NFC Champion Carolina Panthers than did any other offense in the NFL that season.

But for years media members, fans, even other NFL players never seemed to know quite what to make of Eli and his placid demeanor. He was still an inveterate jokester like he had been at Ole Miss—one time a Giants coach messed with Eli's car keys, and the next day Eli made sure that coach's bike ended up in a net fifty feet above the gym floor; other times Eli was known to switch his teammates' cellphone keyboards to Spanish—but there were so many questions about Eli. Did he really care about the game? Did he study like Peyton? Was he a good guy like Archie? Did he ever feel . . . anything at all? The answers always seemed to be hidden behind his expressionless face.

But Eli's raw emotion during Coughlin's farewell press conference revealed the mind and heart of Archie's youngest boy. Far from being aloof and happy-go-lucky—the usual portrayal of Eli by the New York media for over a decade—Eli, the best big-game quarterback of his generation, cared deeply.

Indeed, Archie's youngest son had always been driven by one emotion:

Love.

———

The date was February 3, 2008. The game was Super Bowl XLII at University of Phoenix field in Glendale, Arizona, against the 18-0 New England Patriots.

With 1:15 left in the fourth quarter, the Giants trailed 14–10 and faced a third and 5 at their 44. New England needed one more victory to fossilize its status as the greatest team in NFL history. But now Eli, playing in his first Super Bowl, squinted his eyes toward the sideline as the play call was relayed into his helmet receiver: *62 Y Sail Union.*

The play featured a four-wide-receiver set—two on each side of the offensive line—a running back, and Eli in the shotgun formation. The primary target was Steve Smith, who lined up in the right slot and would run a corner route. The last option, Eli's fourth, was right wideout David Tyree, who would run a post pattern. In the dozen times the Giants used this play in the regular season, Tyree acted only as a decoy to entice defenders to follow him deep.

Eli approached the line of scrimmage, carrying with him nearly three decades of football knowledge. The Patriots were in dime coverage—meaning six defensive backs, three linebackers, and two defensive linemen. Four of the defensive backs were evenly spaced across the field, 15 yards behind the line of scrimmage.

Eli immediately recognized the coverage, but his facial expression remained Mount Rushmore stoic, as if he was completely unaware that more than 148 million people around the globe were watching his every move in a game that was then the most highly viewed Super Bowl in NFL history. Archie taught his youngest boy years ago never to show the slightest bit of emotion at the line because it could tip off the defense on what he planned to do. Now only Eli knew: this was the moment he planned to break New England's bend-but-don't-break defense.

From his shotgun position, he called the signals: "Five-eighty, five-eighty, set, hut!"

Archie stared down at his youngest boy from a private luxury suite. He liked that Eli looked like he always did—as animated as a mannequin—and that his body language wasn't negative. Cooper stood nearby, a slight grin on his face and confidence gleaming in his eyes. He had seen this show before in his backyard, in sandlots across New Orleans, in high schools across Louisiana, and in college stadiums throughout the South.

Farther down, in another suite, Peyton, the Super Bowl MVP the previous year with the Colts, tried to calm himself by scanning the field, checking the defensive coverage and guessing where Eli should throw the ball. Peyton was a tangle of nerves and pride, and he had to hunch over and put his hands on his knees to quell his anxiety.

Eli dropped five steps back into the forming pocket. The Pats' Richard Seymour was the first to terrorize Eli, grabbing his jersey. Then nose tackle Jarvis Green wrapped his arms around Eli, sandwiching him between the two Pats in a 630-pound maw. A sack was imminent. Green had spent two weeks watching film of Manning, and he was shocked at how quickly Eli would take a sack. "All year long," Green said, "somebody just touches him, he falls to the ground."

But Eli didn't hit the turf this time. He broke free and lurched away from the tidal wave of defenders. He scampered to his right. Up in a luxury suite, Olivia thought she was seeing a ghost down on the field. To her, Eli suddenly looked like a young Archie scrambling at Ole Miss.

Eli was desperate now. He knew that an incompletion would set up a do-or-die fourth-and-5 play. The defense would have the upper hand in that scenario because the Giants would be limited by the plays they could call to gain five yards with the game on the line. In a series of split seconds, Eli looked at each of his receivers in a one, two, three sequence. He spotted Tyree 42 yards down the middle of the field. Eli understood that if he unleashed a heave it would be a 50-50 ball at best, but given his options—more on-rushing Patriots defenders were closing in on him fast—Eli reared back and threw the ball. Not his usual arching rainbow, but a near-flat fastball.

It was right out of the book, the precise throwing motion that Archie had learned at Ole Miss in the late 1960s from Johnny Vaught's instructional manual on the art of throwing a football, which read, in part: "Stand tall and balanced; ball high; step with the left foot and point with the left arm; dart the ball—put RPMs with fingers; follow through with right foot." Vaught's method of throwing, which Archie taught his boys, was now on display on the University of Phoenix field, as Eli unleashed a long-distance dart in the direction of Tyree.

As the fourth option on this play, Tyree had struggled in recent practices. During the Friday before the Super Bowl, Tyree dropped nearly every pass thrown to him. Afterward, Eli, who estimated that Tyree muffed eight easy catches, approached the wide re-ceiver. "Hey, just wipe this day away," Eli said. It was a little thing, but the interaction displayed Eli's style of leadership—personal, concise, and instructional.

In their luxury suites, as the dart spiraled through the Arizona night, Archie, Peyton, and Cooper all put their hands on their heads. Every practice, every drill, every game of Eli's athletic life had been building to this moment, and now, as the ball neared Tyree and four New England defenders, the anticipation was un-like anything the Manning family had ever experienced. The baby of the family, the one so like Olivia, the one who used to go an-tiquing with his mom, now had his own legacy on the line. At age twenty-seven, he had reached his moment of reckoning. Now was his chance to fully emerge from the shadow of his famous football father and brother.

Tyree leaped high into the air, snagging the ball with two hands. Patriots safety Rodney Harrison punched at the ball, but instead of knocking it away he actually helped pin it against Tyree's helmet. As the two players fell to the ground, Tyree kept the ball pressed against his blue Giants helmet.

The crowd *oooaah*ed as the replay flashed on the stadium's video screens, re-creating the once-in-a-lifetime catch and confirming that the ball never touched the turf. Archie, Olivia, and Cooper jumped up and down like cheerleaders at a high school game, hugging each other and fist-pumping. Peyton did the same a few boxes down. But there was still work for Eli to do. The Giants still trailed.

Four plays later, with the ball on the 13-yard line with 39 seconds left, Eli noticed at the line that the Patriots had single coverage on Plaxico Burress, who was lined up out wide to his left and would be running a slant-and-go route to the left corner of the end zone. Eli immediately knew he had it. He received the snap in the shotgun, took two steps back, pump-faked to get cornerback Ellis Hobbs to bite on the in-route to the post, then floated an I've-done-this-1,000-times-before thing of beauty to Burress in the left corner for the game-winning touchdown.

Up in the luxury suite Archie, wearing a blue sweater, embraced Olivia tight. They had done it: the first parents to ever raise two kids who each quarterbacked their teams to Super Bowl victories. Peyton raised his arm in the air as if he had just thrown the touchdown pass.

As Eli dressed in the locker room, Peyton cut through a crush of reporters to hug his brother. Peyton was so choked up he could barely speak.

"That play to Tyree will go down as one of the all-time greats," Peyton said. "I love that you looked down the field. They brought seven."

"That was the look we were hoping for," Eli said. "That was the look."

"I love you, man," Peyton said. "I'm proud of you, man."

At the pinnacle of Eli's professional life, the two brothers talked ball—just like always.

The date was February 5, 2012.

There was Eli bounding toward the exit of the field at Lucas Oil Stadium in Indianapolis—known locally as "the House that Manning Built"—waving one hand in the air to the crowd and picking confetti from his hair with the other. With two police officers jogging next to him, Eli looked up into the stands at the New York Giants fans, who now yelled, "Hall of Fa-mer! Hall of Fa-mer!"

For the first time in his career, Eli was worthy of that chant. Minutes earlier, with time running out in the fourth quarter of Super Bowl XLVI, Eli approached the line of scrimmage at the New York 12-yard line facing a first and 10. The Giants trailed the New England Patriots 17–15. Looking out at the Patriots' cover 2 defense, Eli replayed his mental catalog of New England defensive schemes and tried to pinpoint when he'd seen this formation before—just like Archie taught him to do back when he was in high school.

One, two, three seconds passed—then the image appeared. Recalling what he had seen in film study, Eli knew that New England's safeties typically didn't play very wide in cover 2. This meant he might have a small window to complete a deep pass along the sideline.

Eli received the snap and dropped back. He first looked right, but defensive backs blanketed his two wide receivers—Hakeem Nicks and Victor Cruz—on that side of the field. Then Eli scanned to his left, where Mario Manningham was running a go route up the sideline. Manningham had beaten cornerback Sterling Moore off the line of scrimmage, and safety Patrick Chung had slid into the middle of the field, just as Eli's mental movie forecast.

In a suite above the field, Peyton—Eli's longtime teacher—saw the same thing his little brother did. He knew this moment was freighted with possibility.

Eli considered Indianapolis a home away from home. He'd been coming to Indy for nearly half of his life to visit his brother, who was now in his fourteenth season with the Colts. Eli was familiar with the rhythms of the city, and he made sure to show his teammates a good time in the days leading up to the Super Bowl.

Six days before the big game Eli escorted twenty of his teammates to St. Elmo's Steak House in downtown Indianapolis, buying steaks for all. Tom Brady had taken a few of his teammates to St. Elmo's the same night, but it was clear who felt most in his element, as Eli challenged his teammates to gulp down the restaurant's shrimp cocktail sauce—a notoriously incendiary sauce laced with horseradish. "I told them to load up on the sauce," Eli said. "We had some people start sweating, half-choking. No major injuries."

On Wednesday, Eli headed to Peyton's downtown condo and enjoyed a dinner of chicken, shrimp, and sliders from Harry & Izzy's. Peyton and Eli talked about old times, old games, and old friends as Archie and Olivia sat nearby and watched their two boys joke like they were back on First Street in New Orleans.

"I don't think people understand our relationship," Peyton said. "I always used to look after him. I used to drive him to school. He used to come to all my games. Our relationship is so much one of support and help. I've given him every piece of knowledge I've had about playing quarterback, and he gives it to me. Love is what that is."

At his own 5-yard line, Eli reared back and lofted a gorgeous strike to Mario Manningham, dropping it perfectly into his hands for a 38-yard gain—the longest of the Super Bowl. It was the kind of read and throw that Peyton had made hundreds of times, and now Eli looked just like his older brother as he charged up the field after the completion and immediately looked to the sideline for instructions on what the coaches wanted to do next.

Eight plays later, the ball on the New England 6-yard line, Eli handed off to running back Ahmad Bradshaw, who fell into the end zone with only 57 seconds to play. The Giants won the game 21–17, the eighth time in the season that Eli had led New York to a winning score in the fourth quarter.

After the game—after Eli had won his second Super Bowl MVP trophy and had been awarded the keys to a 2012 Corvette, the same make of car his dad drove forty-one years earlier when he was a rookie QB with the Saints—Eli ran off the field and into the concrete tunnel at Lucas Oil. He neared Archie, who was leaning against a wall holding ten-month-old Ava Manning, the first child of Eli and his wife, Abby. Wearing a red bow in her hair, Ava repeated, "Dada, Dada, Dada."

Next to Archie stood Cooper, who was holding the game ball that Eli had thrown to him during the postgame celebration. Cooper caught the ball with ease, joking that it was his first reception in two decades.

Olivia and Peyton joined the family reunion. Soon they all were hugging the youngest Manning boy, who had once declared he could be kissed only on Sunday nights. This was a Sunday night to remember; the hugs and kisses continued well into the small hours of the next day—and Eli never stopped any family member from planting a wet one on his cheek.

A month later Archie and Olivia were sitting in their den on a weekday evening. The television was on, but Archie's head was buried in a book and Olivia was flipping through the pages of a magazine.

Then a story about Peyton and Eli flashed on the television. Archie shut his book and Olivia put down her magazine. Without uttering a word to each other, they watched as the piece recounted Peyton's and Eli's combined success: four trips to the Super Bowl, three victories, and three MVP trophies. The parents, experiencing a full-body shiver of tingles, looked at each other in disbelief.

"Do we need to pinch ourselves?" Archie asked. "What's going on here?"

Then, for several minutes, they talked for one of the few times about how they had raised two sons who were champion quarterbacks in the NFL.

They recounted how it began with the front-yard games played when their three boys could barely grip a miniature football. There were years of skinned elbows, knots on their heads, and rips in their shirts. There were trips to the emergency room. There was carpooling to pee-wee league games. And there were the mounds of mud-stained clothes and uniforms and jockstraps loaded into the washing machine week after week.

Archie and Olivia looked at each other with shock and pride. They never imagined that Peyton and Eli would rise from their house on First Street to win multiple NFL championships. Their wildest dreams just hadn't stretched that far.

CHAPTER 28

―――
―――

The Thinking Man's QB

Santa Clara, California. Winter 2016.

He stood in front of the Denver Broncos team in a conference room at the Santa Clara Marriott. With the start of Super Bowl 50 only twenty-four hours away, Peyton Manning scanned the room filled with the faces of teammates. He was the oldest player on the roster—he would turn forty soon—and against the Carolina Panthers at Levi's Stadium on February 7, 2016, he would be going for the 200th win of his career as a starting quarterback, which would be the most in NFL history and break his tie with Brett Favre, the former Green Bay Packer, New York Jet, and Minnesota Viking.

Peyton's body was breaking down. He had admitted a week earlier that he would eventually need hip-replacement surgery. He was sidelined for the entire 2011 season with a neck injury, and in 2015 he had missed six of the final seven games of the regular season recovering from a rib injury and a torn plantar fascia in his left foot. His medical chart was now as detailed and lengthy as Archie's had been when he limped away from the game in 1984, and Peyton's conditions robbed him of his arm strength and foot speed. But Peyton still was the leader of the Broncos. So on the eve of Super Bowl 50, Denver coach Gary Kubiak asked his aging quarterback to address the team.

Peyton began by telling a few jokes to lighten the mood—a seasoned public speaker, Peyton now excelled at delivering pitch-perfect punch lines—and he thanked everyone from the coaches to the trainers to the equipment managers for making the season so special. As he recapped the year, Peyton's voice cracked with emotion. He told his teammates how much football meant to him—it was his first true love, the air he had breathed for over two decades—and he emphatically asked them to play for one another, not just themselves. Tears welled in the eyes of several Broncos players.

Peyton didn't say directly that Super Bowl 50 would be his final game, but everyone in the room knew the end was near for their quarterback. "Life is fair," Peyton told his teammates. "Keep working." Peyton felt so at peace with his own life that, on the night before the Super Bowl, he slept ten and a half hours—far more rest than he normally enjoyed before a game.

In the week leading up to Super Bowl 50, Peyton was unusually nostalgic. Even though Peyton told Archie that he didn't think about retirement or what he might do in the next chapter of his life, because it would take away from his preparation, he took time to relish the entire scene at the Super Bowl—from media day to quiet dinners with his family to the practices with his teammates. For the player who had always combined players' hours with coaches' hours, he now tried to cherish each moment, each interaction.

About sixty minutes before kickoff, Peyton walked around the field. Alone, he gazed up into the stands for several seconds, as if he was taking mental snapshots that could be stored away in his memory. Down on the field he spotted Eli, posing for photos with past Super Bowl MVPs Tom Brady and Joe Namath. Peyton's instinct was to talk to the trio—he wanted to chat about quarterbacking, his favorite subject—but instead he decided to allow Eli to enjoy the occasion without the interference of big brother. As Peyton watched Eli, he smiled and savored the sight as though he was looking at a magnificent still life.

Peyton then threw a few more warm-up passes. His arm had clearly lost strength compared to his prime-time days, but his mind still operated at the pinnacle of its powers. Heading into what would be the final hours of his football life, Peyton remained an intellectual six-shooter.

For nearly two decades in the NFL, Peyton set the standard for being mentally prepared to play every game. Applying the lessons he learned from Archie at their home on First Street, Peyton wasted no time in establishing the work ethic that would both define and propel his career. After he was selected the first overall draft pick by the Colts in 1998, he began spending more time in the quarterbacks' meeting room than did his coaches. During some late-night sessions, rather than stopping to order dinner, he'd raid the refrigerator for the coaches' leftovers.

He installed a film projector in his two-bedroom apartment that featured a Beta dock so he could watch every rep he took at every practice. Sitting alone in the darkness, he'd jot down copious notes in a spiral notebook, constantly looking to improve his mechanics and better understand the designs of every play in the playbook. When he climbed into bed he'd have another spiral notebook by his side—just in case something popped into his head in a dream. By the end of his career the notebooks with his scribbled words and diagrams would fill an 18-wheeler.

On Saturdays after practice he'd lock himself in the equipment room with the equipment manager and carefully rub his hands over dozens of footballs—the surgeon at work—gripping and squeezing each one to see which twelve felt best and could serve as game balls the next day. Peyton became extremely close to the Colts' equipment managers—Archie, who was especially tight with the managers in New Orleans, taught him the value of that—and over the years they would catch thousands of Peyton's passes in private workout sessions and watch film with him countless nights, sometimes examining a single play for over half an hour.

As a rookie, Peyton, who had bought gloves for each of his offensive linemen at Newman, asked that his locker be placed next to those allotted to his offensive linemen. He wanted to make sure he had his finger on their collective pulse.

"No one worked harder than Peyton," said Bruce Arians, the Colts' quarterback coach from 1998 to 2000. "After we drafted him we had a minicamp the next weekend. He shows up for that first practice and he knows the whole damn playbook. He starts rattling off everything to everyone. Players were like, 'Whoa!' He took over the team by the third practice. It was all his. And if you were going to sit down with him at a meeting, you better be ready, because the questions were going to come at you fast and furious."

After his rookie season, Peyton and Archie went on a hunting trip in the open Mississippi countryside not far from Drew. Before they started back for home in New Orleans, they stopped in Drew to visit Archie's mom, whom everyone still called Sis and who was still living in the little wooden house of Archie's boyhood days on the corner of Third and Green. Father and son looked at yellowed newspaper clippings that detailed Archie's long-ago athletic exploits. Peyton was spellbound.

After saying their goodbyes, they drove around town. Archie pointed out where he used to play sandlot football games, where he got his haircuts, where he went to church, and where "the best hamburger joint in Mississippi" was located.

Before heading south to New Orleans, Archie turned the car into the town cemetery. Archie guided Peyton to the graves of several Manning family members, including Uncle Peyton, his namesake, the man who had taken little Archie in his Studebaker to so many high school football games on Friday nights.

Finally they walked to Buddy's grave. For several minutes, father and son stared down at the headstone in silence, the only sound the wind rustling the oaks that shaded the grounds.

Archie had never discussed with any of his children the day he found his dad slumped over in his bed, a pool of blood spreading beneath him. Peyton had earlier asked Olivia for details, but now he wanted to hear them from his dad.

"What was it like, Dad?" Peyton asked. "What happened with your dad?"

Archie revisited the worst moment of his life, telling his son everything about that late afternoon when Archie was twenty years old. He spoke about finding Buddy, how he cleaned him up, how he wanted to protect his sister and mom from the horror of seeing him. Tears fell like raindrops as he spoke.

Archie revealed how Buddy didn't make it to all of his high school football games, because he had to work. Buddy traveled to the Ole Miss games if he could reach them by car, but he never stepped onto an airplane to see Archie play. Archie was never bitter about his dad's absences; he understood Buddy was deeply worried about the business and the family finances. But it still stung.

There were thousands of times throughout the years since that Archie thought, *I wish Buddy was here to see this.* There was so much Buddy missed—the family events, holidays, Archie's own games and graduation, Archie's success in the NFL, and the games of his grandkids. Every milestone moment prompted memories of Buddy to rush back at Archie. Archie intuitively knew his dad loved him, but Buddy never told him. That hurt, Archie told Peyton. That hurt.

As his father spoke, Peyton began to understand Archie like never before. No matter if Archie was in an important business meeting, at a crowded restaurant with friends, or even in the presence of a mayor, a governor, or an NFL head coach, when Archie ended a phone conversation with any of his boys, his last words were always the same: "I love you." Peyton figured his dad said those three words more than any other father in the world.

Now Peyton realized why Archie made it to virtually all his sons' games. For so many years Archie had felt empty without his own dad, so much so that Archie swore he would always be there for his boys, present in their lives and at their games. It didn't matter how difficult it was for Archie to make it to a school play or a Friday night football game or a college game hundreds of miles away, he would be there—usually with his video camera rolling, a loving smile on his face.

In February 2007, in the days leading up to what was at the time the biggest game that anyone named Manning had ever played in, Peyton stayed in his routine as he prepared for Super Bowl XLI against the Chicago Bears.

Six days before the game at Dolphin Stadium in Miami Gardens, Florida, he took twenty teammates to dinner at a Fort Lauderdale hot spot, but that was his only indulgence—and the only deviation from his norm—during the week. For the next five nights he lay low in the Marriott Harbor Beach Resort. Peyton even replicated his home in the hotel. In Indy, Peyton watched film at night alone in his basement. In South Florida, Peyton had the Colts cordon off a room on the hotel's third floor—two floors below the off-limits level—so he would feel like he was watching late-night cut-ups back in his mansion.

But the long hours of preparation didn't pay immediate dividends. The Bears' Devin Hester ran the opening kickoff 92 yards into the end zone. On Indy's first offensive play—a play the team had practiced repeatedly for two weeks, a play everyone on the offense knew would be their first of the game—tight end Dallas Clark was supposed to run a seam route underneath the safeties, but instead cut it inside. Bears linebacker Brian Urlacher deflected the pass at the line of scrimmage. Frustrated, Peyton later in the drive forced a deep throw to Marvin Harrison; the ball was intercepted by strong safety Chris Harris.

For as long as Peyton could remember, Archie had preached a mindset of taking "one play at a time." It was one of the oldest and most overused clichés in football, but Peyton lived by it. He quickly wiped the interception from memory and settled down, and with 6:58 left in the first quarter, on a play called 66 D-X-Pump, he stepped up in the pocket to avoid the rush and threw a beautiful, high-arching deep ball to Reggie Wayne for a 53-yard touchdown. In his private suite, Archie raised his hands in jubilation. He'd seen Peyton make that exact rainbow throw dozens of times at Newman.

For the remainder of the Super Bowl—a sloppy game, the first to be played in a rainstorm—Peyton was in full command and control. He finished 25 of 38 for 247 yards and 1 touchdown in Indy's 29–17 win. Peyton was named the MVP.

More than ninety minutes after the game had ended, Peyton finally emerged from the locker room in a dark suit—the last player to have showered. He'd been caught up in media interviews and now was in a hurry to reach the team bus, anxious to celebrate his first title of any sort in his football career. But as soon as he boarded the idling bus he looked around and asked, "Where's Archie?"

Through the bus window Peyton saw his dad and Cooper walking through the rainy South Florida night, approaching the bus. No celebration at this hour could start without his dad and his brother—his two best friends. Peyton, his suit drenched by the driving rain, stood at the doorway.

Peyton greeted his dad and brother. Their smiles were as wide as the Mississippi River. The bus then disappeared in the darkness, the Manning family champions at last.

After his third neck surgery, when he woke up from the anesthesia in Northwestern Memorial Hospital in Chicago in May 2011, Peyton tried to push himself up in his hospital bed with both of his arms. But his right arm gave out. He tried again—and again his right arm failed him. The surgery on a herniated disk in his neck, which had forced him to the sideline for the entire 2011 season after making every start in fourteen years with the Indianapolis Colts, was supposed to strengthen his arm. But now his throwing arm felt dead.

Two weeks later, a zipper scar visible on his neck, Peyton could barely grip a football and he was haunted by an overwhelming thought: *I may never play again.*

He had a heart-to-heart with Cooper, who had to give up football after being diagnosed with spinal stenosis. After Cooper's surgery nearly two decades earlier Archie took both Peyton and Eli to a doctor to determine whether they had the same condition. Their necks weren't picture-perfect, the doctor told Archie, but they were stable enough to keep playing football. Ever since, Peyton understood his neck put him at risk.

Peyton left the hospital carefully avoiding reporters and fans, not wanting anyone to see that his golden right arm looked atrophied. Unable to return to the Colts' headquarters due to the NFL lockout, Peyton needed somewhere to recuperate and rebuild his arm. Todd Helton, then a first baseman with the Colorado Rockies who had started at quarterback in front of Peyton at Tennessee at the beginning of the 1994 season, encouraged Peyton to come to Denver, where they could play catch at a place no one could see them: in the underground batting cage beneath the Rockies' stadium.

Once in the Mile High City, Peyton held a ball in his hands in the underbelly of the stadium. Helton stood ten yards away. Peyton, for the first time since the surgery, fired a pass with all his strength. It wobbled five feet and nosedived to the ground. Helton figured Peyton had pulled a joke on him.

"C'mon, quit kidding," Helton said.

"Man," said Peyton, "I wish I was."

In July, Peyton flew to New Orleans and went to his childhood home. He played catch with Eli in their old backyard—the place where Peyton had taught Eli to throw. Before the surgery, the brothers threw the ball with nearly identical velocity. But when Peyton reared back and tossed his first pass, it fluttered in the air like a paper airplane.

Peyton talked again with Cooper, asking him about his neck. Peyton had seen up close the complications of Cooper's surgery—

the temporary paralysis, the days in a wheelchair, the learning how to walk again—and now he wondered if the risks of playing again outweighed the reward. He flew to Europe several times for various therapies. He talked to one American doctor after the next, soliciting their advice.

(It was around this time, according to an *Al Jazeera* report in the fall of 2016, that human growth hormone had allegedly been sent to Ashley Manning at the Mannings' home in Florida. Peyton vociferously denied using any illegal performance-enhancing drugs during his recovery, calling the report "completely fabricated, complete trash, garbage.")

In November, after a fourth surgery to stabilize his neck, Peyton flew to Durham, North Carolina, to spend time with the man he considered his second father: Duke University football coach David Cutcliffe. But when Cutcliffe and Peyton started to throw the ball around, the coach had to tell his student to stop. He was afraid that Peyton, whose mechanics were woefully disjointed, was going to hurt himself.

Peyton had to relearn how to throw like the Peyton of old. First he and Cutcliffe spent days in the film room studying old Indianapolis tapes and the nuances of his throwing motion, analyzing every minute detail from his footwork to how he held the ball during his drops to the position of his left arm as he prepared to cock his right arm. Cutcliffe had to teach everything again.

For the better part of three months, Peyton holed up with Cutcliffe at Duke. One evening, when Peyton rode with Cutcliffe back to the coach's house, Peyton wondered aloud if his career was over and if he was just wasting his time. The teacher told his pupil to keep fighting and pushing the boulder up the hill. Peyton had been listening to Cutcliffe's syrupy southern drawl for years, and the advice from Coach Cut—Peyton's name for his mentor—was precisely what he needed to hear.

Slowly, Peyton's arm returned to life. During a Duke spring practice Peyton donned a Colts helmet and ran several plays. He invited old teammates to Durham for pass-catch sessions: Dallas Clark, Brandon Stokley, and Austin Collie flew to North Carolina to run routes for their recovering quarterback.

Peyton was so encouraged by his improving arm strength and throwing motion that on March 3, 2012, he decided to make things a little more interesting for his trio of Colts receivers: they re-created the 2010 AFC championship game against the Jets, down to the specific plays they had executed in Indy's 30–17 victory. Peyton threw for 377 yards and 3 touchdowns that day against New York, and in this mock game he was nearly as sharp. He was close to being Peyton again.

On that day when Peyton felt so good about his comeback, the Colts were about six weeks away from selecting Andrew Luck with their number one overall pick in the 2012 draft. Peyton told owner Jim Irsay he would help develop Luck and be his mentor. But on March 7, the Colts cut Peyton. Hearing the news, Peyton cried.

Three weeks later, Peyton signed a five-year, $96 million contract with the Broncos. Still, he didn't know if he would ever be as good as he once was—or if he'd ever return to the playoffs, much less another Super Bowl.

On the first play of Super Bowl 50, Peyton lined up under center. Scanning the defense while calling the signals, he saw the Carolina safeties and linebackers creeping toward the line of scrimmage. Peyton knew the blitz was coming—and he knew he had the perfect play to beat it. Even though his arm wasn't what it once was—he hadn't thrown a ball longer than 40 yards in the air all season—he still had enough pop in it to make 30-yard and shorter throws, especially over the middle of the field.

Peyton took the snap. As the Panthers defensive line pressured Manning, he took three steps back and hurled the ball over the middle to tight end Owen Daniels, who caught it in stride for an 18-yard gain. This was exactly the type of tone-setting play Peyton wanted to start the game with—and the exact opposite of how Denver and Peyton had begun Super Bowl XLVIII against the Seahawks two years earlier, when the opening snap sailed over Peyton's head and resulted in a Seahawks safety. The favored Broncos lost the game 43–8.

On the next three plays of Super Bowl 50 the Panthers blitzed Peyton each time. First Peyton threw a quick 6-yard out to Emmanuel Sanders. After an incompletion, Peyton then looped a beautiful 22-yard pass to Andre Caldwell on the right sideline. In the face of oncoming rushers, Peyton kept his eyes down the field—just like Archie had preached to him years ago—and, more important, he knew precisely where he was going to throw the ball before he even received the snap. It was quintessential Peyton, the Peyton of the past. His ability to dissect the defense threw the entire Panthers team off balance, as if no one on Carolina believed Peyton and the Denver offense could move the ball through the air.

Six plays later Brandon McManus kicked a 34-yard field goal to give Denver a 3–0 lead—a lead the Broncos never surrendered.

Peyton nearly retired a year earlier. After losing in the divisional round in the playoffs to the Colts 24–15 in January 2015—Andrew Luck threw for 265 yards; Peyton only 111—Peyton flew home to New Orleans to confer with Archie and Olivia about his future plans, a normal course of action for the Mannings' middle child. He had torn a muscle in his right quad earlier in the season, and the injury further limited his already decreasing mobility. Yet he had tossed 36 touchdown passes that season, and he felt he still had one more season of throws in his right arm.

But then, early in the 2015 season, Peyton aggravated the plantar fascia near his left heel. He no longer could generate the power in his legs to launch the ball with the needed velocity, a skill Cutcliffe had taught him at Duke. The low point came on November 15 against the Chiefs, when Peyton threw four interceptions in Denver's 29–13 loss. In the third quarter Bronco coach Gary Kubiak benched him.

Peyton was inactive six of the next seven weeks. He spent his days in the training room and on the practice field throwing to either trainers or practice-squad players. Peyton was suddenly cast into an unfamiliar role in his pro career: an injured backup hoping for one more chance to play. On most days his mood was dark. For the first time as an NFL player, Peyton ran the scout team.

Peyton suited up for the final game of the regular season against the Chargers, a must-win for the Broncos to maintain home-field advantage in the playoffs. It was the first time since his freshman year at Tennessee he was listed on the active roster as a backup. But now the time away from the team—Peyton watched the games either in street clothes from the sideline or on television—forced Peyton to embrace what he was: a game manager, not a gunslinger.

Down 13–7 midway through the third quarter against the Chargers with Brock Osweiler behind center, Kubiak summoned Peyton from the bench. "My gut told me to turn it over to Peyton and let him lead the football team," said Kubiak. Peyton guided Denver to 20 points and a 27–20 win. He was only 5 of 9 for 69 yards, but he consistently read the Chargers defense at the line of scrimmage and put the Broncos offense in the right pre-snap play call and position. Peyton led the team not with his arm but with his long-learned smarts.

As Archie and Olivia watched Peyton from home on First Street in New Orleans, the father was relieved that Peyton was part of the team again. Olivia, as usual, was most thrilled about one thing: that her boy didn't get hurt.

The final pass of Peyton's NFL career was a 2-yard toss for a 2-point conversion to wide receiver Bennie Fowler. The score put Denver up 24–10 late in the fourth quarter of Super Bowl 50.

As soon as Fowler caught the ball, Peyton pumped his right fist into the air. Up in a luxury suite on the seventh level of Levi's Stadium, Olivia and Archie hugged, the proudest parents in America. Cooper, now a partner in an energy investment firm in New Orleans, raised his right fist in the air just like his brother, smiling like he had just caught a pass from Peyton, like a man who was living out his dream through his brother. And Eli gazed in awe down at Peyton, as if, after all these years, he was still amazed by his big brother.

As the clock ticked down, Peyton stood alone at the end of the Broncos' sideline, staring stoically into the distance, his chin up, his eyes squinted, his face equal parts Archie and Olivia and 100 percent a Manning. It was his image for posterity—the thinking man's QB deep in thought, his mind always pondering what was to come.

After the final whistle blew, Cooper, Olivia, and Eli walked onto the field to find Peyton. Archie, recovering from knee-replacement surgery, waited for Peyton outside the Denver locker room.

"I'll take some time to reflect," Peyton said to the crush of reporters surrounding him. "I have a couple of priorities first. I want to go kiss my wife and my kids. I want to go hug my family. I'm going to drink a lot of Budweiser tonight, I promise you that."

Hours after the 200th and final victory of Peyton's NFL career, Peyton was reunited with his family outside Levi's Stadium. As darkness fell and the stars above twinkled in the nighttime sky, the middle Manning child hugged them all, long and hard and lovingly.

Peyton didn't say it at this moment, but here, in the warm embrace of his family, the end had finally arrived.

Acknowledgments

Archie Manning always answered the phone with a warm hello when I called his office in Oxford, Mississippi. Before I wrote a word of what you now hold in your hands, I discussed the project with Archie. The Mannings declined to actively participate, but Archie did help me fact-check portions of the book, treating me not like an intrusive writer examining his life, but as a past acquaintance he was happy to catch up with.

Yet Archie and Peyton did speak to me at length through the words they penned with author John Underwood in their book, *Manning,* published in 2000 by HarperEntertainment. This autobiography was an essential resource in piecing together the sprawling family history and re-creating the day that Archie lost his father, Buddy.

I'm in debt to dozens of folks who know the Mannings well and spoke to me on the condition of anonymity. These sources provided background details on the family and colorful anecdotes from when the Mannings boys were young. Scores of others talked to me on the record. Sarah Braslow, a former student of mine at Alabama, conducted several of these interviews, and her disarming personality and winning smile always put her subjects at ease.

Over the years reporters from across the country have written thorough examinations of the Manning family—the Mannings may very well be the most covered family in the history of sports journalism—but I want to acknowledge 10 writers whose works I especially leaned on in crafting this book: John Ed Bradley, William F. Reed, Tim Layden, Paul Zimmerman, S.L. Price, Michael Silver, Lee Jenkins, Paul Attner, Sam Borden, and Chuck Culpepper.

My literary agent, Scott Waxman, has been with me for fifteen years. Scott helped shape the idea for this project in its earliest stages and fine-tuned the book proposal—just like always. Scott continues to be the best in the business.

Mark Tavani was my initial editor at Ballantine, and his big-picture ideas for the narrative were spot on. Ben Greenberg at Ballantine deftly shepherded the manuscript through the editing process and Caitlin McKenna always made sure deadlines were met. I'm fortunate to be on such a talented team.

My stepfather, Gordon Bratz, edited several drafts of the manuscript and his careful reads improved the narrative one paragraph at a time. A retired Army colonel, Gordy's literary fastball is as lively as ever. Cary Estes—a Birmingham, Alabama–based writer and close friend—also poured over the manuscript and stamped his flourishes onto the pages.

Langston Rogers, an associate athlete director at Ole Miss, graciously opened up the school's archives and allowed me to spend days digging through long-ago accounts of Archie's and Olivia's time in Oxford. These yellowed clippings were instrumental in re-creating Archie's early life.

Finally, none of this would have been possible without my

wife, April. During the reporting and writing of this book we had our first child, Lincoln, who has his mom's soft blue eyes. When I had to travel or spend late nights in my office tapping on the keyboard, April always was there to care for Lincoln and make sure the wheels of our life never spun off the rails.

I am beyond lucky to have April by my side.

Notes

PROLOGUE: PEYTON'S FINAL PASS

xiv **both parents grew emotional**: Greg Bishop, "Wild Ride: Tale of Super Bowl 50 Champs Broncos," *Sports Illustrated*, February 15, 2016.

xv **Peyton used his influence to change the game**: Kevin Van Valkenburg, "After the Perfect Ending, What's Peyton Manning's Next Rodeo?," *ESPN.com*, February 8, 2016.

xvi **he verbally recounted**: Lee Jenkins, "Peyton Manning: Sportsman of the Year," *Sports Illustrated*, November 23, 2013.

CHAPTER 1: DESPERATE FOR A HERO

4 **The images of his trip to the Farm**: Charles Pierce, "Legends of the Fall," *GQ*, September 1996.

CHAPTER 2: THE PEE-WEE QB

7   **"A convict is out!"**: Archie and Peyton Manning with John Underwood, *Manning: A Father, His Sons, and a Football Legacy* (New York: HarperEntertainment, 2000), 17.

8   **Two policemen patrolled during daylight**: Chuck Culpepper, "Quarterback Central," *Newsday,* July 27, 2004.

8   **an adult could grab**: Ronnie Virgets, "The Sporting Life," *New Orleans Magazine,* December 2000.

8   **kids would sled around on top of old car hoods**: Culpepper, "Quarterback Central."

9   **"When the fights broke out, Buddy was there"**: Archie Manning, *Manning,* 19.

9   **if he received a shirt with only one pocket**: Ivan Maisel, "Archie Manning Faces Family History," *ESPN.com,* September 24, 2013.

11   **Always be humble, Buddy implored**: Virgets, "The Sporting Life."

11   **He had dance lessons**: Paul Zimmerman, "The Patience of a Saint," *Sports Illustrated,* June 8, 1981.

13   **He dreamed of how his scouting report**: Archie Manning, *Manning,* 17–18.

15   **he'd repeatedly look across the street**: Ibid., 21.

15   **After little Archie stole some plums**: Anthony L. Gargano, "Archie Manning: What I've Learned," *Esquire,* December 20, 2013.

15   **"Okay, you're the fullback"**: Archie Manning, *Manning,* 22.

16   **he often forgot to eat**: William F. Reed, "Red-Letter Year for Quarterbacks," *Sports Illustrated,* September 14, 1970.

CHAPTER 3: "MY BOY WILL BE THERE"

18   **"I am told I was born"**: Paul Zimmerman, "The Patience of a Saint," *Sports Illustrated,* June 8, 1981.

19   **Archie viewed his weekly trips**: Archie and Peyton Manning with John Underwood, *Manning: A Father, His Sons, and a Football Legacy* (New York: HarperEntertainment, 2000), 31.

21 **Archie spent most of the fall standing next to Morgan**: Article of unknown origin contained in the Ole Miss archives.

24 **"Son, is it worth it?"**: Article of unknown origin contained in the Ole Miss archives.

24 **Throughout Sunflower County he was now known**: Article of unknown origin contained in the Ole Miss archives.

25 **"This might surprise you"**: Archie Manning, *Manning*, 34.

26 **Before the game the seniors**: David Bloom, "The Loser Becomes a Winner," *Commercial Appeal*, September 9, 1968.

27 **The mayor of Drew even got involved**: Archie Manning, *Manning*, 36.

27 **"They've passed Ruleville"**: Ibid.

28 **Archie drained his first shot**: William F. Reed, "Red Letter Year for Quarterbacks," *Sports Illustrated*, September 14, 1970.

29 **That sorry performance**: Ibid.

31 **Buddy heard Archie crying**: Interview with Archie Manning contained in the Ole Miss archives.

31 **Archie memorized the names**: Ronnie Virgets, "The Sporting Life," *New Orleans Magazine*, December 2000.

31 **That validation from Buddy**: Interview with Archie Manning contained in the Ole Miss archives.

32 **Archie couldn't remember the last time**: Reed, "Red-Letter Year for Quarterbacks."

32 **The note arrived**: Letter from John Vaught contained in the Ole Miss archives.

33 **Mississippi had an unmistakable link to slavery**: Frank Deford, *Land's End*, September 2002.

33 **"When you started sports"**: Zimmerman, "The Patience of a Saint."

34 **his heart silently ached**: Ibid.

CHAPTER 4: THE REDHEADED SHOW-OFF

36 **After checking in to the Benwalt Hotel**: Chuck Culpepper, "Quarterback Central," *Newsday*, July 27, 2004.

37 **fans standing on the sidelines of the court**: Ibid.

38   **A young woman named Olivia Williams**: Ibid.

38   **the biggest show-off she'd ever seen**: Archie and Peyton Manning
     with John Underwood, *Manning: A Father, His Sons, and a Foot-
     ball Legacy* (New York: HarperEntertainment, 2000), 54.

40   **He threw four touchdown passes**: Robert Fulton, "North Plasters
     South," *Meridian Star*, July 30, 1967.

CHAPTER 5: THE CEREBRAL SIGNAL CALLER

42   **"I don't care how successful you are"**: Paul Zimmerman, "The
     Patience of a Saint," *Sports Illustrated*, June 8, 1981.

43   **Boland, overcome with pride, felt moved**: Letter from Boland
     contained in the Ole Miss archives.

45   **"You ready to go?"**: Archie and Peyton Manning with John Un-
     derwood, *Manning: A Father, His Sons, and a Football Legacy*
     (New York: HarperEntertainment, 2000), 47.

45   **He was strolling across campus**: Ibid., 54–55.

49   **"I've got a boy"**: Zimmerman, "The Patience of a Saint."

49   **One evening Sigma Nu**: Archie Manning, *Manning*, 57.

49   **"Hey, Daddy, guess who"**: Ibid., 56.

50   **On passing, Vaught instructed**: Passing manual from Vaught con-
     tained in the Ole Miss archives.

51   **From early in the morning until late in the afternoon**: Article of
     unknown origin contained in the Ole Miss archives.

52   **"What happened?"**: Archie Manning, *Manning*, 64.

52   **"How do you compare him with Joe Namath?"**: John Vaught,
     Rebel Coach (Memphis, Tenn.: Memphis State University Press,
     1971), 141.

53   **"Everything is fine now"**: Charles Cavagnaro, "Bouncy Vaught
     Aims His Rebs with a Cause," *Commercial Appeal*, July 21, 1968.

53   **"We are in the process"**: Article of unknown origin contained in
     the Ole Miss archives.

53   **"I'm finding it fun to coach again"**: George Bugbee, "New Soph
     Blood Revitalizes Rebs," *Memphis Press-Scimitar*, September 3,
     1968.

53   **"You had to consider what Manning had"**: David Bloom, "The
     Loser Becomes a Winner," *Commercial Appeal*, September 9, 1968.

56   **"Boys, we're going to Tiger Stadium"**: Article of unknown origin contained in the Ole Miss archives.
56   **"Wheh's AWWW-che Mannin"**: Article of unknown origin contained in the Ole Miss archives.
57   **"I'll take him right now"**: Zimmerman, "The Patience of a Saint."
58   **The son copied the film**: Archie Manning, *Manning*, 52.

CHAPTER 6: A STORM GATHERS

64   **Buddy never believed in doctors**: Archie and Peyton Manning with John Underwood, *Manning: A Father, His Sons, and a Football Legacy* (New York: HarperEntertainment, 2000), 60.
64   **He was only fifty-nine, but he was a worn-down fifty-nine**: Ibid.
64   **Though before the games he'd tell his son**: John Ed Bradley, "Like Father, Like Son," *Sports Illustrated*, November 15, 1993.
65   **Buddy appeared to be happy**: Archie Manning, *Manning*, 61.
65   **"I hope my son"**: Ibid., 60.
66   **"cook steaks"**: Ibid., 61.
66   **"I want to go on home"**: Ibid., 61.
66   **Out of the corner of his eye, Archie noticed**: Ibid.

CHAPTER 7: WHY NOW?

67   **there was a big blood spot**: Paul Zimmerman, "The Patience of a Saint," *Sports Illustrated*, June 8, 1981.
67   **"I think Buddy's dead"**: Archie and Peyton Manning with John Underwood, *Manning: A Father, His Sons, and a Football Legacy* (New York: HarperEntertainment, 2000), 61.
68   **He then burned**: Sam Blair, *Dallas Cowboys Star Magazine*, December 17, 2011.
68   **On the hull**: Zimmerman, "The Patience of a Saint."
69   **Olivia was in awe of her boyfriend's strength**: Archie Manning, *Manning*, 59-60
70   **Archie made a decision**: Ibid., 61.

CHAPTER 8: THE BIRTH OF A FOLK HERO

71   **It began with a man**: William F. Reed, "Archie and the War Between the States," *Sports Illustrated*, October 12, 1970.

73   **Vaught always was suspicious**: Pat Putnam, "Answer to a Foolish
Question," *Sports Illustrated,* November 24, 1969.

74   **Cutcliffe dreamed of playing quarterback**: Kevin Armstrong, "A
Cut Above," *New York Daily News,* September 14, 2013.

78   **Back at the team's Birmingham hotel**: Charles Cavagnaro, "Tide
Victory Washes Away Proper Description," *Commercial Appeal*,
October 6, 1969.

78   **church buses took detours**: Paul Zimmerman, "The Patience of a
Saint," *Sports Illustrated,* June 8, 1981.

80   **Rebel trainers found a trough**: Paul Atkinson, "He's an 'Unreal'
Quarterback," *Christian Science Monitor,* November 22, 1969.

83   **The red-and-blue buttons**: William F. Reed, "Red-Letter Year for
Quarterbacks," *Sports Illustrated,* September 14, 1970.

84   **"The only thing I can figure out"**: Ibid.

84   **A young man from Gholson**: letter contained in *Sports Illustrated*
archives.

86   **a small plane roared across the blue sky above**: Putnam, "Answer
to a Foolish Question."

89   **the Ole Miss players started taunting**: Ibid.

90   **A guitar-twanging group**: Reed, "Red-Letter Year for Quarterbacks."

CHAPTER 9: THE BEST I EVER SAW

93   **If he was introduced**: William F. Reed, "Red-Letter Year for Quarterbacks," *Sports Illustrated,* September 14, 1970.

96   **Archie never trained to be a drop-back passer**: Bill Pennington,
"Mannings Follow Father, but Not in His Footsteps," *New York
Times,* February 5, 2012.

97   **"What's the matter, Billy?"**: stringer file contained in *Sports Illustrated* archives.

98   **"Well, young man"**: Reed, "Red-Letter Year for Quarterbacks."

CHAPTER 10: THE FEAR OF FAILING

99 **Most days Cooper Williams remained**: Sid Salter, "Cooper Williams More Than a Famous Grandfather," *Franklin County Times,* April 27, 2002.

100 **Following the team was his favorite hobby**: Frank Deford, *Land's End,* September 2002.

100 **His boyish face beamed**: William F. Reed, "Red-Letter Year for Quarterbacks," *Sports Illustrated,* September 14, 1970.

100 **"I've never seen anything like it"**: Ibid.

101 **he would come up with 95 percent**: Peter Finney, "Sharp Mind, Rifle Arm—Rebs' Archie," *Sporting News,* November 7, 1970.

102 **Vaught enjoyed watching Archie**: John Vaught, *Rebel Coach* (Memphis, Tenn.: Memphis State University Press, 1971), 140.

102 **"He has a great football mind"**: Reed, "Red-Letter Year for Quarterbacks."

102 **Have a daily work schedule**: Joe David Brown, "Babes, Brutes and Ole Miss," *Sports Illustrated,* September 19, 1960.

104 **He was so engrossed**: William F. Reed, "Archie and the War Between the States," *Sports Illustrated,* October 12, 1970.

104 **"I've never seen him like this"**: Ibid.

105 **Though he was emotionally crushed**: Bubba Burnham, "Between the Goalposts with Archie," *Clarksdale Press Register,* October 4, 2001.

107 **Standing in front of his locker after the game**: Reed, "Archie and the War Between the States."

107 **The coach was normally low-key**: Finney, "Sharp Mind, Rifle Arm."

CHAPTER 11: WHAT MIGHT HAVE BEEN

109 **He was so battered**: Rick Cleveland, "USM's 1970 Upset of Ole Miss Changed Course of Events," *Clarion-Ledger,* April 5, 2012.

109 **Vaught's labored walk**: Article of unknown origin contained in the Ole Miss archives.

112   **Archie always called collect**: Fred Katz, "Manning, Plunkett, Kern and Theismann Sound Off," *Sport Magazine,* October 1970.

113   **Archie stuck out his left arm**: David Davidson, "Joy Turns to Gloom in Rebeland," *Clarion-Ledger,* November 8, 1970.

113   **"I hurt my arm, Coach"**: Davidson, "Joy Turns to Gloom in Rebeland."

114   **a nurse kept it as a souvenir**: Article of unknown origin contained in the Ole Miss archives.

115   **The eighth-floor secretary, Mrs. L. Franklin**: Bob Phillips, "Memphis Hospital Remembers Manning," *Clarion-Ledger,* November 18, 1970.

115   **"Archie Manning is the greatest"**: "Ailing Johnny Vaught," *Knoxville News Sentinel,* November 13, 1970.

117   **On doctor's orders**: Peter Finney, "Archie Will Revolutionize Pro Football," *States-Item,* May 7, 1971.

117   **"I look for him to revolutionize"**: Ibid.

117   **One agent was particularly aggressive**: Paul Zimmerman, "The Patience of a Saint," *Sports Illustrated,* June 8, 1981.

118   **Archie couldn't stop imagining Rudoy**: Ibid.

CHAPTER 12: A MARRIED MAN BECOMES A SAINT

120   **Archie met with Crosthwait for two hours**: Paul Zimmerman, "The Patience of a Saint," *Sports Illustrated,* June 8, 1981.

120   **stopped for a few cold ones**: Archie and Peyton Manning with John Underwood, *Manning: A Father, His Sons, and a Football Legacy* (New York: HarperEntertainment, 2000), 84.

121   **When Sis saw people swiping bottles**: Ibid.

122   **The Saints graded players**: John Vaught, *Rebel Coach* (Memphis, Tenn.: Memphis State University Press, 1971), 140.

125   **After the conference call**: Bobby Hall, "When the Saints Call," *Commercial Appeal,* January 29, 1971.

126   **Ten words in the story**: Archie Manning, *Manning,* 85.

126   **"You're 0 for 0 up there when you start"**: Bobby Hall, "A Hit, On and Off the Field," *Commercial Appeal,* February 8, 1971.

127   **"When you're a star player"**: Ibid.

CHAPTER 13: "I'LL ALWAYS BE FROM DREW"

129 **On Main Street all twenty**: David Bloom, "And What a Day," *Commercial Appeal,* March 1, 1971.

132 **Even black children at the parade**: Bobby Hall, "Drew's King Returns," *Commercial Appeal,* February 28, 1971.

132 **After the parade the crowd of ten thousand**: Sue Dabbs, "Home Folks Honor Archie," *Jackson Daily News,* February 28, 1971.

133 **Archie took a moment to talk to Money Lockett**: Bloom, "And What a Day."

CHAPTER 14: THE BEAT-UP QUARTERBACK

136 **Archie rammed into the back of a car**: Sam Borden, "A Saint in His City," *New York Times,* January 26, 2013.

137 **New Orleans assistant coach Don Heinrich**: Dave Anderson, "The Saints Raise the Roof," *New York Times,* January 3, 1988.

137 **Dempsey spent the off-season**: Ibid.

138 **"Wow, this guy must be really good"**: Paul Zimmerman, "The Patience of a Saint," *Sports Illustrated,* June 8, 1981.

138 **Archie nicknamed him Sudden Sam**: Ibid.

139 **"C'mon, men, let's play!"**: Archie and Peyton Manning with John Underwood, *Manning: A Father, His Sons, and a Football Legacy* (New York: HarperEntertainment, 2000), 99.

140 **Archie and Olivia began to sink their roots**: Borden, "A Saint in His City."

CHAPTER 15: ARCHIE ONE AND ARCHIE TWO

142 **"You have my sympathies"**: Archie and Peyton Manning with John Underwood, *Manning: A Father, His Sons, and a Football Legacy* (New York: HarperEntertainment, 2000), 95.

142 **when his smiling face would appear**: Ibid., 113.

142 **"You suck, Manning!" they screamed**: John Ed Bradley, "Like Father, Like Son," *Sports Illustrated,* November 15, 1993.

143   **She was going to tell every soul in that building**: Ibid.

143   **"Boo," the Manning boys yelled**: Ibid.

143   **"I don't know whether the weight is an NFL record"**: Stringer file in the *Sports Illustrated* archives.

144   **One night Dick Brennan**: Archie Manning, *Manning*, 116.

144   **Archie was carrying him into the Superdome**: Ibid., 117.

145   **"There are a million suburbs"**: Sam Borden, "A Saint in His City," *New York Times*, January 26, 2013.

145   **Archie often played a game he called "knee football"**: Archie Manning, *Manning*, 138.

146   **"Cooper Manning. Six years old."**: Bradley, "Like Father, Like Son."

146   **"You need an attitude adjustment"**: Ibid.

147   **During a Thanksgiving football game**: Rick Reilly, "Nothing Is Out of Bounds," *Sports Illustrated*, November 28, 2005.

147   **"He thinks we're stupid"**: Lee Jenkins, "Peyton Manning: Sportsman of the Year," *Sports Illustrated*, November 23, 2013.

147   **"Hey, everybody is not like you"**: Steve Springer, "Well-Bred Colt," *Los Angeles Times*, December 12, 1999.

147   **"A quata-back"**: Ibid.

148   **Archie would take the boys to Domilise's**: Borden, "A Saint in His City."

148   **Cooper often wandered away**: Archie Manning, *Manning*, 140.

149   **Years later, when he would drink beer**: Wright Thompson, "Peyton Manning," *Kansas City Star*, January 11, 2004.

150   **"Well, who do you play next week?"**: Archie Manning, *Manning*, 119.

151   **Peyton was in the Saints' weight room**: Ibid., 139.

151   **After practice they would jump into the whirlpool**: Ibid., 140.

153   **He grabbed a ball from his trophy case**: Paul Zimmerman, "The Patience of a Saint," *Sports Illustrated*, June 8, 1981.

153   **Archie couldn't even walk down the stairs**: Charles Pierce, "Legends of the Fall," *GQ*, September 1996.

154   **"I can't do it to that boy"**: Zimmerman, "The Patience of a Saint."

154   **"You better get out of this place"**: Ibid.

CHAPTER 16: THE COMMUTER QB

155   **On his way to the stage**: Larry McMillen, "Award Packed with Emotion for Manning," *Sporting News,* September 2, 1978.

156   **"I'd like to win"**: Ibid.

157   **"It's hard to describe this thing"**: Larry Fox, "Is It Time for Archie to Leave the Bunkers?," *New York Daily News,* December 12, 1980.

158   **"Let's beat 'em 70–7"**: Dave Anderson, "The Saints Raise the Roof," *New York Times,* January 3, 1988.

158   **Archie lit a cigar and played poker**: George Vecsey, "For Manning and Dispirited Saints, It's 0–14 and Counting," *New York Times,* December 14, 1980.

159   **"Richard, old buddy"**: Archie and Peyton Manning with John Underwood, *Manning: A Father, His Sons, and a Football Legacy* (New York: HarperEntertainment, 2000), 136.

159   **saw what he later described as "a huge black cloud"**: Anderson, "The Saints Raise the Roof."

159   **"Jesus Christ could be back there"**: Gordon Forbes, stringer file contained in *Sports Illustrated* archives, October 16, 1981.

160   **"The number one question people ask me"**: Paul Zimmerman, "The Patience of a Saint," *Sports Illustrated,* June 8, 1981.

161   **"Dad," Peyton said, "could you hold out"**: Hal Lundgren, stringer file contained in *Sports Illustrated* archives, September 29, 1982.

161   **Archie decided to lease an apartment**: John Ed Bradley, "Like Father, Like Son," *Sports Illustrated,* November 15, 1993.

162   **Oliver would chaperone Cooper and Peyton**: David Fleming, "Luck-Manning Link Goes Way Back," *ESPN.com,* October 17, 2013.

164   **Wilson looked at Archie with sincere sympathy**: Peter King, "Survival Test," *Sports Illustrated,* October 22, 1990.

164   **"This has been especially hard on my boys"**: Ibid.

165   **"Where are all the ducks?"**: Sam Borden, "A Saint in His City," *New York Times,* January 26, 2013.

165   **"You ever think of retiring?"**: Archie Manning, *Manning,* 173.

165   **"I think they thought their daddy could play forever"**: Rick

Cleveland, "Olivia Gets Archie Back," *Jackson Daily News,* August 27, 1985.

165   **"It's been a good trip"**: Ibid.

166   **"I don't want to live anywhere in Mississippi"**: Rick Jervis, "Conflict for Archie Manning," *USA Today,* February 5, 2010.

CHAPTER 17: TEACHING LIFE—AND FOOTBALL—LESSONS

167   **perform five-step drops**: *Athlon's Monthly,* April 5, 2011.

167   **little Peyton would climb onto his dad's lap**: Ibid.

168   **Archie went to a school event**: Paul Attner, "The First Family," *Sporting News,* March 22, 2004.

168   **Peyton asked Rickey to come upstairs**: John Ed Bradley, "A Glimpse of the Future," *Sports Illustrated,* December 23, 2013.

168   **he kicked him in the stomach**: Sean Gregory, "The NFL's Royal Family," *Time,* December 5, 2005.

169   **Peyton was the only player who could control the ball**: Bill Watkins, "Like Father, Like Sons," *Clarion-Ledger,* December 1, 1991.

169   **"Why did you draft these guys?"**: Sam Borden, "A Saint in His City," *New York Times,* January 26, 2013.

170   **"The reason you lost"**: Steve Springer, "Well-Bred Colt," *Los Angeles Times,* December 12, 1999.

171   **Peyton reared back and threw his first pitch**: Ibid.

171   **Fitzgerald called Peyton into his office**: Tim Layden, "Matinee Idol," *Sports Illustrated,* August 26, 1996.

172   **"Daddy, I've got to watch more film"**: *Athlon's Monthly,* April 5, 2011.

172   **a young caller who referred to himself**: Watkins, "Like Father, Like Sons."

173   **he didn't even know what constituted a good college player**: Angus Lind, "The Manning Boys to Men," *Times-Picayune,* April 4, 2004.

173   **Cooper began his high school career**: John Ed Bradley, "The Older Brother," *Sports Illustrated,* November 10, 2003.

174 **"You didn't beat me"**: Ibid.

174 **Cooper's hands were strong and reliable**: Watkins, "Like Father, Like Sons."

CHAPTER 18: THE MOST MAGICAL FALL

176 *If you're going to watch film, do it the right way*: Tim Layden, "Matinee Idol," *Sports Illustrated*, August 26, 1996.

177 **he would imagine he was in the crowd**: Ibid.

177 **Archie and Olivia told their curious son**: Ibid.

178 **When Peyton was a teenager, he also found a few dust-covered videos**: Bill Pennington, "Mannings Follow Father, but Not in His Footsteps," *New York Times*, February 5, 2012.

178 **"Why aren't I fast like that?"**: Ibid.

179 **One day Cooper spotted Peyton**: John Ed Bradley, "The Older Brother," *Sports Illustrated*, November 10, 2003.

179 **He would warn his boys**: Anthony L. Gargano, "Archie Manning: What I've Learned," *Esquire*, December 20, 2013.

180 **"I'm eight and you're ten and I beat you"**: Bradley, "The Older Brother."

180 **"You know how lucky you boys are"**: Ibid.

180 **Mora's breath was taken away**: Wright Thompson, "Peyton Manning," *Kansas City Star*, January 11, 2004.

181 **"You've got to know what you're doing out there"**: Lee Jenkins, "Peyton Manning: Sportsman of the Year," *Sports Illustrated*, November 23, 2013.

181 **On the various tapes Archie's voice**: Bill Watkins, "Like Father, Like Sons," *Clarion-Ledger*, December 1, 1991.

183 **"What was that?"**: John Ed Bradley, "Like Father, Like Son," *Sports Illustrated*, November 15, 1993.

183 **"Have some fun out there"**: Gargano, "Archie Manning: What I've Learned."

184 **In the huddle Cooper was constantly jabbering in Peyton's ear**: Bradley, "The Older Brother."

184 **a defensive back covering Cooper began talking trash**: Watkins, "Like Father, Like Sons."

184 **Reginelli returned to school and spied a tall, lanky teenager**: Vin-

cent Coppola, "In the Mirror," *Dunnavant's Paydirt Illustrated,*
Fall 1996.

185 **Peyton wanted to treat his offensive linemen to lunch**: Watkins,
     "Like Father, Like Sons."

187 **"Blame it on the sophomore!"**: Archie and Peyton Manning with
     John Underwood, *Manning: A Father, His Sons, and a Football
     Legacy* (New York: HarperEntertainment, 2000), 194.

187 **"I definitely want Peyton to come with me"**: Watkins, "Like Fa-
     ther, Like Sons."

CHAPTER 19: A NOTE FOR PEYTON

190 **"He runs great routes"**: Mike Strom, "Breaking from the Shad-
     ows," *Times-Picayune,* July 24, 1992.

190 **"My whole hand seriously has atrophy"**: Ibid.

191 **"It's better to be a good person than a good player"**: Archie and
     Peyton Manning with John Underwood, *Manning: A Father, His
     Sons, and a Football Legacy* (New York: HarperEntertainment,
     2000), 211.

192 **Five-year-old Cooper once surprised a group of strangers**: John
     Ed Bradley, "The Older Brother," *Sports Illustrated,* November 10,
     2003.

194 **"I can't," Peyton said**: Ibid.

194 **his "finest gathering of thoughts"**: "Olivia Manning Is the Back-
     bone for Busy Sports Family," *Knoxville News Sentinel,* August 24,
     1997.

195 **Cooper left behind a note**: Tyler Conway, "Cooper Manning's In-
     jury," *Bleacher Report,* September 25, 2013.

CHAPTER 20: "THE BAD THING HAPPENED
TO THE RIGHT GUY"

197 **When Peyton brought his new football jersey home**: Ron Hig-
     gins, "Peyton's Place?," *Commercial Appeal,* January 16, 1994.

198 **"What I'd do to have you back again"**: John Ed Bradley, "The
     Older Brother," *Sports Illustrated,* November 10, 2003.

198 **"He took it hard but he took it good"**: Jim Kleinpeter, "Manning's Career Ended by Ailment," *Times-Picayune*, September 29, 1992.

199 **"This is just not fair"**: Don Yaeger, "Raising Champions," *Success Magazine*, October 5, 2010.

200 **"What the hell are you doing here?" the burly**: Bradley, "The Older Brother."

200 **For one of the few times in his life**: Ibid.

200 **"Peyton, you need to go with my wife"**: Archie and Peyton Manning with John Underwood, *Manning: A Father, His Sons, and a Football Legacy* (New York: HarperEntertainment, 2000), 205.

202 **He kept a picture in his wallet**: Dave Scheiber, "The Other Manning," *Tampa Bay Times*, November 7, 2004.

202 **"Maybe the bad thing happened to the right guy"**: Ibid.

CHAPTER 21: THE DECISION

205 **"The way he looks, the way he throws"**: Archie and Peyton Manning with John Underwood, *Manning: A Father, His Sons, and a Football Legacy* (New York: HarperEntertainment, 2000), 222.

205 **believed there were four common fundamental mistakes**: Ibid., 224.

206 **He raised his hand and was called on**: Ibid., 223.

206 **Before putting his hands under center**: Lee Jenkins, "Peyton Manning: Sportsman of the Year," *Sports Illustrated*, November 23, 2013.

207 **"Hey, stripes!"**: John Ed Bradley, "Like Father, Like Son," *Sports Illustrated*, November 15, 1993.

208 **"The blind bootleg"**: Ibid.

208 **"Did you see my blind bootleg?"**: Ibid.

208 **Standing near midfield, Archie threw a few short passes**: Ibid.

209 **Just before Peyton was hit, he dumped the ball**: Ron Higgins, "Peyton's Place?," *Commercial Appeal*, January 16, 1994.

210 **He stored the missives**: Ibid.

211 **Archie secretly hoped that Peyton would stay in the South**: Charles Pierce, "Legends of the Fall," *GQ*, September 1996.

212 **Peyton and Archie took another long car trip**: Higgins, "Peyton's Place?"

212 they sprinted down the tunnel from the dressing room: Ibid.

214 The Rebel staff even made an audiotape for Peyton: Archie Manning, *Manning*, 234.

214 "Peyton's a player who will have the most impact": Ron Higgins, "Mannings Not Pressuring Peyton," *Commercial Appeal*, January 16, 1994.

215 "I couldn't believe Archie Manning": Kevin Armstrong, "A Cut Above," *New York Daily News*, September 14, 2013.

215 The father demanded it be spotless: Ibid.

215 "Ya know, I didn't really talk to Peyton": Ibid.

215 She left a hot dish for them to eat: "Olivia Manning Is the Backbone for Busy Sports Family," *Knoxville News Sentinel*, August 24, 1997.

216 He had arrived early in the afternoon: Archie Manning, *Manning*, 231.

216 "Tennessee or Notre Dame," Eli replied: Higgins, "Peyton's Place?"

218 "Dad, I've decided I want to go to Tennessee": Archie Manning, *Manning*, 235.

218 "Yessss," Cooper said: Ibid., 239.

219 He was slumped on the couch and fast asleep: Armstrong, "A Cut Above."

CHAPTER 22: THE MAMMA'S BOY

220 Her hope for a girl suddenly changed: Archie and Peyton Manning with John Underwood, *Manning: A Father, His Sons, and a Football Legacy* (New York: HarperEntertainment, 2000), 312.

221 he didn't say any intelligible words: Peter King, "Destiny's Chill," *Sports Illustrated*, January 28, 2008.

221 he essentially spoke in monosyllables: S. L. Price, "The Big Easy," *Sports Illustrated*, December 17, 2012.

222 reading was difficult: Ibid.

222 if he had a test on Friday: Ibid.

223 he removed the pillows from a living room couch: Paul Attner, "The First Family," *Sporting News*, March 22, 2004.

223 He insisted on eating his peanut butter and jelly sandwich: Billy

Watkins, "Eli Who?: Many Sides to This Manning," *Clarion-Ledger*, 2002 Football Magazine.

224 **Eli walked through the front door after playing**: Michael Silver, "May the Best Manning Win," *Sports Illustrated*, September 11, 2006.

224 **"you don't even have to play football"**: David Jones, "Seems Like Old Times," *USA Today*, October 5, 2002.

225 **he could be kissed only on Sunday nights**: Archie Manning, *Manning*, 310.

CHAPTER 23: EASY RIDER

228 **"This is what we're learning at Tennessee"**: S. L. Price, "The Big Easy," *Sports Illustrated*, December 17, 2012.

228 **he sometimes drove Eli in the mornings**: Rick Reilly, "Talking Football and Archie, Peyton and Eli," *ESPN.com*, April 27, 2011.

229 *What is wrong with this kid*: Ibid.

229 **Over and over, little Eli launched bricks**: Seth Wickersham, "Eli: An Absolute Possibility," *ESPN The Magazine*, December 24, 2012.

231 **Eli claimed he won when he blew past Peyton**: Ibid.

232 **He'd board the Saints' charter flight**: Rick Jervis, "Conflict for Archie Manning," *USA Today*, February 5, 2010.

232 **Alas, Archie picked up the phone at home**. Michael Eisen, "Giants vs. Steelers," *Official Game Program of the New York Giants*, December 18, 2004.

CHAPTER 24: "I ONLY HAD DOGS AND CATS NAMED AFTER ME"

234 **"It wasn't pretty, was it?"**: Paul Attner, "Rare Heir," *Sporting News*, August 21, 1995.

235 **"Hey, Peyton!" one yelled. "What are you doing?"**: John Ed Bradley, "The Older Brother," *Sports Illustrated*, November 10, 2003.

236 **The coaches started calling Peyton "the Computer"**: Ibid.

236 **"Damn it, Peyton"**: Ibid.

236 **Peyton and the members of his class**: Lee Jenkins, "Peyton Manning: Sportsman of the Year," *Sports Illustrated,* November 23,
2013.

237 **"If God is willing and I live long enough"**: Ibid.

237 **Wearing a pastel shirt, he was introduced to Ashley Thompson**:
Michael Silver, "Thoroughbred," *Sports Illustrated,* November 22,
1999.

237 **On their date Peyton was the perfect gentleman**: Ibid.

238 **He once arrived for a date with Ashley**: Ibid.

239 ***"What the hell are you doing here, Peyt?"***: Curry Kirkpatrick,
"Sons of Gun," *ESPN.com,* November 29, 2001.

239 **"Oh, I'm just getting drunk and chasing women"**: Archie and
Peyton Manning with John Underwood, *Manning: A Father, His
Sons, and a Football Legacy* (New York: HarperEntertainment,
2000), 259.

240 **"Hey, Peyton! Get your ass in gear!"**: Ibid., 259.

240 **Fulmer walked over to Peyton and said, "Be ready"**: Ibid., 250.

241 **"Peyton's going in!"**: Ibid.

241 **"Shut the fuck up and call the play!"**: David Clymer, "High Expectations," *The Tennessean,* Athlons 1995 College Football Annual.

241 **She had a one-word response: "young"**: Archie Manning, *Manning,* 251.

244 **"Now, son, when you go back to school this year"**: Attner, "Rare
Heir."

244 **Peyton would walk up to the center slightly bowlegged**: Ibid.

244 **"Quit being so hard on yourself, Peyton"**: Ibid.

245 **"Peyton," he wrote, "you have screwed up my fleeting fame"**:
T. J. Quinn, "Proud Papa," New York *Daily News,* January 8, 2006.

246 **parents were naming their newborns Peyton**: Jenkins, "Peyton
Manning: Sportsman of the Year."

246 **"I only had dogs and cats named after me"**: Ibid.

247 **Peyton was far from a sure bet to make it as an NFL player**: Ibid.

248 **"Peyton has this ideal of college life"**: Vincent Coppola, "In the
Mirror," *Dunnavant's Paydirt Illustrated,* Fall 1996.

248 **The just-completed game would be replaying**: Wright Thompson,
"Peyton Manning," *Kansas City Star,* January 11, 2004.

249 **"I was clowning around in the training room"**: "Manning Puts
End to Jokes," *Philadelphia Daily News,* May 3, 1996.

249 **"I know that around the country"**: "Trainer's Settlement Involved More Than Manning's Mooning," Associated Press, August 20, 1997.

251 **After an overweight Florida Gator fan heckled him**: Thompson, "Peyton Manning."

251 **He slapped Peyton on the shoulder pads**: Ibid.

252 **"I've counted every day of football"**: Tim Layden, "A Most Willing Volunteer," *Sports Illustrated,* December 23, 2013.

253 **He wanted to be able to walk around campus**: Tim Layden, "Thank You, Peyton!," *Sports Illustrated,* March 17, 1997.

253 **Peyton sat in front of his locker and read the official program**: Tim Layden, "Matinee Idol," *Sports Illustrated,* August 26, 1996.

254 **"I always see us playing Georgia"**: Ibid.

CHAPTER 25: A COACH JUST LIKE ARCHIE

257 **"Looks like I'm going to be starting Friday night"**: Archie and Peyton Manning with John Underwood, *Manning: A Father, His Sons, and a Football Legacy* (New York: HarperEntertainment, 2000), 340.

258 **after the first quarter Eli rose to his feet**: Ibid., 316.

258 **"On first and 10, there's a completion out there"**: Kevin Armstrong, "A Cut Above," *New York Daily News,* September 14, 2013.

259 **"How much money you got for me if I do?"**: Archie Manning, *Manning,* 315.

259 **"I don't think I can go to Tennessee"**: William Gildea, "At Ole Miss, Passing the Torch," *Washington Post,* August 4, 2002.

259 **"I'm recruiting you again"**: Ibid.

259 **"fast-twitch thinking ability"**: Paul Attner, "The First Family," *Sporting News,* March 22, 2004.

CHAPTER 26: THE PAST IS NEVER DEAD

262 **Eli never was as engrossed in the entire process**: Joe Drape, "Eli Manning Inherits the Reins," *New York Times,* October 19, 2001.

263 **"Why don't you ask him?"**: Archie and Peyton Manning with

John Underwood, *Manning: A Father, His Sons, and a Football Legacy* (New York: HarperEntertainment, 2000), 346.

263 **"Where's Dad?"**: Ibid., 347.

264 **"This really didn't have anything to do with my father"**: Ibid.

266 **"What if I went out there my first game"**: Billy Watkins, "Eli Who?: Many Sides to This Manning," *Clarion-Ledger,* 2002 Football Magazine.

266 **he was now more frightened of failing than ever before**: Allison Glock, "Easy Does It," *ESPN: The Magazine,* December 19, 2005.

267 **"I need to know, and I need to know the truth"**: Albert Breer, "Unflappable Eli," *NFL.com,* February 2, 2012.

267 **"I want to be able to say that I went for it"**: Glock, "Easy Does It."

268 **when Eli's teammates saw him driving his SUV**: Michael Silver, "May the Best Manning Win," *Sports Illustrated,* September 11, 2006.

268 **he wanted Eli to sit on the bench**: Chris Dufresne, "Can't (Ole) Miss," *Los Angeles Times,* August 29, 2001.

269 **Cutcliffe agreed that it would be in everyone's best interest**: Ibid.

269 **"We got us one"**: Steve Greenberg, "Pro Athlete of the Year: Eli Manning," *Sporting News,* December 22, 2008.

270 **In the year that she died she penned a letter**: Billy Turner, "The Tiny Town That Gave Birth to the Manning Legacy," *Times-Picayune,* January 27, 2008.

270 **In the midst of the funeral celebration**: Watkins, "Eli Who?"

271 **Archie would tidy up by putting magazines in stacks**: Michael Lewis, "The Eli Experiment," *New York Times Magazine,* December 19, 2004.

274 **swore he had traveled back in time**: Ian Thomsen, "Out of the Shadows," *Sports Illustrated,* November 12, 2001.

274 **"fast-twitch mental fibers"**: William Gildea, "At Ole Miss, Passing the Torch," *Washington Post,* August 4, 2002.

274 **"Eli has great football thinking ability"**: Ibid.

275 **"It's like an out-of-body experience"**: Bill Campbell, "Eli Shares Manning Name, Has His Own Style," *Dallas Morning News,* September 11, 2002.

275 **Eli, in his boxer shorts, bouncing up and down on the bed**: S. L. Price, "The Big Easy," *Sports Illustrated,* December 17, 2012.

276 **One would signal the play**: Ibid.

276 **"We hit Manning a lot of times"**: Joe Drape, "Some More Manning Magic," *New York Times,* October 14, 2001.

276 **"I don't know of anyone since I've been here who studies as much film"**: Watkins, "Eli Who?"

277 **Accorsi had hoped to sit in the press box**: Michael Lewis, "The Eli Experiment," *New York Times Magazine,* December 19, 2004.

277 **"Rallied his team from a 14–3 halftime deficit"**: Ibid.

278 **"He's the complete package"**: "Ernie Accorsi's Scouting Report," *Giants.com,* June 18, 2013.

278 **Eli would eventually score a 39 out of 50 on the Wonderlic**: Michael Lewis, "The Eli Experiment," *New York Times Magazine,* December 19, 2004.

CHAPTER 27: A COMBINATION OF ARCHIE AND PEYTON

281 **"Thank you, Coach, for being that role model"**: "More Than a Coach," *The Players' Tribune,* January 8, 2016.

282 **one time a Giants coach messed with Eli's car keys**: S. L. Price, "The Big Easy," *Sports Illustrated,* December 17, 2012.

284 **"All year long"**: Tim Layden, "Remember?," *Sports Illustrated,* August 4, 2008.

284 **To her, Eli suddenly looked like a young Archie**: Tim Layden, "They're History!", *Sports Illustrated,* February 11, 2008.

285 **"Hey, just wipe this day away"**: Larry McShane, "Don't You Forget about Eli Manning," New York *Daily News,* August 9, 2008.

287 **"Hall of Fa-mer! Hall of Fa-mer!"**: Seth Wickersham, "It's Time to Celebrate Eli," *ESPN.com,* February 6, 2012.

288 **On Wednesday, Eli headed to Peyton's downtown condo**: Damon Hack, "One Giant Leap for Manningkind," *Sports Illustrated,* February 12, 2012.

288 **"I don't think people understand our relationship"**: Ibid.

289 **"Dada, Dada, Dada"**: Wickersham, "It's Time to Celebrate Eli."

289 **Cooper caught the ball with ease**: Ibid.

290 **"Do we need to pinch ourselves?"**: Mike Lupica, "Manning Family Doesn't Take Success for Granted," New York *Daily News,* January 25, 2014.

CHAPTER 28: THE THINKING MAN'S QB

292 **"Life is fair"**: Peter King, "A Super Bowl Sunset," *SI.com*, February 8, 2016.

293 **he'd raid the refrigerator for the coaches' leftovers**: Michael Silver, "Thoroughbred," *Sports Illustrated*, November 22, 1999.

294 **he'd lock himself in the equipment room**: Lee Jenkins, "Peyton Manning: Sportsman of the Year," *Sports Illustrated*, November 23, 2013.

295 **Archie pointed out**: Archie and Peyton Manning with John Underwood, *Manning: A Father, His Sons, and a Football Legacy* (New York: HarperEntertainment, 2000), 65.

295 **"What was it like, Dad?"**: Ibid., 66.

296 **when Archie ended a phone conversation**: Ibid.

297 **Peyton even replicated his home in the hotel**: Michael Silver, "Bringing It Home," *Sports Illustrated*, February 12, 2007.

298 **No celebration at this hour could start**: Ibid.

298 **Peyton tried to push himself up**: Sally Jenkins, "Peyton Manning on His Neck Surgeries," *Washington Post*, October 21, 2013.

299 **Archie took both Peyton and Eli to a doctor**: Archie Manning, *Manning*, 206–7.

299 **Peyton needed somewhere to recuperate**: Sally Jenkins, "Peyton Manning on His Neck Surgeries."

299 **"C'mon, quit kidding"**: Ibid.

299 **Before the surgery, the brothers threw the ball**: Ibid.

300 **He flew to Europe several times**: Ibid.

301 **Peyton donned a Colts helmet**: Lee Jenkins, "Peyton Manning: Sportsman of the Year."

301 **they re-created the 2010 AFC championship game**: Ibid.

302 **Peyton flew home to New Orleans**: Greg Bishop, "Von Trapped," *Sports Illustrated*, February 15, 2016.

Index

ABOUT THE AUTHOR

LARS ANDERSON is the *New York Times* bestselling author of six books, including *The Storm and the Tide*, *Carlisle vs. Army*, and *The All Americans*. A 20-year veteran of *Sports Illustrated*, Anderson is a senior writer at *Bleacher Report* and an instructor of journalism at the University of Alabama. He lives in Birmingham, Alabama, with his wife, April, and their son, Lincoln.

@LarsAnderson71